THE B.S. SYNDROME
by
VICTOR SALUPO

First published in MCMLXXXV
Copyright MCMLXXXV / Victor Salupo
Library of Congress Catalog No. 85-070347
All Rights Reserved
Designed by John Citraro
Printed In The United States of America
The Bull Buster Press / Publishers / 1701 East 12 Street,
Cleveland, Ohio 44114
ISBN 0-933219-00-8

ACKNOWLEDGEMENT

Thanks to my family for loving, encouraging and supporting my every effort to speak my heart and mind. And to Laura Greene, a beautiful, talented and loyal business partner and friend who daily set an example of courage despite feeling that the end of the world was right around the corner. To Bert Andrews, Jack Krause, Cy and Charlie Porter, always true, kind and generous friends. To Sharon Friedman for editing with a strong yet gentle hand and with an innate respect for authors. And last but not least, all the wonderful people I have not mentioned who have at one time or another illuminated and deepened the meaning of my life.

THE B.S. SYNDROME
TABLE OF CONTENTS

The world is composed of five elements:

1. Earth
2. Fire
3. Air
4. Water
5. BULLSHIT

— Laurence Sanders
"Tenth Commandment"
1980

If you can't dazzle them with brilliance, baffle them with bullshit.

Anonymous

"You can call it what you will, but to me, it's DISHONESTY IN DRAG."

Florynce R. Kennedy
1981

When my love that she is made of truth,
I do believe her, though I know she lies,
That she might think me some untutored youth,
Unlearned in the world's false subtleties.
Thus vainly thinking that she thinks me young,
Although she knows my days are past the best,
Simply I credit her false-speaking tongue;
On both sides thus is simple truth suppress'd.
But wherefore says she not she is unjust?
And wherefore say not I that I am old?
O, love's best habit is in seeming trust,
And age in love loves not t'have years told.
    Therefore I lie with her, and she with me,
    And in our faults by lies we flattered be.

— Shakespeare, Sonnet 138

. . . one ought to recognize that the present political chaos is connected with the decay of language, and that one can probably bring about some improvement by starting at the verbal end . . . Political language — and with variations this is true of all political parties, from Conservatives to Anarchists — is designed to make lies sound truthful, and murder respectable, and to give an appearance of solidity to pure wind.

—George Orwell,
"Politics and the English Language"
1946

PREFACE

The moment the subject of BULLSHIT arises, there is universal recognition of what it means. The experience of bullshitting, or having been bullshitted, is so common that everyone feels compelled to relate his or her experience.

Yet, as common as this experience is, even the sophisticated are still mystified as to why others do it and what others get out of it, particularly when there is no material gain.

In the short space of several months a number of sad tales were related to me. An experienced businessman in need of expansion capital but in a risky business described how he had wasted six months of precious time with a person representing himself as a "deal maker" who supposedly had contact with Arab investment money. During the six month period, the deal maker, while being wined, and dined, and sexually satisfied (paid for by the businessman's credit card), continually asked the businessman for additional and/or new information. It was a never ending request. Finally, the victim concluded he was being bullshitted. But why?

A young woman deeply in love with her fiance of a year discovered he was not quite the person he had appeared to be. Although he had not lied, neither had he offered some important information: he was divorced, had a child, and was deeply in debt due to a business failure. The negative information would not have made any difference to her, but deliberately creating an opposite impression of this was disappointing and puzzling. Why had he done it? What had he gained?

A music composer in the course of composing a score for a motion picture producer, was "flashed" by her diamond ring, Rolls-Royce, expensive designer clothes, and was led to believe she wanted to produce a Broadway musical he had written. He was not only enticed into sex which was not bad, but into a business partnership. A year later when no real exploration or effort had transpired toward the production of the musical he concluded she was "stringing" him along. Painfully, he wondered why? If she hadn't been serious, why did she waste a year of his time, as well as a year of her time? Was it just for the sex?

A lay-educator had what he considered the key to an improved educational system. He tried to sell his idea to private companies and foundations. He was rejected. He eventually ended up at the Health, Education, and Welfare Department of the Federal Government, where he was granted a hearing. He espoused his ideas, was given great encouragement, and was told to leave his proposal. Several months later, he discovered the person he had spoken to was not the correct person. Then, after finding the right person and wasting three more months, he was told the HEW could not implement educational programs because legally and jurisdictionally it was a state or city function. Why had he not been told immediately? Why? Why? Why?

What none of these people understood is that bullshit is so pervasive, it has permeated every aspect of our lives. It is no longer just a spot on the fabric, or part of the design. It has become the entire cloth. It is so much a part of the system, if not the system itself, that the only defense some people find possible is to believe nothing of what other people, institutions, or media say — or worse, believe exactly the opposite of what is being said!

BULLSHIT results in great frustration, confusion, anger, pain — ultimately to cynicism. It reduces our ability to trust, believe, accept words and people at face value, and severely damages our effort to act efficiently and effectively. It causes such an insecurity that it has devastated, possibly to an irreversible extent, the foundation of human relations which forms the basis of human existence. Although BULLSHIT is probably as old as man, it is doubtful whether, with the sophistication of our media, complex technological developments, and the examples set from on high by our "leaders," that it was ever as pervasive as it is today.

Because the author of this book does not want to add to the disillusionment or degeneration, I am saying in advance that his book might possibly be construed as bullshit too. The crux of all bullshit is that the perpetrator lays down one set of impressions to the victim for other than the apparent motivation. Should you receive the impression that this book is being printed and sold solely for the benefit of the reader, you would be sadly deceived. It is more accurate to say I wrote it for my own pleasure, therapy, ego gratification, and monetary reward. In reality, you might be my tenth motivation, not my first.

But even if I should accept the charge that this book might be bullshit, I maintain it is hopefully an antidote – a vaccination – and the best possible defense against bullshit. Like a vaccination, there must be a certain amount of the live, but diluted disease. My hope, by shedding some light on the subject, is to be able to weaken the disease sufficiently to allow the patient to survive in good health and with more happiness.

It must be understood that I am not writing this book to eliminate bullshit, because I firmly believe it will never be eliminated. Nor is this book a "bible" on bullshit; but if someone were to ask, "What is the bible on bullshit?" I'd hand them my book. And should you look to this book to make you a better practitioner so that you can become rich, successful, or famous, which may be an inadvertent result (no promises), you would again be mistaken. The bottom line is that this book is primarily designed for my benefit, and secondarily, as some defense for you against being buried alive and drowned in BS.

If you are intrinsically happy, this book is not for you. If you are an expert "slinger," this book is not for you, for there will be nothing new, and many things not welcomed. This is a book for the fools of the world. And we're not saying "fools" should not be a word to become elevated, along with words like whore, bitch, bastard, and a host of other words which have been used to often-times denigrate innocent and honest people. Fools are sometimes honest. Honest people are sometimes fools. Maybe it is time the fools of this world united and became proud they were "taken" before they began to "take" someone else and became "winners."

Foremost, we should not despair. In spite of it all, I am idealistic enough to believe there is an inherent strength in our system that allows for the correction of most imbalances. It is not perfect by any means, but it has dealt with serious problems like Watergate, Vietnam, Peace, Justice and Disease, and has emerged wiser, stronger, and victorious. It is also wise to remember that the clothes we wear, the food we eat, the cars we drive, the electric power we use, and the buildings we live and work in were created with solid, factual knowledge – not BULLSHIT. This splendid work was done by common, decent, honest, straight-forward people. I believe they still outnumber the others.

PART I

CHAPTER I

FORMS OF DECEPTION

As this book took shape, I was constantly challenged, "Can you write a book about BULLSHIT without using the word "bullshit?" It was implied that use of this word lacked taste, was vulgar and offensive; that it indicated the range of my vocabulary and literary craft was limited; that I would be censured on radio, TV, and in the press, thereby hurting my chances of promoting and publicizing the book. So, while the answer to their queries could have been, "Yes, I can try to write this book without using that word," I have chosen otherwise. I did not want to sacrifice the negative implication, nor the richness of "bullshit" as a word-symbol of unique color, force and impact.

Of all the words in the English language, the effect of the word "bullshit" on many people is unlike any other. Frequently, not even sexual profanities and stigmata can approach the same level of intensity or impact provoked by this word—in many instances, even violence. Some might say it's not the word that is so devastating but the "virgin ears" which are so "fragile." With today's extensive graffiti, open discussion of sex, and contemporary language in books and films, this is highly unlikely. Yet, there is something inherent in the word which has enabled it to retain its strength. If not to "devastate," at least to deflate. There are, however, exceptions. I've observed the true bullshitter, when called that, to take the epithet as a decoration bestowed upon him. Some people are proud of being bullshitters!

Arthur Herzog in his book, "The B.S. Factor," made a valiant attempt to deal with this word and subject. I believe, however, by avoiding the actual use of the word, he mitigated much of its effectiveness: and by simply illustrating various effects of the subject without dealing with its basic principles, left it in an unresolved quandry. The same applies to William Lambdin who calls it "Doublespeak," and others who skirt the consequences of

3

the head-on confrontation which its utterance provokes. Therefore, it is imperative we take a close look and try to understand the *underlying* implications of this word, and why it is so avoided.

THE RANDOM DICTIONARY OF THE
ENGLISH LANGUAGE

Bullshit (bool'shit) N.V. — shit — shitting Amterj — slang (Vulgar)
n.   1. nonsense, lies, or exaggeration.
vt.   2. To lie or exaggerate to
vi.   3. To speak lies or nonsense
interj 4. (used to express disbelief, disapproval, or the like)

I'm sure that not many people would get upset if accused of talking nonsense, lies, or in an exaggerated way. After all, much of what we hear and see today is nonsense, lies, or exaggerated. We have become quite conditioned to it. However, if you start by honing in on "shit" and "shitting," the sparks begin to fly. Psychoanalysts have written countless books explicating the many psychological and emotional meanings of the anal, i.e., feces. Their research and knowledge have great validity. Yet, it still does not explain the total impact of the word. For this, I believe, one has to go to the "street" meaning. On the street, when you are "talking shit," you are not only talking about something that is a waste, that smells bad, that must be contained and disposed of, that is physically and psychologically repugnant to most everyone over a certain age — you are literally talking about less than nothing — a zero.

When you connect this word to the image of the bull — a big, mindless stud — the conflagration is immediate. I don't mean to denigrate the bull who is an integral performer in the Art of Bullfighting, with all of its sense of pageantry and its ritual meaning. Sadly, the bull is most often the victim. Nor do I wish to denigrate the bull's procreative function which is necessary to the continued health and enjoyment of nonvegetarian humans. I simply suggest that a facet of the bull is a "force" that can be dangerous, has a narrow purview and a "blind spot," and will oftentimes attack without provocation (at least it seems that way to those of us who are not bulls). It is also interesting to note the word "bully" is a derivative meaning a person who hurts, frightens, or tyrannizes over those who are smaller or weaker. Or "bull-headed," as blindly stubborn and headstrong. So, while it is

4

the latter part of the word, SHIT, that is the main thrust of denigration, it is the BULL which provides the motive power that carries the denigration to its target.

To get serious, to know the "street" interpretation is to know only the tip of the iceberg. One can begin to know the composition of a cancer cell but until one comes to know its mechanism, structure, and how it spreads and develops to the point of ravishing the entire body, you won't know cancer in its true reality. Therefore, it is imperative there be a clarification and distinction made between BULLSHIT and other forms of deception. Too often, these other forms of deception—LYING, THE PUT-ON, THE CON GAME, ADVERTISING, PROPAGANDA—are seen as interchangeable and are classified (wrongly) as bullshit. While there is some overlapping, it is important to understand that each activity has its own unique form, functions by its own principles, and has a different payoff.

Bullshit is the laying down of a set of impressions by the perpetrators to the victim for other than the apparent motivation. In other words, the victim is led to believe certain things, and that the motivation for the things said or conveyed is the true (honest) motivation of the perpetrator. The victim may be led to believe, for example, that the perpetrator is rich, powerful, influential, important, loving, or some other impressive quality, and that the perpetrator's motivation is to give the benefit of these qualities to the victim, when that is not the case at all.

Although the payoff for the perpetrator may be a material gain, most often it is a gain of power he seeks. The end transfer of power occurs because the perpetrator intimidates, the victim is intimidated; the perpetrator controls, the victim is controlled; the perpetrator dominates, the victim is dominated; the perpetrator's ego is enlarged, the victim loses self-esteem; the perpetrator wins, the victim loses.

LYING VERSUS BS

Sissela Bok in her book, "Lying," defines lying and the lie "as any intentionally deceptive message which is stated." Most often, such statements are made verbally or in writing, but they can of course also be conveyed with smoke signal, Morse code, sign language, etc. Significantly, the intention of the liar is obviously to mislead, particularly where he knows what he is communicating is not what he believes, and where he has not deluded himself into believing his own deceits. Delusion, of course, implies

5

belief in something that is contrary to fact or reality, resulting from deception, a misconception, or a mental disorder (to have delusions of grandeur). An important factor in lying, therefore, is a conscious awareness—without the distortion of a mental disorder—whereby the person "objectively" knows what he is doing. Up to this point, the bullshitter and the liar are similar in that they both function by design.

"Any number of appearances and words," says Bok, "can mislead us but only a fraction of them are intended to do so. A mirage may deceive us, through no one's fault. Our eyes may deceive us all the time. We are beset by self-delusion and bias of every kind. Yet, we often know when we mean to be honest or dishonest . . . We must single out, therefore, from the countless ways in which we blunder misinformed through life, that which is done with *the intention to mislead*: and from the countless partial stabs at truth, those which are intended to be truthful." The distinction then between bullshitting and lying is while bullshit is a distortion, it stops short of lying—the *stating* of an untruth. If not careful, however, it can easily turn into a lie. A good bullshitter will almost never lie if he can possibly help it!" (Italics Mine)

In a social context, BS is far more permissive than lying. Only when Nixon was found to be a liar did people think badly of him. Nixon's friends *and* foes, if they thought about it at all, probably thought his modus operandi (bullshitting) to be standard operating procedure. It was only when Nixon was trapped in his lies that the House of Representatives moved toward impeachment. Had Nixon not fallen prey to the idea that one gets out of a lie by covering up with another lie, and realized that a good BS artist can only weasel out of a lie with bullshit, he might still be President today. But in terms of gravity, when the courts address themselves "to the truth, the whole truth, and nothing but the truth," there is definitely a heavier moral and legal implication to lying than there is to BS. As a matter of fact, bullshit is generally not legally prosecutable!

Ultimately, however, the key distinction between lying and bullshit resides in the intended end result desired by the perpetrator. Excluding "white lies" (well intentioned lies of little moral import), *lying* is specifically vicious in that it is often done with *maliciousness for the purpose of leading to the destruction of the victim*. It is hostility and violence almost out of control. Bullshit, on the other hand, aims at intimidation, control, domination, or ego enlargement, and is a power transaction. It does not necessarily want to see its opponent destroyed.

THE PUT-ON VERSUS BS

THE PUT-ON, as a form of deception is primarily a game in which the perpetrator *confuses* the victim first and then let's him know he's been fooled or "taken." Jacob Brackman characterizes the put-on as malicious but stopping at the door of complete harm, except as a sadistic assault on the ego. He positions it in the lexicon of deception thus:

> . . . more and more often we suspect we are being tricked. What was once an occasional surprise tactic—called "joshing" around the turn of the century and "kidding" since the twenties—has been refined into the basis of a new mode of communication . . . it occupies a fuzzy territory between simple leg pulling and elaborate practical joke, between lampoon and free floating spoof.

The put-on is most like lying and BS in that it, too, must lay down a series of impressions which deceive. However, it differs from those forms in that it must *reveal* the deception to the *victim* for its pay off—the sadistic pleasure of the perpetrator. Brackman describes how it works in this manner:

> . . . At first, the victim believes the false (impressions) to be true, whereas the kidder knows the "truth." Then the gulling accomplished, the kidder lets the victim know he's been taken for a ride. *This payoff is the kidder's goal.* With kidding and other hoax-derived precedents, the perpetrator smooths the rug out, has you stand on it, and then suddenly yanks it out from under you . . .

> . . . As the put-on artist draws out the derisive moment, the gull has time to reflect (What's he up to? How should I respond? Is he trying to make a monkey out of me?), and the joke's latent malice wells close to the surface (and) it becomes clear that the victim is the butt of a generalized ridicule. (Italics Mine)

Brackman concludes that a conversation with a put-on artist is a process of escalating confusion and distrust. He doesn't deal in isolated little tricks; rather, he has developed a pervasive style of relating to others that perpetually casts what he says into doubt. The put-on artist doesn't want you to take him seriously for any length of time.

The Put-On, in contrast to Lying or Bullshitting, is almost a reverse process. The put-on artist's payoff is in letting you *know* you've been *had*. He must *reveal* his trick to get complete gratification.

THE CON GAME VERSUS BS

In the examination of these various forms of deception, it should become more evident that a clear understanding lays, to a great extent, in comprehending what the payoff of each unique form is. The techniques of these forms may overlap but their results and rewards remain distinctly their own. In the CON GAME which most closely resembles bullshit in technique and form, the payoff is the only distinction. Erich Berne describes the CON GAME as:

> . . . Games (that) are sets of ulterior transactions, repetitive in nature, with a well-defined psychological payoff. Since an ulterior transaction means that the agent pretends to be doing one thing while he is really doing something else, all games involve a con. *But a con only works if there is a weakness it can hook into, a handle, or "gimmick" to get hold of in the respondent, such as fear, greed, sentimentality, or irritability* (Italics mine)
>
> After the "Mark" is hooked, the player pulls some sort of switch in order to get his payoff. The switch is followed by a moment of confusion or crossup while the mark tries to figure out what has happened to him. Then both players collect their payoff, which is mutual, and consists of feelings (not necessarily similar) which the game arouses in both agent and respondent. Unless a set of transactions has these four features, it is not a game—that is, the transaction must be ulterior so that there is a con, and the con must be followed by a switch, a crossup, and a payoff.

I differ from Berne on two points: (1) I believe that on the "street," where the con game is consistently performed by a criminal mentality, it is performed for material gain: (2) I do not believe it is performed as a "game," or that a mutual benefit exists between parties. As Berne explains these points, they may serve as a description of psychological, emotional elements of a process, but from my perspective they are not an accurate reflection of reality. Intimidation, domination, ego enlargement—winning and losing—reflect serious business far more than "game playing." So, while the con game and bullshit may have very similar techniques, they differ in that the primary objective of bullshit is always power, the primary objective of the con game is material reward.

ADVERTISING VERSUS BS

Of all the forms of deception, the distinction between ADVERTISING and BULLSHIT is probably the most difficult to make. Lying, The Put-On, and The Con Game share a similar characteristic; they function on a one-to-one basis. That is, each person is responsible for retribution or payment from the other. Advertising, however, appears to be a general (mass) activity because it is transacted through the mediums of film, TV, radio and print.

In addition, companies utilize the technique of "propogandizing" a publicly held idea such as "Every housewife wants a better kitchen utensil . . . here it is! Tupperware . . . Tupperware and you!" Or, it can extrovert itself and appropriate entire epochs such as the "Pepsi Generation," or create "new" cities such as "Shaefer City" for the beer company of that name.

Further, because the messages are coming at you from early morning to late at night the illusion is that they are more important than they really are. All that remains is to add the "weight" of the medium itself, that is, if something is printed it is thought to be the truth; if on television we think we are protected by the government with FTC—"Truth In Advertising." But even more insidious is McLuhan's observation that "The medium is the message."

Though these distortions may obfuscate the picture, it remains that while advertising messages are beamed over media to the masses, they are written by individuals, received by individuals, and must be interpreted by individuals. Advertising is *single* messages sent to many individual people in large numbers: that some decide to buy and others do not adds proof that advertising like other forms of deception functions on a one-to-one basis.

A more important similarity that advertising has to bullshit is that it, too, creates a set of impressions for other than the apparent motivation. Advertising messages promise the individual a sense of personal achievement, accord him a feeling of equality with his neighbors, divert his mind from thought, serve sexual aspirations, promise social acceptability, and enhance his subjective feelings of health and well being, if the consumer will just buy Tide detergent, Lite Beer, Johnson floor wax, or any one of a thousand products.

Advertising, like bullshit, does not have to *state* an untruth because as Christopher Lasch points out: "The rise of mass media makes the categories of truth and falsehood irrelevant to an evaluation of their influences. Truth has given way to credibility, fact has given way to statements that sound authoritative without conveying information. Statements announcing that a given product is preferred by leading authorities without saying what it is preferred to, statements claiming a product's superiority to unspecified competitors, statements implying that a given characteristic belongs uniquely to the product in question when in fact it belongs to its rivals as well, *all serve to blur the distinction between truth and falsehood in a fog of plausibility. Such claims are "true" yet radically misleading.*" (Italics Mine)

The difference between advertising and bullshit lays essentially in its primary purpose and payoff. At one time, the simple purpose of advertising was to call attention to the product so the consumer would be aware of it and buy it. The payoff was measured in simple monetary gains. For many years now, as John Galbraith points out, the purpose of advertising has greatly expanded. It is now the essential element necessary to create a "Planned Market"; that is, creating a desire for a product *before* it is manufactured, and then producing it to the demand created. In this new role, advertising functions as a control mechanism. With the application of "Management of Demand"—making the consumer buy the product when the manufacturer wants and at the price it wants—the control of the consumer is complete. So, while the public perceives the primary purpose of advertising to be the sale of goods, in reality, it is to promote economic stability in industry and the country through the *manipulation* of the consumer.

This function is not only an integral factor of our economic system but is an example of how advertising develops into PROPAGANDA. In a simpler time, advertising merely called attention to the product and extolled its advantage. Now it manufactures a product of its own; the consumer, perpetually unsatisfied, restless, anxious, and bored. Advertising serves not so much to advertise products as to *promote consumption* as a way of life. It educated the masses into an unappeasable appetite, not only for goods, but for new and personal fulfillment.

PROPAGANDA VERSUS BS

Lasch describes modern propaganda as an art which long ago incorporated the most advanced techniques of modern advertising. He says, "The Master Propagandist . . . does not circulate "intentionally biased" information. He knows that partial truths serve as more effective instruments of deception than lies. Thus he tries to impress the public with statistics of economic growth that neglect to give the base year from which the growth is calculated, with accurate but meaningless facts about the standard of living—with raw and uninterpreted data; in other words, from which the audience is invited to draw the inescapable conclusion that things are getting better and the present regime therefore deserves the people's confidence, or on the other hand that things are getting worse so rapidly that the present regime should be given emergency powers to deal with the developing crisis. By using accurate details to imply a misleading picture of the whole, the artful propagandist, it has been said, makes truth the principal form of falsehood."

Propaganda got its name during the seventeenth century when it was first recognized that public opinion was important and that steps could be taken to modify, bias and direct it in certain ways. Propaganda is any systematic, widespread dissemination or promotion of particular ideas, doctrines or practices to further one's own cause or to damage an opposing one. It is basically an "engineering of consent" by an appeal to the emotions using images and statements that are neither true nor false but merely credible. Within this context Lasch points up an existing irony; "It sometimes becomes necessary to suppress information even when it reflects credit on the government, for no other reason than the facts sound implausible . . . In 1942 the Germans did not reveal that the invincible General Rommel had been absent from North Africa at the moment of Montgomery's victory: everybody would have considered it a lie to explain the defeat and prove that Rommel had not really been beaten. The Office of War Information in the United States, eager to use atrocities to inflame public opinion against Germany, deliberately avoided the most horrifying atrocity of all, the extermination of Jews, on the ground that the story would be "confusing" and misleading if it appeared to be simply affecting the Jewish people. Truth has to be suppressed if it sounds like propaganda." An Allied handbook used in World War II says, "the only reason to suppress a piece of news is if it is unbelievable."

As Jacque Ellul in "Propaganda" brilliantly reveals, propaganda, despite what appears to be a group or national function, converts or persuades on a one-to-one basis. In this regard it is like other forms of deception. Propaganda, however, is most like bullshit in its objective, which is to diminish the opponent's power while increasing its own.

Generally, the degree to which any form of deception utilizes a series of impressions contrary to what seems like the "honest" motivation for those impressions, and which is used for the purpose of modifying or retaining power, is the extent which determines when these forms have been transformed into bullshit.

BS: THE UNSEEN DANGER

When the forms of deception other than BS are articulated, studied, researched, analyzed, defined and brought out into the open, their destructive qualities can be opposed with some sort of defensive action. Lying and The Con Game, for example, can be prosecuted in court; Advertising mitigated by "watch-dog" agencies. Bullshit, on the other hand, goes stark free, unopposed, discounted as "harmless," and is treated like some whores in contrast to some wives. A whore conducts an illegal business transaction, and in doing so is outside the law and can be prosecuted. Socially, she is also a subject for scorn, study, and thought and is constantly under scrutiny. Yet, a "wife" who marries for "security," "status," or "money" is given moral sanction by the church and state, and in the majority of instances, is revered and honored. This raises the question, How was the blurring accomplished? Was it sheer hypocrisy or was bullshit involved?

Dee Brown in his book, "Bury My Heart At Wounded Knee," makes the historical point that the U.S. government broke every major treaty held with the Indians, and that these treaties numbered in excess of one hundred. The American public during this time, however, believed themselves to be "honorable" people. They also believed themselves to be "civilized," and the Indians to be "savages." And in the name of "honor," "safety" and "progress" they righteously committed genocide of an entire race. History verifies that the *Indians* were lied to, but by what means did the White American population come to see themselves as "honorable," "peace loving," etc. Were they victims of bullshit?

I'm sure there are many who "speak no evil, see no evil, hear no evil," who Flo Kennedy calls the "innocent"—those who cop out of their responsibilities as human beings, such as the Germans who disclaimed any knowledge of Dachau although they lived but a few miles away. I don't mean to absolve these "innocent," but was it possible they were "brainwashed" — or bullshitted? If so, why and how was this accomplished?

The distinction between racism in the North and racism in the South is that the South has always been out front and arrogant with its racism. It was well defined, and therefore, a coexistence between White and Blacks did exist for a time, even though this was not a morally justifiable or likeable human condition. But at least the enemy was defined and out in the open — obvious. However, in the North where laws such as equal opportunity, fair housing, plus a "history" for tolerance since the Civil War (all designed to give the North a shining image) camouflaged racism to where a Black person could no longer define his enemy specifically. Consequently, while Black people suffered the reality of racism, the majority of Northern Whites believed it didn't exist to any great extent in their area. In many cases, Northern Whites would get indignant if so accused. Sadly, not only did Black people not have the material benefit of such supposed "tolerance," they were also deprived of the psychological and emotional support that comes from knowing who, what, and where that somebody or something is that hates you. Was this done by design? Who did it? How was the subterfuge accomplished?

Each of these examples is an indication of mendacity raised to an institutional level: if not through an overt conspiracy, certainly through covert actions. It has been firmly implanted in the American psyche and become a "dishonest" way of life according to our constitution and our principles. This deception was accomplished by bullshit and points up the seriousness of the subject.

Bullshit is like cancer, but to make this comparison is to risk being called an alarmist, intellectually dishonest, or more kindly, a fool. However, there was a time when little was known about cancer. Now there is an industry of hundreds of thousands of people, and millions of dollars fighting the war against it.

Until Marshall McLuhan discovered it wasn't so much what was on television that was the danger, but the medium itself, and Gil Scott Heron said, "The revolution will not be televised, television is the revolution," television too, was taken lightly and looked at primarily as an entertainment medium. Today, however, we know differently, though we still do not use it in the most constructive way. The point is that BS is often taken as harmless; we accept it as "standard operating procedure;" some even accept it as playful and entertaining. What we shall hope-

13

fully come to see is that this "harmless" appearance is part of the DECEPTION OF BULLSHIT and is its inherent strength. It is the wolf in sheep's clothing; it can overtake you like cancer long before you're aware you are about to expire.

In a Time Magazine essay, Melvin Maddock cites J.M.G. LeClezio's novel, "The Flood,' in which the anti-hero, a young man suffering from a unique malady—words, the daily deluge of words—has had his circuits overloaded. Even when he is strolling down the street, minding his own business, his poor brain jerks under the impact of instructions (WALK—DON'T WALK), threats (TRESPASSERS WILL BE PROSECUTED), and newstand alarms (PLANE CRASHES AT TEL AVIV). Finally, LeClezio's Everyman goes numb—nature's last defense. Spoken words become mere sounds, a meaningless buzz in the ears. The most urgent words—a poem by Baudelair, a proclamation of war—have no more profound effect than the advice he reads on a book of matches: PLEASE CLOSE COVER BEFORE STRIKING. Maddock concludes, "If one must give a name to LeClezio's disease, perhaps semantic aphasia will do. Semantic aphasia is the numbness of ear, mind, heart—the tone deafness to the very meaning of language—which results from habitual and prolonged abuse of words . . . and when it becomes epidemic, it signals a disastrous decline in the skills of communication, to the numbing low point where language does almost the opposite of what it was created for. With frightening perversity—the evidence mounts daily—words now seem to cut off and isolate, to cause more misunderstanding than they prevent."

This effect is one of a number of symptoms which characterize the syndrome identifying the subject matter. Among the most distinguishing factors of civilization is language—written and spoken. In addition, mankind has always been set apart from animals and other living things by the fact that man thinks—he abstracts, deduces, and synthesizes ideas. And the predominant fact of ideas is that they rest upon and are supported by words. When the accurate meaning of words is attacked and then combined into deceitful impressions, it becomes bullshit. It causes insecurity, a dulling of responses, cynicism, and renders us incapable of believing anyone, or anything, at anytime. Whether this has irreparably damaged our foundation, or whether we can stem the tide, only time will tell. For now, the hope is to shed some light on the subject, pinpoint how it works, place it in proper perspective, and gradually eliminate as much of it from our personal lives as possible, eventually deinstitutionalizing it in society.

CHAPTER II

VICTOR'S VIGNETTES

DISCOVERING BS IN MY LIFE: THE PERFECT VICTIM

When I was a young boy I was taught to respect authority. It seemed everyone in the world exercised some authority over me — my parents, older brothers and sisters, aunts and uncles, school teachers, community leaders, police — even friends of the family living in the neighborhood.

My parents were immigrants, their position in an alien country still new. They believed and taught me that God, country, and family were to be revered and respected at all times. So, whenever I pointed up discrepancies between what persons in authority said and what they did, I was told, "Don't do as I do, do as I (or they) say."

Consequently, when I saw one of our parish priests acting contrary to the image his parishioners held of him, I could only wonder. He drank good wine, ate fine foods, drove excellent cars, and smoked good cigars. As he had a charming countenance, was well-liked, and spoke a stringent morality, he was a trusted member of the community. When the scandal broke and he was exposed as a homosexual with a taste for very young boys, and that he had pilfered the church treasury for other illicit activity outside the city, the shock to the community was great. However, what surprised me was that instead of bringing this knowledge into the open, the community hushed and covered it up. The priest was eventually moved, very quietly, to another city and another parish.

In another early instance, I had discovered music and become an absolute fanatic. I loved it! I practiced the saxophone day and

15

night, with the greatest pleasure I had ever known. My instructor, pleased with my swift progress, suggested I also learn to play the clarinet, a related instrument in the woodwind family. My family was extremely poor (there were ten children), so my mother predictably said "no" to the purchase of the clarinet. The only other person I could turn to was my brother Ben who was in the business of selling appliances, radios, and television sets. I pleaded my case to him in detail. Although he was sympathetic he rejected my request; he needed his money for the growing business. He did, however, suggest I try to borrow the money from the bank. I washed, dressed in my Sunday best, and made the trip to the bank. The manager received me warmly and with respect. He listened attentively as I explained my need. He asked my age and I replied proudly, "I'm eleven years old!" A bemused smile crossed his face as he gave me an application to fill out.

When I had finished, the bank manager said, "Of course, Mr. Salupo, you do understand that at eleven years of age you are legally underaged to secure a loan on just your signature. Therefore, you will have to get a proper co-maker."

Despite my initial disappointment, I became elated, knowing my brother Ben fit the description of a proper co-maker as described by the bank manager. I took the application and hurried over to his store. I confidently explained everything to him, sure that he would support me. When he rejected this request, I went into shock. I'm still not over the disappointment and anger some thirty years later. I asked him why he had made me go through this charade. He replied that it was an important experience that would hold me in good stead in the future; that money was always hard to come by no matter how sympathetic the cause; that no one gives you anything for free; and that you should never put yourself in a position, even with family and friends, where you can get stuck for their debts! Although I half-accepted his explanation, I've always thought there was more to it. Was he just mean? Was he jealous of my musical skills? Or was he just exercising his ego by showing me he was powerful? What I've never been able to accept was the method. It was bullshit.

During my school years in a racially mixed school system, we were taught that regardless of who you were, where you came from, or what your circumstances were, we had equal opportunity to succeed; that if we worked hard, honestly and diligently, we would be rewarded accordingly. However, all I saw was prejudice and discrimination. In my gym class, the taller, stronger, more athletic students were favored over the short, fat, frail ones like myself. In my academic classes, it seemed the White, better dressed students received more attention than the poorly dressed Black students. Also, the more compliant one was, regardless of right or wrong, the better one was treated. When misbehaving students, including myself, were brought before the principal, my Black friends were blamed first while apologies were made for me by the White teachers bringing the charges. It was implied, if not specific, that Blacks were the instigation of trouble.

In high school, when it came time for a group of select students to take college preparatory courses which could put them in first position for college entry and scholarships, this group turned out to be almost exclusively White, although the school population was almost 50% Black. I don't mean to imply that only Blacks were discriminated against. At various times the group included poor Whites, Italians and Jews, etc. Simply, what was preached was not what was practiced.

The bullshit as shown in these examples was constant, and it extended almost to the point of brainwashing. As a matter of fact, to point out any discrepancies of those in power not only tabbed one a trouble-maker, but could have easily caused the person to be labeled unpatriotic or subversive. As a consequence, the victim was subjected to some sort of pressure or punishment.

Upon graduating from high school during the Korean War, I was faced with the draft. I had continued playing my saxophone and had become an excellent musician. In addition, I had become fascinated with motion pictures, and in working with a Cleveland based firm, had become quite proficient in cinematography and film editing. I realized that if I was drafted, I would have little choice over what I wanted to do. So, I quickly set up an audition with the Air Force Band stationed in Washington, D.C. They were impressed with my ability and promised to requisition me once I had finished basic training (8 weeks of physically grueling work). With that assurance, I joined the Air Force. After ten days of basic training (the lowest point of my life), I was summoned to Career Guidance, a facet of the Air Force where an attempt is made to match a serviceman to the job for which he is most qualified. However, it doesn't always mean you get what you want. Since I had noted on my application that my secondary experience included motion pictures, I had been selected by computer for an interview. I quickly learned from the officer in charge that the Air Force, desirous of having their own motion picture unit comparable to that of the Army Signal Corp., had petitioned Congress and received millions of dollars in funds. The Air Force then discovered to their chagrin, that despite having the best equipment in the world, they had no experienced personnel to operate the equipment. As an interim measure, civilians were hired. However, top priority orders were sent to all training camps to secure any qualified servicemen available and get them to Washington, D.C., promptly.

Upon arriving at Career Guidance, I quickly realized that this meeting was going to be most unusual. Just prior to its start, I was offered coffee, a cigarette and treated with the utmost respect. This is *not* like the military, particularly for a recruit: the proof was the sheer hell I had experienced in the previous ten days of basic training where every shred of dignity had been brutally torn from me.

As it turned out, the meeting was not only unusual but extraordinary. The Air Force wanted me for the motion picture unit: I wanted the Air Force Band, knowing there was no better duty to be found anywhere. The band meant travelling the world over in a special plane and playing only for important government functions. The more I insisted on the band, the more and more inducements the officer threw into the pot. It reached the unheard of proportions where I would be doing no KP duty (kitchen police) or patrolling, and I would be living off-base in my own apartment. In addition, I would be promoted immediately and allowed to go home frequently. The negotiation was entirely civilian-like in that it was operating on a supply and demand basis. I was in short supply and the Air Force was in great need. I could hardly believe any of this was really happening because the Air Force literally owned me and could put me anywhere they wanted. When I raised this point, I was informed that the Air Force wanted me now, *that very minute*, not at the end of the eight week period of basic training. For that they needed my consent! At this juncture our interest coincided as I was desperate to get out of the hellish basic training immediately. We struck a deal and within the next two days I was ensconced in Washington, D.C., embarking on a career in the new Air Force motion picture unit.

Most recruits, long before they ever thought of being in the military service, have been conditioned by the "war" stories told to them by family and friends, and reinforced by motion pictures, television and novels. They were taught that everyone in the military was treated equally, i.e., badly! The exceptions, of course, were West Pointers who were political appointees and the officers who made the military their life's work. At the least, we were aware that they were taught differently, acted differently, believed differently: they were an authority placed above us mere draftees, "short termers." I understood this hierarchy. As a consequence, I could not understand their unusual treatment of me at the time. However, I gradually came to comprehend that in innocently following my instinct for survival and happiness, I had gummed up their system. They had secured millions of dollars to bolster their own collective ego, and now had to justify their image. Inadvertently, I had forced them to bend or break firm rules, traditions and procedures—to make an exception of me. What I know now is that they were caught up in their own bullshit and I had breeched their game.

Unfortunately, many of life's actions are returned in kind and I had to pay the price. Ironically, I never learned how to shoot a gun, or how to protect myself from attack. But that wasn't where the danger lay for me. All the protection I ever needed was to be the coward I am and run like hell from any danger. However, because I took great pride in my motion picture craft I became oblivious to danger when in action; consequently, I was severely injured and my duty in the Air Force terminated after one and a half years of service. The Pentagon cited my work as outstanding and awarded me a medal for meritorious work. Incredibly, no one ever knew my true feelings concerning military life or war. Although I never needed to shoot a gun, being in the "game" almost cost me my life!

As I entered civilian life, I was still very naive, idealistic and trusting. I believed in what I had been taught—that the virtues of honesty, loyalty, friendship and the work ethic would bring their own reward. Thus I continued a series of confusing, upsetting and disillusioning experiences bringing me to this book.

—Entering a music conservatory, I found that instead of my musical horizons expanding, they were contracting as a result of the teaching staff's prejudice and snobbery.

—Approaching musically oriented, philanthropic foundations for financial support to advance my career as a concert saxophonist, only to find that none of them gave to an *individual*, let alone a performer who was not legitimatized with "credentials" or sponsored by some authority figure. Not one of the foundations ever got to a point of asking to hear how well I played. They were just not interested in *any* musical contribution I could make, despite the fact that I would have been only one of ten concert saxophonists in the world. Since I had no sponsor to the conservatories either, I was also excluded there.

—A relationship where I was a "son" to a middle-aged man who supposedly had my interest at heart. I divulged a business idea to him that lucky youth sometime hit upon. I was told to keep it a secret, work on it until perfect, and then we would proceed in business together. As the idea came close to realization, my "friend" went ahead with *his* lawyer and formed the business structure. I questioned the fact that my name was not on any of the papers. As a result he accused me of not trusting him, of being ungrateful, of being paranoid! Since I had followed his instructions and told no one outside the family of my idea, it literally was a secret to the outside world. Consequently, as he had the prototype, the design, the application for the patent, the business structure and the capital to produce the product, he effectively put me out in the cold—wiser but poorer.

—Prior to this time, and simultaneous to my entering the music world, I met a very attractive young woman who shared my dedication toward music. Though there were differences in our background—she was a WASP, an only child, and her father was a doctor, her mother a career person—we got along quite well. We had disagreements because we were two strong-willed people, but we were able to resolve them. We even talked marriage. I later learned, however, that a battle was raging between daughter and parents concerning my financial status and background. She defended me, stating I would soon be rich from my business venture. But the pressure continued, weakening the relationship. When my business dream burst, reality set in and I was rejected. My family said "good riddance" to the woman, and "things happened for the best," but I asked, where did the meaning of "love will overcome," and "it doesn't matter *who* you are but *what* you are," disappear. I was once again deeply hurt, broken-hearted, disillusioned, and sadly wiser.

—In another instance, Hollywood, through its major spokesman for film producers, Jack Valenti, put out pronouncements in the consumer press as well as the trade papers (film magazines), and in speeches at various colleges, that Hollywood was desperate for "new blood"—young writers, directors, and other creative talent—and that their doors were wide open. After investing a year and a half of my time and my life's savings to make a short dramatic film that would demonstrate my abilities, and gathering a number of letters of introduction from film professionals in my home town who had seen my film and praised it, I rode a bus from Cleveland, Ohio to Hollywood, only to find every door rudely slammed shut in my face. They were not only disinterested, they were down-right annoyed and antagonized that I was there to begin with. Did I misunderstand all the messages, or was I going crazy? Comparing notes with other young hopefuls I had met, I found it was neither: Hollywood had said it, but Hollywood did not mean it. Furthermore, Hollywood didn't give a damn whether we liked it or not! Now, quite cynical, I returned home.

DISCOVERING THE KEY TO BS

Unfortunately, these experiences repeated until well into my forties. There were times I felt I was congenitally stupid. Oh, I had come to have some defenses like believing only a third of what I saw and less of what I heard, becoming quite wary of anything that sounded too good to be true, of even checking out facts to the best of my ability; still, I found it wasn't sufficient protection. What puzzled me the most was, what had these people gained? Other than the person who stole my idea and profited by it, I very seldom saw anyone gain anything tangible. If they did not gain anything material, why did they do it? There didn't seem to be any logic to it, nor did any answers seem possible. That is, until 1969 when Dr. Laurence J. Peter published "The Peter Principle," the discovery of a new science called hierarchiology, the study of hierarchies which pointed out how incompetence occurs and is rewarded in our society.

As Dr. Peter describes it, the term 'hierarchy" was originally used to describe the system of church government by priests into ranks. The contemporary meaning includes any organization whose members or employees are arranged in order of rank, grade, or class. *Here was my clue.* If all systems have hierarchies where people move up or come down, then someone must dominate and others be dominated. Therefore, a constant in hierarchies had to be power. My next step was to correlate power with "authority" which had run my entire life, from mother to father to priest to school teacher, public figures, business leaders, etc. A further revelation was that in each case something had been imposed on me from on high! The more I examined this thought, the more I could begin to see certain patterns emerging which eventually formulated into principles that could be validated by the same circumstances occuring in all bullshit situations. Initially, these were:

1. EVERY BULLSHIT SITUATION IS A POWER TRANS-
   ACTION.

2. BULLSHIT TRAVELS, MOST OFTEN, FROM THE TOP
   DOWN.

From this point on, to my fascination and joy, other principles and corollaries emerged. For the very first time I now began to understand the mechanics, the structure, the payoffs, the social, psychological, pathological, moral and philosophical implications of this subject. No longer would I have to be a helpless victim. Now I could detect it sooner and end it faster, and overall be more productive and happy.

In retrospect, it is very clear that from the time of our birth, many of us have been trained and conditioned as receptacles for this waste. Whether it came from family and loved ones, or strangers and enemies, bullshit, in addition to all the other things it is, is foremost a control mechanism. When one is controlled, one's power is regulated or suppressed, leaving the person idled and wasted. In other words, impotent, meaningless, and much less than before.

This book then, is a key to an understanding of all deception, and in turn to an understanding of a major facet of the structure of civilization. With many people in business, industry, trade-unionism, politics, government, the armed forces, religion and education using bullshit as coin of the realm, it is almost impossible to escape its snare. Unless you arm yourself well and see bullshit for what it is, you may well be the next victim. Worse, if you are bullshitting yourself, you may be your own worst enemy. Do you have the courage to face the deception of others as well as your own possible self-deception? If so, ahead lies peace of mind through a more honest and accurate communication as well as a more fulfilling and gratifying life experience.

The Five Basics of Bullshit

1. Create a set of impressions
2. for other than the apparent motivation
3. that a second party believes
4. and acts upon
5. resulting in a loss for the second party.

CHAPTER III

PRINCIPLES OF BULLSHIT

PRINCIPLE ONE

EVERY BULLSHIT SITUATION INVOLVES
A POWER TRANSACTION IN WHICH THE
PERPETRATOR INCREASES HIS POWER
AT THE EXPENSE OF THE VICTIM.

Even when there has not been a material gain, the
perpetrator still emerges with the advantage in psychological and emotional terms, which translates as
power: someone dominates, someone is dominated;
someone intimidates, someone is intimidated; someone controls, someone is controlled; someone's ego is
enlarged, someone loses self-esteem—someone wins,
someone loses.

The thing that is most puzzling about BS is not why it is done,
but exactly what has the perpetrator gained. When a perpetrator
has gained some material advantage, particularly money, the
answer seems to be obvious. However, when a direct material
payoff is not in evidence or does not exist, the perplexity
increases.

When a teenage male says to a teenage female, "If you loved
me, you'd sleep with me now," he is using BS to gain pleasure.
Generally overlooked in the situation, however, is the power play

involved in trying to gain his end. In this instance, the boy has utilized pseudo-guilt to intimidate the young lady into the action he desires. Even if she counters by saying, "I do love you but . . .," the male still can maintain his posture, walk away from her, and leave whatever negative implication he wishes. The onus remains on the young lady.

As the perpetrator, he has initiated the action, and utilized intimidation and guilt to effect the result. But mainly, he has kept control even though she may not have acquiesced to his wish. The appearance is that he is determining the action: thus, he still retains his "power" and can continue to try to wrest her "power" by trying again (possibly in some slightly different way) to BS her into the sexual act.

In another example, a young wife who gave up college so that her husband could get his law degree, decided she wanted to complete her education. Since the couple had one child approximately a year old, the husband felt his wife's return to college would be detrimental to the child, and would force him to assume much more responsibility for the child's care. He felt that he would also lose much of the attention his wife showered on him and that much of his freedom would be restricted. Consequently, he wanted to delay, if not postpone permanently, her return to college. But he knew he had no genuine right nor legitimate reason to ask this of her.

The husband realized he had to do something. Not wanting to lie outright, he made inquiries to a law firm in another state. He then rushed home to his wife exaggerating the extraordinary benefits the new job might hold for them. She objected to moving out of state. He then countered by suggesting a move to another firm in the city. In assembling his ploy he had investigated this possibility, too. However, to effect the latter move, he again exaggerated the need to "socialize" extensively with a certain member of that firm. Therefore, the wife would be needed to cover home base and help with the social activities.

For a time, the husband succeeded in his BS. But, when his wife became a little suspect as first "appearances" began to fall apart, he simply continued to create other appearances that she accepted. Although it was possible that something constructive and beneficial could have come out of the husband's actions, it was never his primary objective: his main purpose was to control and dominate his wife so he could gratify his personal needs, retain power, and enlarge upon it at her expense.

In another example, a "consultant" touted connections with

big Arab money looking to invest in American business. In adopting Principle 8, explained in detail later in this chapter, the consultant "looked" prosperous, had a "good" address, and had selected an "impressive" but rather vague company name. As an additional cover, he had made an arrangement with two Arab brothers running a legitimate business; they would receive a percentage of the take should the consultant succeed. In return they would verify they were interested in investing and that the consultant was acting on their behalf.

The consultant approached businesses which were in need of capital for expansion, cash flow, or simply to keep from going bankrupt. The response was immediate. The businesses rushed to provide the consultant with all their confidential and financial data.

As the information poured in, the consultant turned around and approached cash strong companies with the pitch they should acquire "his" companies. If the response from the conglomerates was not forthcoming promptly, and pressure from the businessmen began to mount, the consultant would demand new information from them that would take their CPAs extensive time to prepare and assemble. When the businessmen became really anxious or suspicious, the consultant had them check with his Arab partners. Satisfied, they would allow him even more time.

On the occasions when the consultant succeeded, the deception was never revealed. If the businessmen raised the question of why he had gone to a conglomerate, or why the terms were different, the consultant would simply say the Arabs had changed their minds, so he had found a different source. The consultant used the same story when he failed.

It is important to point out here a refinement of the consultant's technique. At no time did the consultant lie. He made sure in approaching the businessmen, to say his Arab sources "might" be interested in investing if the deal was right. Overall, the consultant not only found this method profitable and safe, but exhilerating as well. In every instance, the businessmen accommodated him on practically every wish. They supplied him with intimate, confidential information, took an obsequious position, made sure he was supplied with lunches, suppers, women, and other perks. In general, they allowed him to be in control. And for as long as the situation lasted, he was in power. He was the winner whether he succeeded or not! He had increased his power at their expense.

26

Whether a material gain is made or not, the constant in each BS situation is that a power transaction has occurred which accrues to the benefit of the perpetrator. Power is defined in the dictionary as the inherent ability to rule, govern, determine, to give commands, make decisions, to regulate, restrain or curb, with the firm ability to enforce obedience to one's orders. The power of power, therefore, resides in its exercise to control and dominate the other party so they comply with the perpetrator's purpose.

Bullshit uses no strong-arm tactic—it is power ruling with the "consent" of the governed through "persuasion." It is the same persuasion by which big business justifies the pollution of the environment, covers up poor automobile engineering responsible for many deaths, and utility monopolies to justify their system of enormous profits. BS allows governments to "rationalize" racism and genocide, call Vietnam a "non-war," and nuclear plants "safe." Bullshit is a big factor in having made these organizations all powerful. They no longer serve the public; the public serves them. Like the magician who performs his illusions—now you "think" you see it, now you don't—the agile artificer skillfully bullshits you out of your power in the same sleight-of-hand/mouth/eye manner.

PRINCIPLE TWO

IN ANY STRUCTURED ORGANIZATION,
BULLSHIT WILL, MOST OFTEN START AT
THE TOP AND TRAVEL DOWNWARD.

Bullshit starts at the top where power resides. To
acquire power, retain it, and to enlarge upon it, one
must either rule by force or rule by persuasion, which
is mostly comprised of bullshit (creating a set of
impressions for other than the apparent motivation).
Bullshit is effective, efficient and the least expensive
way for the powerful to rule. The sheer "weight" of
their power—the general acceptance of authority, the
idea of their omnipotence and omniscience—added to
the "weight" of the media disseminating the "information," and laced with the applications of serious consequences if not followed, forces the bullshit of the powerful at the top down through the ranks.

The first clue to this principle developed when I was able to see
the relationship of authority to hierarchy. As I mentioned previously, I had always been aware of functioning under someone's
authority at all times, starting with members of my family and
extending to school teachers, community leaders, priests, nuns,
policemen, military, or city, state, and federal authorities. Eventually, I became aware that I had to constantly work through
distortion after distortion to arrive at the "truth." The process
began with my family who, I'm sure, were well-intentioned. It
may have been something as simple as having to go to bed at a
certain time (usually earlier than I wished) or eating the same
food together at supper time. Any opposition to the status quo
was rejected, usually in conjunction with the warning that I must
always respect and obey my elders. And since almost everyone
was older than I, it seemed I always had to do what someone else
wanted me to.

In reality, as I later found out, my obedience to authority was
for *their* good. In a family like mine that had ten children, there
would have been virtual anarchy if there were ten separate bed-
times, ten separate suppertimes, and no central authority. In
addition, my parents would have been worn to a frazzle with no

time left for their private use, leaving them "slaves" to the children. I'm not saying that if they had explained the situation "honestly" to me at that time I would have understood, but then again, I just might have. The result was that as an adult, I continued to accept authority unquestioningly, right or wrong, and found it difficult to appraise motives accurately. Consequently, I became excellent prey for bullshit.

In another instance, a friend carried a constant rage for her mother whom she felt sent her out into the world a "cripple." The well-intentioned mother had taught her to live a morally upstanding life; to be loyal, honest, to have integrity, to be a good friend, to work hard and to be sexually stringent. However, when the young lady entered the outside world and found it to be extensively immoral, or at least extremely contrary to the way she was taught, she was nearly devastated by a nervous breakdown. She has, fortunately, many years later, made the necessary adjustments, but the pain was enormous. Interestingly enough, she eventually chose to live as she had been taught; however, her lifestyle was supported by her own reasoning which adhered more closely to reality. In retrospect, she felt she could have accomplished the same thing sooner and more efficiently without much of the pain had her mother presented life to her "honestly" and "accurately." In gaining wisdom, the young lady also realized a mother's altruism may contain a core of selfishness which can lead to the easy way out; the use of BS. A key point, of course, was whether the mother was acting in ignorance or whether she was utilizing "morality" to control the daughter to simplify her own life.

In almost all cases the perpetrators create the image "that they know best what is good for you," and correct or not, they impose it on those with less power; the parent over the child, the community over the individual, the government over the public.

On very rare occasions when BS originates from the lower echelon, the power structure calls it crime and tries to punish it in some way. For example, if a geologist in an oil company did not convey accurate information as to where oil was located, and how much there was, he would face severe penalties from supervisors. However, once the geologist has conveyed accurate information to his superiors, they can distort the information to whatever extent it suits their purpose.

Recently, the public and government were made to believe there was an actual shortage of oil. As a consequence, costs, prices and profits were greatly affected. The oil companies presented a series of impressions to the public which said price increases were unavoidable. However, the billions of dollars of profit were so visible (and obscene) the oil companies felt they had to justify the profit to the public as well as the government. In all their public pronouncements, including extensive television commercials, they tried to "persuade" the audience that the profits were necessary to drill for "new" oil, oil more difficult to extract, so that we would be rescued from foreign domination by OPEC countries.

Although the oil companies were caught in illegal actions and prosecuted, the penalties were something like a flea biting an elephant. Big business knows it doesn't have to be accurate or "honest". They know very few laws can punish them. If any do get to court, even when the government does the prosecuting, they get tied up in the legal system of bullshit and may take years for final action. In the majority of cases, the actions are resolved in the company's favor anyway. Big business is a family apart, and unlike individuals or smaller companies who have to reconnoitre more directly with the IRS, the cops, the legislators, etc., they act autocratically.

To fully understand this principle, however, one must understand that in order to have become a top power in the first place, bullshit had to be the prime weapon. Later, we shall examine the use of "morality" in religion, propaganda in government, and advertising in business to show how BS delivered the power. But once the power was established, and to avoid the expensive and messy use of force, BS had to come into even more extensive use to keep things in control. Therefore, BS most often originates prior to and with power at the top, and consequently travels downward to the lower echelons.

PRINCIPLE THREE

WHEN A PERPETRATOR CAN'T BULLSHIT UP (VERTICALLY), HE WILL ACT IN A SIDEWAY OR DOWNWARD MANNER, TO THE ONE WITH LESS POWER.

Bullshit that makes an attempt to travel upwards is labeled by those at the top (the power structure) as crime, or at the least, lies which are prosecutable by law. However, one can BS someone on the same level or someone less strong or powerful without punishment because it can be made to stick even if force has to be employed. The reason middle or lower echelon people bullshit is that a portion of the power is better than nothing.

Flo Kennedy in "The Pathology of Oppression" points out that if someone cannot vent their anger and hostility vertically toward the party who is causing the pain, they will vent it horizontally to a peer, or downward to someone who is weaker, because they are well aware that those with the power are capable of punishing them with the loss of jobs, security, imprisonment, death, or in some other way. Quite often, the powerful don't have to take any action because the victims they dominate are already *intimidated* by the *fear* of such punishment. However, the victim's pent up anger and hostility must find an outlet. It doesn't just dissipate itself. It is unloaded horizontally to the person closest to the victim which is most likely to be his/her lover, wife, husband, or child. Studies of violent crime, for example, point out that most of the violent crime is committed by the poor and disadvantaged. Those same studies also point out that most of the victims are the same poor and disadvantaged people. In other words, victims are hurting other victims. It is not the poor hurting the rich, nor the weak hurting the strong.

The powerful isolate themselves by design, not only for the reason of status, but because it removes their person from imminent danger of violence. They have also designed it so that the potentially dangerous parties remain divided and violent toward each other while they monopolize the power and continue to rule unmolested. In addition, it allows them to perpetrate the same crimes of theft and violence while appearing "innocent," and without being prosecuted or incarcerated.

They make the rules. Whenever bullshit attempts to go from the bottom up, it doesn't happen for long because this is the stuff of which top honcho bullshitters have created as modern "no no" categories, labeled as crime, and persuaded society to punish as such. The people at the bottom instinctively know this; that is why so many turn to tyranny. A teenager, for example, may grab Grandma's bag rather than rob Chase Manhattan Bank because he lacks the ability to bullshit. The difference between tyranny and bullshit is, tyranny is grabbing the bag, and bullshit is conning her out of it. Whether it is tyranny or bullshit, it should be considered crime and equally punished, but it is not. The teenager, if caught, will go to jail. If Chase Manhattan utilizes bullshit, and steals the amount of the purse and much more, that is called "good business." For example, Chase Manhattan may steal the value of Granny's house which may be situated in a neighborhood that has been redlined by the bank. When attrition finally sets in and the neighborhood has decayed, the bank steps in, buys cheap and erects expensive housing or apartments which they sell or rent at even greater expense to Granny's grandchildren or someone else.

To feel powerless is intolerable; consequently, those on a lower rung must try to grab it whenever they can. However, there is an inherent danger. When the downward stress is too severe, the victim on the lower rung will turn the conflict into violence, and tyranny will prevail. As an example, a bus driver in New York's public transit system took to taking longer breaks at the end of the line than were allotted by the rules. To make up the time, he passed up passengers who had been waiting for long periods at the bus stop, and was surly with the rest. The passengers filed complaints with the management of the transit system. However, management could not fire him. They had to go to the union and file grievances. The union supervisor went to the bus driver who denied all charges. The supervisor gave him the benefit of doubt but kindly suggested he "cool it." And for a while, the driver modified his behavior until the incident was almost forgotten. Then he reverted back to his bad behavior. Again, more passengers filed complaints. This time, the supervisor called a meeting of all drivers and warned everyone that severe punishment would be forthcoming if anyone was caught mistreating passengers. He also withdrew several discretionary privileges they had earned.

The drivers, knowing the real culprit and angry as hell, "lined him up against the wall." The culprit once again denied all charges, and further, reminded them of their own complaints against the passengers. They commiserated for a while and dispersed. Although they too asked him to cool it, the culprit had successfully diverted the issue away from himself, removing the peer pressure.

But then came an unexpected turn. One day the driver chose to abuse a man twice his size who had a short temper. The huge man pulled the driver from the bus, beat him to a pulp, and calmly walked off. Someone called the police who questioned the passengers. They told the truth — the driver had abused and provoked the man — and when they could not (or would not) give a very good description of him, the police shrugged and left. Tyranny had triumphed. After the incident, the union supervisor suspended the driver for a few days, more to impress management and other bus drivers that the problem had been dealt with stringently, than to discipline the culprit.

On a different level, the Moral Majority illustrates this principle even more fully. The Moral Majority are not a new group, nor are their ideas recent. They are typical of the righteous throughout history who want to eliminate any opposing viewpoint in order to dominate. Recently, they have strongly turned to politics to effect their ends. In the 1980 presidential election, Reagan, desperate to rebound from the blow Nixon had dealt the Republican Party and needing all the support he could garner to beat Carter, implied to the Moral Majority that he would give them special consideration if elected. The office of the presidency, however, is such that it must try, or at least give the appearance, of being even-handed. In addition there are a number of real checks and balances in government that operate to limit the power of the president. As a consequence, the Moral Majority could not secure the degree of power they wanted from Reagan once he was elected, even if Reagan wished to give it. Taking another approach the Moral Majority directed their effort horizontally, and downward to the public. This was accomplished through intimidation, which the Moral Majority uses extensively. One of its key weapons has been to distort the image of the pro-abortionists and provoke guilt with such tag words as "murderers." In addition, they liken abortion and abortionists to death in the German concentration camps, or to other violent crime. The rhetoric of the Moral Majority has so inflamed a fringe element of society as to cause arson of abortion clinics, kidnapping of pro-abortion doctors, and other illegal acts.

Those who are most affected by the Moral Majority, however, are the poor and disadvantaged who are least able to bear the cost of children. The Moral Majority is not only economically conservative but reactionary. They spearhead opposition to any social help such as aid-to-the-dependent, welfare, food stamps, and other social programs. In their pro-life stance they do not suggest that if these unwanted children are born that the government financially support both the mother and child. Instead, they lobby and apply political pressure to cut off the little federal funds that go to pro-abortion organizations like the National Planned Parenthood which dispenses sexual information and abortion assistance. This is but one of the dichotomies of the "Right To Lifers"; they do not, for instance, oppose capital punishment, or violent death perpetrated in war, or death caused by alcohol, drugs, tobacco, and automobiles. It seems to be that either the forces of government or big business are too strong for the Moral Majority to oppose, or the Moral Majority may have a vested interest in big business, or their position is hypocritical. Whatever the reasoning, they have attempted to impose their will on poor, defenseless women to effect their righteous moral beliefs. More importantly, it is their way to control and dominate a large, potentially restless segment of the public. So, the Moral Majority having failed to bullshit upwardly for the power they desire, bullshit horizontally and downward to the defenseless and powerless.

There are, of course, rare instances when bullshit travels from the bottom up, but this is more exception to the rule and only reinforces it. For example, my mother was the sole boss of the household, and if necessary, ruled by force. Her word was the law. Therefore, I either obeyed or I had to circumvent it with bullshit. However, it first required that I BS horizontally.

During my youth, my Sunday afternoons were spent watching the most exciting performers and movies of the time at the Palace Theater in downtown Cleveland, Ohio. The Palace was everything my life was not — luxurious, opulent, regal. Its lobby was incredibly long with red carpet so thick it felt as if one were floating instead of walking. Sitting against both walls were enormous velvet couches, so soft one did not sit on them but gently melted into the folds. Above the couches hung a series of large, imposing pictures of regal personages and exotic places framed in gold. And at the end of the lobby stood a marble staircase that led from both sides into an auditorium of three tiers that contained plush red seats in the thousands.

For three weeks all I could think about was seeing Blackstone The Magician. The intensity was so all-consuming it was as if nothing else mattered. But my anticipation was shattered when my mother told me I had to take my sister Grace, 13, and my brother Nick, 7, to the theater with me. By the time they would be ready to go, it would blow my early lead for first position in line. The shows were so popular they sold out hours in advance. Worse, my mother gave me only enough money for carfare and admission for those under 12 years of age. My sister Grace was 13 and big for her age. However, my mother insisted we could get by. As we left for the theater, she gave us solemn warning to be back by five, or after the first complete show. Any violation would bring a severe beating.

The first obstacle was the bus driver. I told Nick and Grace to move to the rear of the bus immediately upon entering and that I would pay the fare. As I dropped the fare in the box, the driver tried to call Grace to the front. I insisted she was under twelve but that she was big for her age. Since I was blocking the entrance, the passengers who were anxious to get on, ridiculed the driver for picking on "kids." The driver was so embarrassed he allowed the incident to pass.

The next confrontation occurred with the ticket taker at the theater. I had instructed Nick and Grace to get as far into the theater as fast as possible before I gave him the tickets. Again, the ticket taker called Grace back but I argued strenuously. Fortunately, the backed up crowd whom I was blocking put pressure on him, and he relented.

Since we had come late and the theater was already sold out, we had to settle for seats way up in the third tier of the theater. The movie came on first and it was wonderful. It was an exotic adventure film that transported us across the world into a fantasy land. Then came the newsreel and a serial which lifted the festive spirit of the audience higher. The lights went up a little as the curtain closed over the screen. The audience made last minute changes for better seats, others rushed out to buy refreshments. Then the orchestra struck up the overture and the master of ceremonies announced the first live act. It was a dance team that moved with exceptional grace. The next act was a family of acrobats that performed feats on the trapeze as well as creating pyramidal forms of strength, with each standing astride the other's shoulder. Then came a unicycle act of performers who weaved in and out of each other's way and played basketball on the enormously high unicycles. And then with a flourish and fanfare, the MC announced Blackstone The Magician. Blackstone executed one astounding illusion after another. The audience was vociferous in its appreciation. At one point in the act, Blackstone asked for a volunteer to help out. Several people raised their hand and Blackstone selected one. The spotlight focused on the volunteer as he proceeded up the stairs onto the stage. Blackstone then performed several more illusions which included pulling a large loaf of bread out of the air, breaking it open and pulling a white rabbit from it that was so adorable the audience oooohed and awed. To my astonishment, Blackstone then *gave* the white rabbit to the volunteer as a reward. I just couldn't believe it. All of a sudden, I too had to have a white rabbit! My desire was so strong I wanted to fly over the railing and take it from him. At that moment, I decided that no matter what it took, I was going to volunteer and get my own rabbit.

The first problem was to move as close to the stage as possible. I gathered Nick and Grace and we moved to the second tier. Of course, we had to sit through another complete show. Nick was getting impatient so I used our carfare to buy him chocolate and popcorn. Grace reminded me that if we didn't leave right away we would face hell at home. I told her if she didn't shut up I would beat her. She pouted but kept quiet knowing my threat was not idle. The magic of the show took over once again with the time passing quickly. Of course, when Blackstone reached the point of the white rabbit, I poured every ounce of my being onto the stage. That moment passed and we made our next move to the back of the first tier, sitting through still another show. Nick was whining, Grace was terrified (my threats had escalated to death), but they obeyed. Nick was a bit more difficult because he was only seven and a baby. I sort of felt bad for him because I didn't have any more money for candy.

Finally, we moved to the first row of the theater, and not a moment too soon because this was the last show of the day. By this time, Nick was asleep in his seat and Grace was squirming in hers. But the magic moment came. When Blackstone asked for the volunteer, I jumped on my seat and shouted "Here I am Blackstone. I'll help!" His eyes rested in my direction. But lo and behold, he wasn't pointing at me but at Nick who was asleep! I woke Nick with a jolt, practically lifted him out of his seat, and pushed him toward the stage. The spotlight hit him and the audience roared with laughter. Nick had hair that stood up on his head, an overcoat that was two sizes too large for him, and a pair of untied brogans also much too large for him. I shoved him toward the stage. He was still in a daze. Blackstone did his tricks which Nick could not follow bringing more laughter. But then came the loaf of bread and the white rabbit. My heart stopped beating. I was oblivious to everything except Blackstone handing the white rabbit to Nick. As he came off the stage, I grabbed the rabbit and tucked him inside my coat. People close to me wanted to pet him but I put them off. Gradually, we found our way out of the theater and into the night.

Since I had spent our carfare, we had to walk home in the cold. Nick was shivering and Grace kept reminding me that we would be facing a beating. As we walked in the surrounding darkness, and with the rabbit firm against my heart, I was struck with guilt for the pain I would be causing Nick and Grace. I said to them, "When we get home, you two get behind me and let me talk to ma." The least I could do would be to take the first blows while they tried to escape.

As we walked in silence, I saw my father coming toward us. Again I instructed Nick and Grace to get behind me while I explained our situation to him. As soon as he got close enough, I held out the white rabbit and shouted, "Look pa, look what we won. Isn't it beautiful!" I went into the explanation so fast he couldn't get a word in edgewise. He gently reminded us we had done wrong and that mother was furious because the police and my other seven brothers and sisters were out looking for us. My father broke the silence as we continued along, and said to us, "When we get home, you all get behind me while I explain to your mother."

Upon entering the house, I could hear my mother's roar but I couldn't see her as we were trying to fit our three bodies behind my father. I did have the presence of mind, however, to hold the rabbit out so she could see it while my father was explaining. About the same time, the rest of the family was returning from the search, and they too had to hear the story and pet the rabbit. The family prevailed on my mother and we escaped punishment.

Encouraged by this victory I really became bold. I asked for permission to sleep downstairs in the kitchen (it was so large we did everything there), on the couch next to the potbellied stove, so I could put coal in the stove for heat so the rabbit would not be cold. I was being bold because no one slept downstairs; it was an iron rule set by my mother. However, the family prevailed once again. It's hard to win any battle when there are 11 to 1 against you, and as dominant as my mother was, she was no exception and granted the O.K. reluctantly. The family dispersed to the bedrooms, and as I lay on the couch I could hear the rustle of the rabbit in the box. The stove was aglow with a warm red color. I got drowsy. I fought to keep my eyes open. The next thing I knew I was awakened by the cold. I looked around and saw that the fire in the stove was out. I ran to the rabbit which lay stiff in the box. I brought him close to my heart and caressed him vigorously, but there was no sign of life. Suddenly, the tears flowed from my eyes, and I was struck with horror. I was a murderer! I had killed him! I couldn't move. I must have been frozen in that position for at least two hours before my dad came down. He was usually the first to awake. He asked me what I was doing and I blurted out through my sobs that I had killed the rabbit, that I was a murderer! My father tried to calm me but my sobs grew louder waking the rest of the family. As each one came into the kicthen I had to repeat the story, and the more they tried to comfort me, the louder I sobbed.

Finally, my father explained to me that God had come to take the rabbit; that ultimately God comes for us all. But that it was not bad. The rabbit was going to heaven which was the most beautiful of all places. And when the rabbit got to heaven, he would be peaceful, happy, and unbelievably content. It was the perfect place. More importantly, the rabbit would be serving God's wonderful purpose of doing good. But there was a condition. We had to bury the rabbit so that he would have a safe trip, and we had to say a prayer for him so that he would be blessed. I looked around and saw the others nodding their heads in agreement. My mother was silent and the fact that she was not recriminating made me know she too was affected.

My dad found a shovel, took me by the hand, and we went to a nearby field. As he dug a hole, I held the rabbit gently and stroked him. We put the rabbit in the hole and my father shovelled the dirt over him until it formed a mound. He then found two sticks and made a cross which he stuck above the grave. We then said a prayer together asking God for a safe trip and special consideration. My father then prompted me to ask for God's forgiveness, although I was not guilty or bad. It was to let God know I was humble. I made my last request and we walked home in silence. Nonetheless, I still felt like a murderer for many weeks, but found comfort in the thought that the white rabbit was safe and happy.

This is a long way around to illustrating an exception to the rule, but it is appropriate because it also brings into play the fact that BS, most often starts from the top anyway, and though I was able to mitigate it in this instance, it still took more BS from the top to assuage my guilt. It had all come back to where it began. I manipulated the power structure for a moment but it would not really change, nor would I necessarily be able to continue my BS toward the top in the future. The magic of a white rabbit is rare and so are the instances when one can BS from the bottom up.

PRINCIPLE FOUR

WHERE TWO EQUAL BULLSHIT POWERS EXIST, THE ORIGINAL POWER MOST OFTEN DOMINATES.

A bullshit power is a power which uses all its resources to be "persuasive." This may be accomplished through public relations which will bias public opinion in one's favor. The BS power also utilizes the complexity and the high cost of the legal system to cause confusion and attrition, and may attempt one form of bribery or another. Most often, the defensive position rather than the offensive position carries a greater inherent strength, as it forces the opponent (the attacker) to fight on the other's turf.

The term "bullshit power" does not imply that power is not real, or that it doesn't have force, or doesn't rule; it simply means that when a power controls or dominates by "persuasion," it is using bullshit to retain or enlarge upon its power. When two such powers are in conflict, unless force is used, the original power will retain its dominance.

A parent will create the illusion for a child that he has a choice between cookies or playing, knowing full well the cookies are irresistible to the child and will be his choice. The parent is controlling and dominating the child with "persuasion" — by trickery — because the parent does not want the child to play at that particular time. However, should the child resist the trickery and choose playing, a standoff might occur; that is, unless the parent goes back on his word which will turn the proposition to the child into a lie that carries other attendant risks. And should the child "flatter" the parent, winning the cookie and the opportunity to play, he is definitely an exception to the rule.

A parent may also use "persuasion" in the form of "guilt," such as accusing the child of some failure: "You misbehaved and disappointed me." If the child counters by creating "guilt" in the parent by saying "And you're never around when I need you," a standoff is possible. In both situations, however, the parent is most likely to win because he has the more persuasive weapons, the ultimate being the implied threat of withholding love.

At one time a man could rule on the sheer basis of the male-dominated tradition. In marriage and family, his word was law: his need of "persuasion" minimal, if at all. The courts, business, and religious institutions, over many years, backed the male so insistently, the BS became institutionalized. In this context, the wife, in order to escape sex had to feign "illness," or some urgent matter, such as the care of an infant. If the wife was successful with this tactic she might create a standoff for a while. However, since the advent of women's liberation, the male has been forced to use "persuasion" to a far greater degree. Sex is no longer automatic. A wife may state her tiredness or lack of desire and make it stick. If the husband uses force as he may have been wont to do in the past, he may have to face the law, charged with rape. If the husband tries to unload too much of the family responsibility onto the wife, she can possibly cite her involvement in the community, or the fact that she works part-or-fulltime and is also a breadwinner. Therefore, the male, lacking automatic obedience from his wife, has had to go to the use of, what for him, are "new" techniques of persuasion. For example, the husband might create pseudo-guilt by accusing his wife of neglecting the children or the house. If she should want to continue her education, he may accuse her of selfish desires. The conflict is not new, of course, and the battle of the sexes ever since Adam and Eve has always involved subterfuge. What is new is the necessity for the male's increased use of BS. Yet, despite the change, the male, having once been vested with power, still retains his residual potency. And although challenged in his dominance, he still remains so because he was there first, and because he still has the advantage—more weapons of "persuasion."

In a business situation, Scott Paper Company produced a disposable diaper to challenge Proctor and Gamble's Pampers. On the battlefield, their common weapon of persuasion was advertising. The full battlefield, of course, included marketing, distribution, sales, and the respective abilities to secure shelf space in the nation's supermarkets; both had sufficient resources to manufacture the product; both had equal access to the finest creative personnel to produce the commercials.

Once the battle had begun, however, it became quite evident very early on that Scott Paper was no match for Proctor and Gamble in this instance. Not only had Proctor and Gamble situated its product strongly, having been there first, but they unleashed a blitzkreig of advertising. They literally saturated the air waves with commercials. Proctor and Gamble was keenly aware that the quantity of air time was crucial to the battle, and being the world's largest advertiser, they had economic resources to pour into the fray to insure victory. Subsequently, Scott Paper withdrew its diapers and has never reentered the market. Later, Johnson and Johnson, another competitor, entered the market with a diaper some thought to be superior to Proctor and Gamble's and has subsequently been able to hold on in the competition. However, it has in no way challenged Proctor and Gamble's dominance and remains a distant second.

On a broader level, how we perceive power is a big factor in being able to deal with it. Quite often the power of power lies not so much with the power itself, but in what we "think" is power. Flo Kennedy, a Feminist and Civil Rights activist, tells the story of a Black woman who went to a white dentist who was hung over. First he cut her gums, then he sliced her tongue causing her to rent and spit. The dentist suddenly stopped, aware that this Black woman had a grip on his testicles. Afraid that he might become a soprano, and not having had instruction from the college of dentistry as to what to do when a patient grabs your balls, he said: "What is this?" She looked him straight in the eye and said: "We're not going to hurt each other, are we doctor?" Flo Kennedy describes this balancing of power as the testicular method. She points out that every institution has a testicular area, usually involved in money or public exposure. The double whammy is a press conference focusing on budget, and that a squeeze in the testicular area can almost guarantee a change of heart and mind. However, one has to see power accurately and cut through the deception before one can "squeeze."

In government, the Justice Department is supposed to act in support of, and in unity with, other federal departments such as

41

the Federal Trade Commission, the Federal Bureau of Investigation, the Securities Exchange Commission, etc. Unfortunately, this is not quite the way it works. Ideally, the system is supposed to work in this manner: the President sets the policy, then selects the heads of the departments, who in turn convey the tone and the spirit the President indicates to the bureaucracy to be acted on. In practice, however, these departments are individual bureaucracies which inevitably follow and obey their own center of power which may or may not be in line with the President's wishes. Nixon, during Watergate, came to this conclusion a little too late when he tried to bend the CIA, FBI, and the Justice Department to his purpose of the coverup. Ultimately, these departments of government, concerned with self-survival in the Watergate scandal disobeyed "orders." In reality, the departments are often not only in competition with one another, they are in competition with central authority. So, what the public perceives as a monolithic power is often "pockets of power" which have a tendency to neutralize each other.

In addition to the intercine conflict, when the government pursues private companies in antitrust suits or other serious situations like crime, it will often lose because the BS resources of the big companies, which are sometimes larger than sovereign countries, are superior to the "pockets of power" of the government. For example, the Justice Department brought an FTC suit against AT&T in which it sought to break up the Bell System, including sale of all 23 operating companies and Western Electric. As part of the settlement, however, the government granted AT&T permission to enter the fast growing, more lucrative data communications market, of which many other companies wanted AT&T kept out.

A cynical observer says, "It is difficult to judge the winner in legal settlements of this type. Such deals are like labor negotiations: both sides must be able to tell their constituents that, all things considered, they won." And William McGovern, chairman of MCI Telecommunications Corporation, one of Bell's main competitors, has said, "It was just a slap on the wrist."

The irony is that under any circumstances, Bell would have come out the winner. While one agency of the government was prosecuting AT&T, another government agency was giving them every rate increase requested, allowing AT&T to show the highest net profit of any business in the world!

The case of the Justice Department versus IBM, a twelve-year-old suit charging IBM with monopoly in mainframe computers, was bogged down in legal wrangles so long, technological advances dated the substance of the case and made it meaningless. Since IBM is not a monopoly sanctioned by the government as is AT&T, they must use another form of persuasion. Therefore, the IBMs of the world work on the idea of attrition by court involvement. They literally wear the plaintiff out with time and expense. The IBM/Justice Department case was originally filed in 1969. It went to trial in 1975. It was resolved in IBM's favor in 1981! The government originally estimated it would take 60 days to present its case. It took three years. In addition, just before the settlement, the Justice Department was on its third lead counsel. Robert H. Bork, a Yale law professor has dubbed the case, "the antitrust division's Vietnam." All in all, it took 12 years in court with IBM finally winning.

The bottom line is that the public is being bamboozled. What appears to be a battle between private and public interest is in reality simply a *show* performed for the public. In almost all instances, the public winds up paying for the wasteful and inefficient efforts, as well as all increased costs. Unlike theater, where the protagonist and antagonist seem to progress toward a resolution of conflict, "bullshit power" knows that before the show even begins, everything will remain the same: the original power will most often retain its dominance against the aggressor.

UNTIL ONE BULLSHITTER THREATENS
THE POWER OF ANOTHER, A
CONSPIRACY WILL MOST LIKELY EXIST
BETWEEN THEM AND AGAINST A THIRD
PARTY.

As long as individual territories remain defined and
each person, company, or country stays within its
proper boundaries, a cooperation can exist, often in
conspiracy against a third party. However, when a
transgression occurs, it becomes each entity for
itself, with public opinion becoming a large factor in
determining the outcome.

As long as individual territories remain defined, and each person, company or country stays within the proper boundaries
agreed upon, (articulated or presumed), a cooperation between
bullshitters will most likely exist, often in conspiracy against a
third party.

It is inherent in the nature of relationships that a constant
power struggle occur. It may be subtle and benign, or it may be
violent, but in all cases it is there. On a personal level it is
between husband and wife, which is a microcosm of the eternal
male/female conflict. At first, the physical alone was sufficient
to determine who dominated; man was bigger and stronger so he
prevailed. Society then reinforced man's domination legally, reli-
giously, politically, socially and economically; he was well nigh
invulnerable.

One of the few ways women were able to create a semblance of
a balance of power in certain situations was through the use of
bullshit. Women literally had to fool, outsmart and deceive the
male. However, despite being dominant, the male, too, has
resorted to BS, and in recent times increased its use. I deal more
thoroughly with this view in the upcoming chapter, "Lovers &
Spouses." The point for now is that bullshit was mutual even
though it was more of a necessity for women.

With the advent of children in a marriage, however, a major
change occurs. Totally helpless, children imbue parents with a
sense of enormous power; so much power, in fact, it is sufficient

to satisfy both their needs. So, although the basic male/female conflict may continue, it becomes far more muted because their focus is now on the power exercised over the children. Where they once were mainly adversaries, they now become conspirators. This is, of course, an oversimplification and may be considered extreme. However, many wish to see the family in idealized terms — togetherness, unity, loyalty, love — and refuse to see clearly, or admit to underlying tensions, all of which tend to obscure base motivations.

Once a husband and wife mute their opposition to each other and direct their focus on to the children, it becomes incumbent upon the child who is basically powerless to gradually acquire it through opposition to the parents. Sometime this is done fairly, honestly, equitably, through direct communication and compromise, but very often it is done with bullshit. And though the appearance of cooperation may exist between parent and child, underlying the relationship are adversarial tensions. And when either party wishes to avoid the adversarial and take, for what is at the moment, the path of least resistance, they go to bullshit. This is particularly true of parents. With children, it may be they have no other alternative.

Many parents of this generation, involved with their own self-fulfillment or other self-interest, do not want the work nor the stress of imposing their will on children. Consequently, they utilize deception. The dichotomy of their morality, for example, was strongly challenged by the 60s generation and exposed. The point is, that where the struggle originally existed between husband and wife, it shifts with the advent of children. Adversaries become conspirators, and the bullshit once exercised against each other now becomes focused against their children. But should the parents conflict too strenuously with each other, mother or father will try to make an ally of the children so as to oppose the other partner with greater support and strength. A father may demand and order his son to mow the lawn. It may be a direct power order, it may be done by imposed guilt, or may be accomplished by some other method. If he and his wife are unified, the son may have no alternative but to mow the lawn. However, if the wife is angry with her husband for some breach, she may, in conspiracy with her son, pay someone else to mow the lawn and simply not tell the husband/father how the lawn got mowed. They simply leave him with the impression that the lawn was mowed by the son as ordered. Children, on the other hand, often band together in forbidden situations against the parents, and sensing one parent's dissatisfaction with the other, may easily include that parent in a conspiracy; together thev mislead or deceive the remaining parent.

In a different area, owners of major league baseball teams banded together to virtually keep baseball players "slaves," albeit well paid slaves. The rules were worked out in such a manner that baseball players were drafted out of college and sent to a minor league club controlled by the owners. The baseball players, as a consequence, were kept confined to a particular club, in a system that served as a prison. The players could not, on their own, put their services up for sale in a "free market." If they did not play for their original owners, the only alternative was not to play in the major leagues at all. Conversely, when the owners decided to get rid of a player they either traded him away to another owner, or they fired him. The owners were "legally" allowed to function in this manner because they were exempted from the antitrust laws by Congress. Baseball owners are the only exception to this law in the country. All in all, the owners were in conspiracy with each other, and the conspiracy was reinforced and extended by Congress.

But as the baseball players organized into a union, and gained strength they gradually began to correct the imbalance of power. They increased minimum wages, created a pension fund and accrued a number of other benefits. Eventually, the crucial issue of "free agency" arose, that is, the players wanted to be able to sell their services on a free market basis. They wanted to be able, after they had delivered the agreed upon services of their original contracts, to put their services up for bid by all owners. Eventually, the player's union broke the stranglehold and forced the owners to compete with each other for top quality baseball players who qualified for free agency.

If we introduce an economic factor—winning teams draw more people which increases the value of the franchise—we have the final factor that divided the owners. Once the bidding began for free agency players, the price of these players went sky high. Within the last few years, for example, a player like Dave Winfield of the New York Yankees was able to secure a twenty million dollar, ten year contract! Instead of the owners continuing to band together by quietly maintaining an agreed upon ceiling on salaries, individual owners breached the "silent" understanding between themselves and wooed certain star players. In effect, the owners encroached on each other's territory. Ironically in the baseball strike of 1981, the owners, in trying to make free agency more stringent, were in effect asking the baseball players to protect them against their fellow owners!

Standard procedure, of course, by both sides during the strike was to wage an intensive press campaign to win the support of sports fans to their side. The intent was to have the public apply pressure so that one or the other capitulated on the issues.

Although the baseball owners gained a slight modification of free agency from the strike action, most clubs still engage in it heavily. Those that utilize free agency frequently, of course, make hay in the press by presenting the image they "care" for their fans and want to bring them a winner at all costs!

In the more basic product and service industries such as steel, automobiles and transportation, the principle works in this manner: before the labor unions came along, big business had a monopoly on power which was, to a great extent, originally secured with bullshit. It was based on THE BIG BULLSHIT ILLUSION of "economic necessity," and "economic progress," (see chapter, "Bullshit in Business"), and was reinforced in the general public by constant exposure of their message and philosophy in the media. Ultimately, it became part of the foundation and was embedded and reflected in every institution of the system. The balance of power was so inequitable that the formation of unions was inevitable.

As the unions gained in strength they were not only able to defend themselves, but they were able to cause severe economic damage. As a consequence, they were allowed to share the power with Capital. But as the unions became institutionalized, like all institutions, leaders of the union had to BS their own constituents to maintain their leadership, in effect, corrupting the organization. They no longer serve the members; members serve them.

Eventually, as labor and capital achieved a balance of power, they now entered into a conspiracy against a third party. In this case they entered into a conspiracy against the public. The union goes through every appearance of fighting management for higher wages and benefits, etc. Capital gives every appearance of opposing demands. Both parties know, however, that capital will eventually give into the demands of the union. In turn, capital will raise prices that cover the cost of labor's demands, and in addition, raise it further to assure their profit. Capital will then pass the entire cost on to the consumer.

In the meantime, labor leaders report to their members that they have won; management reports to its stockholders they have won. And the public which is imprisoned by the need of their services or products know they have lost — they are paying for all the increases. In the "adversarial" battle between labor and capital, labor did not subtract from capital's profit; in fact, capital gained. All in all, labor and management leaders, showing well to their constituents, maintain their power and increase it in the process.

Ultimately, power aligns itself with other power. They will co-exist as long as there is no encroachment by either party on the other's territory. In fact, they are most likely to form a conspiracy against a third party. Quite often, the third party is the very source of their original power — the worker, the consumer, the party member, the public.

PRINCIPLE SIX

THE GREATER THE POWER, THE GREATER THE NEED TO BULLSHIT TO MAINTAIN IT.

A "police state," always on the alert is extremely costly to maintain. Also, the logistics required by the minority to dominate the majority are impossible to maintain for any length of time without the cooperation of the governed. Therefore, persuasion in the form of BS is the least expensive and the most effective instrument in creating the proper response among the governed.

Over 400 years ago, Machiavelli raised the question of whether a head of state should use force or persuasion to execute his designs. He concluded that the element of force, or the ability to apply force, was an essential element necessary to dominate and rule. He says, "Entreaty succeeds ill, and accomplishes nothing; but when they can depend on their own strength and are able to use force, they rarely fail. Thus it comes about that all armed prophets have conquered and unarmed ones failed; for besides what has already been said, the character of people varies, and it is easy to persuade them of a thing, but difficult to keep them in persuasion. And so it is necessary to order things so that when they no longer believe, they can be made to believe by force." However, a little later on, he modifies his position saying, "Man must either be caressed or else annihilated; they will revenge themselves for small injuries, but cannot do so for great ones; the injury, therefore, that we do to a man must be such that we need not fear his vengeance. But by maintaining a garrison instead of colonies, one will spend much more, and consume all the revenues of that state in guarding it, so that acquisition will result in a loss, besides giving much greater offence, since it injures everyone in that state with the quartering of the army on it, which being an inconvenience felt by all, everyone becomes an enemy, and these are enemies which can do mischief, as, though beaten, they remain in their homes. In every way, therefore, a garrison is as useless as colonies are useful." In other words, force alone is not sufficient to rule or keep the peace.

Yet, observing the world situation today, it would seem that the capacity to use force is still the "ultima ratio regum"—the final argument of sovereigns: Jews against Arabs, Arabs against Arabs, civil war in Latin American countries, Russia against its dissidents, France against its colonies and England the same, to name a few. It seems that force is as universal today as it ever was in the past. However, if we go beyond appearances we shall find that this impression is no longer accurate. Dating from the time the United States dropped the atomic bomb on Japan, or since the rapid development of technology in general, the super powers have just about been excluded from engaging in the use of force on each other directly. In addition, they have had to mediate many of the conflicts in other parts of the world. The two most prominent technologies which have made these changes imperative are nuclear energy and the incredible development of communications.

Twentieth-century development has, for the first time in history, required world power to act consciously in and upon an undivided world theater. Only following World War I did radio, and later television, come to blanket most, if not all of the earth. Now, the world lives in the presence of and with the consciousness of events in most of Asia, Africa, and South America, or even with conditions in great parts of Europe and North America. Contrast this condition with the past by skimming the output of our electronic and printed media for a short period and you can see instantly, right as it is happening, graphic images of starvation in Africa and India, genocide in Asia, rebellion in

Poland, terrorism in Germany, Italy and France, war in the Falkland Islands, Iranians running through the streets mad with hate of America while they hold our people hostage, the bombing of Lebanon by the Jews, and massacre in Beirut, or assassination in the United States. As Marshall McLuhan has shown, the world has become a global village.

But technology has brought an even greater change. Until recently, it was thought that war could be limited or "contained" within isolated countries or geographic regions. In the later twentieth-century, few make that assumption. Brush-fire wars anywhere can escalate into roaring world-wide disaster. Almost nostalgically one thinks of the Franco-Prussian War of 1870, in that happy Victorian century when one nation could make war on its neighbor while surrounding countries remained ceremoniously neutral. In 1914, the United States watched the unexpected outbreak of World War I with the strong conviction that it was not responsible for it and with the ill-founded conclusion that it was not and ought not be involved. National power holders did not then consider themselves responsible in whole or in part for chaotic situations outside their balliwick. But that attitude has changed forever more. It is now imperative that super powers mediate these conflicts lest they escalate to where they must involve each other in direct use of force. It is universally accepted today that should direct warfare occur among the superpowers it would eventually lead to the use of intercontinental rockets that would destroy the world. Everyone knows there would be no victors and no world to rule. Ironically, the incredibly destructive power of technology has brought an uneasy "peace" to the super powers. At the least, it has ruled out the likely use of force between them in any kind of direct combat. Smaller powers may engage each other with force, a super power may engage a weaker power with force, but no longer can a super power engage another super power with force. Consequently, the battlefield has had to shift to another area. Of necessity, the primary focus today is now on the battle for the mind of the world. This is not a new battle, of course, for it has been going on for centuries. It has just become more imperative. And long before it was an international necessity, mind control was an essential element used internally within each country to keep citizens in control and persuaded that their leaders and philosophy was the best.

Machiavelli noted that ecclesiastical principalities in his time were acquired either by ability or by fortune but were maintained without either, for they were sustained by ancient religious customs, which were so powerful and of such quality, that they kept their princes in power in whatever manner they proceeded and lived. He says, "These princes alone have states without defending them, have subjects without governing them, and their states not being defended, are not taken from them; their subjects not being governed do not resent it, and neither think nor are capable of alienating themselves from them. Only these principalities, therefore, are secure and happy, but as they are upheld by higher causes, which the human mind cannot attain to, I will abstain from speaking of them; for being exalted and maintained by God, it would be the work of a presumptuous and foolish man to discuss them." In other words, "God" and/or "higher moral principle" (a form of bullshit in my estimation), not only created an inner strength that kept the principalities unified, but allowed for a temporal accumulation that was powerful enough to dominate all other powers at that time. The Christian ideology that Machiavelli describes which unified the ecclesiastical states was also appealing enough to be spread around the world by propaganda. As a matter of fact, the word propaganda originated with the catholic church which sent missionaries everywhere to disseminate its dogma.

Organized propaganda consists primarily in the delivery of words or symbols by radio, television, newspapers, books, magazines, posters, or talk carried on by agents. It can become effective only when it energizes action in a foreign country, when it stirs up political approval of or opposition to policies and power holders the sending country likes or dislikes. With increased effectiveness, it can perhaps induce armed revolt. Almost every substantial power in the world uses propaganda to some extent, if only to induce support for its policies, both externally as well as internally.

Propaganda can run the entire range from offering legitimate popular presentation of a country's point of view to stimulating outright subversion or undermining the receiving country's system of order. In the hands of skillful operators, the propaganda instrument may have substantial effect. This is usually accomplished over a long period of time, though it may, depending on conditions, cause immediate results.

Internally, particularly in totalitarian countries where repression and force is ever present and fear dominates, the core idea of the system must be constantly sold to the people under its control, or it will perish. It must be acceptable, and have the kind of appeal that gives the system an attractiveness above and beyond its negative qualities. It must encourage and motivate those in control to obey without force, if possible. Even in a democratic country where freedom is permitted, similar conditions must prevail. If it is absent, for example, a policeman may be able to keep a juvenile gang in check, but it will be only for as long as he is on the spot. The moment he is gone an anarchic juvenile will stop nowhere; plate-glass windows have been smashed on the streets of New York, old men have been beaten to death in Brooklyn parks, youngsters and other people have been stabbed or assaulted "just for kicks."

Most individuals have a high degree of internal restraint based on the system of ideas and morals in which they were brought up or to which they agree. Power holders know this; hence the concern with the system of ideas and morals. To extend their power beyond the sweep of the fist, they must foster a situation in which the people within their scope of their power act predictably, follow instructions, and maintain a degree of order. If need be, of course, order can in limited measure be produced by force. A mother knows that in the case of ultimates she can spank her smaller children. However, she can do this only occasionally; domestic order must hold together most of the time without that resort. Because of this, as well as because of moral conviction, she tries to instill principles of obedience, consideration, regard for orderly life. So, in different application, does every power holder in great or small affairs. This, of course, is not to say that what the power holder espouses is right, or in the best interests of the one being controlled.

The reality is that no matter how the core idea may be clothed, or whatever it is called — religion, government, morality — it is there because it maintains a status quo of power which originally became power by virtue of a lot of bullshit. For example, institutions, or any power holder usually claim to act under some authority or mandate. But the source claimed by absolute authority usually is not reachable — or, at all events, not readily available for consultation. Their word alone attests where they got power, and what they are authorized to do.

In earlier centuries power holders familiarly claimed a mandate from God. Genghis Khan, whose thirteenth-century empire covered much of Europe and Asia, did so; he claimed God had given him the entire earth — all resistence was contumacious and criminal rebellion. Virtually all kings, princes, and princelings, down to the end of the eighteenth-century — some throughout the nineteenth — asserted divine right. Absolutists find it convenient to claim a mandate from God — few, if any, are in a position to disprove or get an effective ruling on the point. And where divine right leaves off, secular, political, or economic authority or mandate picks up. And once power is secured in this manner, other bullshit is created to maintain it. In fact, it must be created. It is very much like having to tell a second lie to cover up the first lie. Bullshit must also accompany the use of force. During the Crusades, it was the idea of Christianity that lent support and thrust to the violence. People "willingly" killed others, and in the process were killed themselves because they felt God was on their side; that their cause was righteous. And until the American public had worked through its "patriotism" and opposed the war in Vietnam, thousands of American lives, along with many Orientals, were lost fighting the "menace" of communism.

The latter is an example of leaders having to act in what Adolph Berle describes as a "field of responsibility." That is, power must seem to participate in a "dialogue" with its constituents, and act as if in accordance with its mandate. As long as American leadership was able to persuade the public that war in Vietnam was necessary, it received support. When the "persuasion" broke down, leaders were removed from office, and general support of the public was withdrawn. The "dialogue," or what was passing for dialogue, lost its effectiveness in direct proportion to the loss of credibility of its leaders; news reporters kept revealing discrepancies between what they said and the facts. Berle says, "Recognition of the field of responsibility and the organization of an orderly dialogue between it and the power holders are, precisely, the qualities of democracy. A dictatorship does not admit its responsibility, does not, at least in form, accept a dialogue as important, and seeks to control its functioning as completely as it can. Even when the dictator does that, he nevertheless accepts its existence. He cannot do otherwise. He carries on a dialogue through his secret police and his propaganda people, rather than through argument; but the dialogue is there all the same. The feelings and emotions within the field are reported to him by his spies or his police rather than through open argument and expression of views. His answers may take the form of repression, of public announcement, of propaganda, or of measures designed to alleviate discontent or please his adherents, even though he declines to acknowledge interest in the views to which he responds. Where there is also an institutional means of dialogue, he may, outside that framework, use indirect discourse. Even a president of United States reads and reacts to opinion polls." In other words, power, no matter how absolute, must keep its constituents "persuaded" if it is to continue to rule. If it is successful, word alone is effective with little force or compulsion. It then has "authority," actual as well as formal. If it does not, its power is reduced; it must use compulsion, with immense waste of effort and usually with continually diminishing effectiveness. In a democratic state, the next election may displace him. In a non-democratic state, he may be eliminated by growing power combinations built up against him by his rivals or by men who fear for their own safety.

Power, quite often, has a way of lining up with other power. The power holders have more of a propensity for each other than for the source of their power. The individual, whether he be worker, consumer, party member, or citizen, always seems to wind up as the adversary. Therefore, he must be tamed—controlled, directed, motivated and made obedient—to the power holders. Although, as a group they have the power to topple its leaders (which the power holders know and fear), they are kept duped. Like a ferocious animal that has been tamed, they remain quiescent as long as they are fed (some are fed better than others), and they are not threatened with extinction. The sheer size of their mass and the infinite variety of personalities, however, demand that it must bullshit them. The interest of the masses must be kept focused on what the power holders want them to believe—must create the proper appearances—a show, a conflict, a rhetoric, a symbol—to divert masses away from the power holder's true motivation—more power.

Some would say that bullshit is more desirable than force in maintaining an orderly society. I don't hold with either position, but force, although brutal, at least has an honesty in its directness. Power and bullshit however, seem to have a symbiotic relationship; it is doubtful whether one can exist without the other. In many cases, power is like the king in the fable, "The Emperor's New Clothes," in which the king is made to believe he is wearing clothes, although naked, by the praise and flattery of his "loyal" subjects. The King's illusion is shattered by one solitary subject either courageous or foolish enough to actually point out his nakedness. Quite often, power is more bullshit than it is true power; its impotence is simply disguised.

Whether it is a simple matter of numbers—there are always far more subjects than rulers, tenants than landlords, workers than management, consumers than businesses—that seem to make

54

bullshit necessary for great powers, or whether it is inherent in people as a group to need it for a sense of well-being, I cannot say. I do know that wherever great power exists it must inevitably use bullshit to maintain itself.

PRINCIPLE SEVEN

IN ANY STRUCTURED ORGANIZATION, OR WHERE A HIERARCHY EXISTS, BULLSHIT WILL AUTOMATICALLY BE KEPT TO A MINIMUM AT THE LOWER ECHELONS.

Because punishment for inaccuracy is extremely severe for the middle and lower echelon in a hierarchy, a stringent control is maintained that minimizes distortion of information within this group. In contrast, the higher one goes in the structure, the greater the probability of BS, if for no other reason than personal political security.

Whenever you have a stringent pecking order, which is common to all hierarchies, you will invariably have little bullshit from the lower echelons. This is true for two reasons. The first is because matters of imposed loyalty are involved. As the parties are generally well known to each other by their proximity, and as the facts and character in most circumstances are generally more well known, there is most often, less room for bullshit. Also, when caught in bullshit, the penalty may be physically as well as emotionally severe, with the loss of respect and possible ostracism from the group.

If your upbringing was anything like mine, then you know that lying was dealt with severely. My mother would not only ask direct questions but insist I look into her eyes when answering. For her, the eyes were an infallible lie detector. Whether there was anything to her method or not, it none-the-less invariably brought the truth. And it wasn't that my mother didn't understand the childish imagination that can be so wonderful, or childish ignorance—not knowing better—because she made allowances for these responses. Where she came down heavily was in the stating of an untruth; knowing the facts and stating otherwise. And for this, the punishment could be spanking, denial of privileges, and most humiliating, shame among the rest of the family which could result in semi-ostracism. It was not uncommon among ten children to "blow the whistle" on each other in the power struggle that was constantly active. In addition, my parents had their own spy network outside the home. Any neighbor or relative—aunts, uncles, cousins—could report misbehavior or lack of truth and almost always be believed over the child. Although I and other children got angry, or even felt betrayed in some instances, there was no stigma attached to a person informing in this system. You just knew that if you lied, you were on your own, and if caught, you would have to suffer the consequences. This system didn't eliminate lying altogether, but I can attest that it certainly cut down on the number of incidences of lying. As a result, we either stayed honest or we tried bullshit.

If I had an errand to do and was ordered not to stop any place, I would run to complete the errand, and with the extra time gained, chat with my friends on the corner. Then I would run home. The errand was thus completed in the time allotted for it. The impression my mother had, however, was that I had obeyed her orders. Because I did not raise her suspicions, she did not ask questions directly, and I did not have to lie. In another instance, if I did not attend church services as I was instructed to do, I would minimally stop by the church, pick up some of the literature dispensed, and upon returning home make sure my mother got it, giving her the impression I had attended the services. No questions asked, no lies given.

However, even this behavior was kept to an absolute minimum because the *risk* of getting caught was so great. More effective in minimizing BS was the fact that we were so intimidated and frightened of the consequences, we put stringent limitations on *ourselves*! And if we were accompanied by another person—a brother, sister, cousin—chances are it would be ruled out altogether because we might be informed on. We literally were our brother's keeper; we were responsible for each other. And, if you knew of a breach and didn't report it, you were as guilty as the party committing it, and were punished, too!

I remember going through great pains to always impress my mother with "honesty" and "goodness." I was so effective I was able to buck some of the adults who informed on me. My mother just could not reconcile the possibility of misbehavior in someone who was so consistently obedient, helpful and constructive in most every other situation.

On the other hand, when we viewed adults, we were able on many occasions to see and expose their duplicity. When challenged, their arrogant response was "Don't do as we do; do as we say." It caused resentment and confusion but nonetheless we had to accept it. They were the power.

In business similar procedures prevail, albeit more sophisticated. However, the penalty may be more severe. If the geologist we spoke of previously is talking to his boss at an oil company like Mobil Oil, for example, he is apt to be very precise about all the facts concerning where the oil is in any region, and how it can best be drilled, especially and as long as his pay check reflects reward for accuracy and honesty, and punishment for sloppy or misrepresented research is perhaps loss of his job and being blackballed. Therefore, in addition to respect, food and shelter, one's total security is at stake.

Essentially, two important factors operate to keep bullshit at a minimum on the lower levels in a hierarchy. The first factor is that those at the top are the ones who set all of the rules by which the others function. The second factor is that most people in the hierarchy are concerned with the security of their job, and are intent on advancing up the scale; as a consequence, they are generally frightened to rock the boat, are easily intimidated, and prefer to conform than rebel.

Not only does top management set the rules of the game, they go to extreme lengths to isolate themselves from the rank and file. Despite the destructive effects of the "enclave" syndrome (isolating themselves at work, at home and in the community), as pointed out by Maccoby in "Gamesmanship" and as I point out in the chapter "Bullshit in Business," management sets up many other artificial barriers to strengthen the mystique of their superiority. They hold out the image of superiority as a carrot, implying to the rank and file that they can attain similar "heights" if only they work hard and follow the "rules." The rules, however, are designed so that almost everyone fails!

Management knows, for example, that those in a hierarchy believe if they move up, they do so by steps: that they have an essentially linear and static view of power, as if life were a ladder to be climbed one rung at a time. Management also knows that almost everybody in the world feels they deserve to be promoted to some higher estate no matter how high they may already have risen. Since the number of positions decline as the level of power increases, most of the world is doomed to live in disappointment and envy. This system has many advantages for management, chief among them the fact that if it were not for the hope of rising, few people would do any more work than is necessary for survival. It is important for people to believe that work will lead to promotion, but in fact, merit is something that most people in power dislike. In reality, those who hang on, get up. Most promotions are based on a system of rewards for faithfulness rather than on any real attempt to assess merit.

The corporation has also promoted the image of themselves in the patriarchal role of the benevolent provider. In the process they intimidate and design actions sure to cause insecurity, and emphasize the idea of a penurious old age if conformity is not forthcoming. However, they are aware that some motivation must be offered for the present. And since what people want most, even more than material rewards, is power over others — "managing people" as the euphemistic business phrase goes — the corporation functions as a kind of power broker, providing those who want power with a certain number of people over whom they can exert it. This costs nothing: every corporation always has plenty of people so unimportant or easily replaceable (assuming they were necessary in the first place) that it is simple enough to satisfy the power cravings of even the most incompetent by giving them someone to tyrannize. For years this has been the real function of secretaries in the minds of many men.

Thus, most corporations find it in their interest to encourage power games. Hence, in every organization there exists a built-in or "house" power game, the rules and rewards of which are established by management. The astute player comes to realize he must play the company game as well as his own, while being aware that winning someone else's game is not necessarily winning his own. Indeed, victory in a game that has been established by the management of a company, or has developed as part of the company's tradition, may ultimately involve losing his own game. The carrot that is held out, however attractive it may seem, is almost always a trap for those who grab it.

But the most pernicious effect on the rank and file is to let them know they are on the outside looking in; that they are inferior! The management objectives then are to establish an insecurity, a lack of self-esteem, a conformity, a desire for what they have.

It was a result of these conditions, along with the inequity of distribution of wealth, that led to the formation of the unions.

However, in the very principle of representation, the rank and file, while gaining in some respect, put themselves under further control. The mere selection of some people to represent others created new members of the elite.

When workers, for example, first fought for the right to organize unions, they were harassed, prosecuted for conspiracy, followed by company spies, or beaten up by police and goon squads. They were outsiders, unrepresented or inadequately represented in the system. Once the unions established themselves, they gave rise to a new group of integrators — the labor establishment — whose members, rather than simply representing the workers, mediate between them and other elites in business and government. The George Meanys and other labor leaders, despite their rhetoric, became themselves key members of the integrational elite. The fake union leaders in the U.S.S.R. and Eastern Europe never were anything but technicians of power.

In theory, the need to stand for re-election guaranteed that representatives would stay honest and would continue to speak for those they represented. Nowhere, however, did this prevent the absorption of representatives into the architecture of power. Everywhere the gap widened between the representative and the represented. Representative government — what we have been taught to call democracy — was, in short, an industrial technology for assuring inequality. Representative government was pseudorepresentative.

The overall effect has been to confine rather than liberate. It has exerted an even more stringent control over the rank and file. It has demanded conformity and gotten it. And in the descending order of the hierarchy, layer upon layer of observation and control is exerted until it comes to rest upon those at the bottom. As a result, those at the bottom must convey accurate information, perform their functions as prescribed, conform and not make waves. Not only does management intimidate the rank and file, labor exerts its own domination. And when the rank and file informs on itself for venal rewards or advancement, there is very little room left for bullshit. And should bullshit be attempted and found out, the punishment will be extremely severe from all three levels of power.

Machiavelli, in the 1500s, made this observation: "Whoever is the cause of another becoming powerful, is ruined himself; for that power is produced by him either through craft or force; and both of these are suspected by the one who has been raised to power." We exist on a double standard in society. Bullshit at the top is called shrewdness; bullshit at the bottom is called crime. Power reserves the right to bullshit and will do all it can to punish those at the bottom who make the attempt to do so. The rank and file, conditioned to insecurity, lacking in self-esteem, frightened, "spied upon," and overwhelmed by the illusions of hope, obey, perform "honestly," and conform. Therefore, they can not be other than "honest" or more accurate in matters of communication internal to the organization. The rank and file simply have no other real choice.

PRINCIPLE EIGHT

CLOTHES ARE TO BS WHAT TOOLS ARE TO A CARPENTER. THE MORE "AUTHENTIC" THE COSTUME, THE GREATER THE PROBABILITY OF SUCCESSFUL BS.

People tend to view other people stereotypically, and as a consequence are more likely to accept what you present as a "front." The more completely clothes become a "costume," the higher the probability of success in bullshitting.

Michael Korda says, "The biggest fool in the world is he who merely does his work supremely well, without attending to appearances." His books, "Power! How To Get It, How To Use It," and "Success! How Every Man and Woman Can Achieve It," provide diagrams on how to sit at a meeting, how a suit coat should fit over the back and shoulders, how to use glasses and cigarettes for rhetorical flourish, all the way down to details of dressing and tailoring that includes advice such as "you can't have too many buttons. Ideally, the sleeve buttons should be real — i.e., you should be able to button and unbutton them — but to get this small, correct touch, you have to go to a tailor."

These books and many others like it have become best sellers. The subject is taken quite seriously, and is so accepted that it extends to daily, syndicated newspaper columns like Harry Newton's "The Apostle of Success." This type of advice, pumped out in torrents, is often contradictory and confusing and sometimes laughable. Newton says, "Better clothes make better shoplifters." He goes on to describe how two women who wore expensive clothes while blatantly shoplifting were caught less often. If this brings a smile to your face, how about these bits of advice?

> Dress for the job you want, not the one you have now. Salesmen should dress like their salesmanager.
>
> Look as though you want to succeed. Your clothes should reflect your enthusiasm, your competence and your general joy in being alive.
>
> If you are small, wear "high authority clothes." Small people can overcome the problem of their height with pinstripes, dark clothes, expensive ties, white shirts, heavy glasses, and perhaps a superb briefcase.
>
> Big people should avoid "high authority clothes." Physically big people often intimidate their customers and business acquaintances because of their size. Big people should mute their size with soft colors, texture and lighter colored clothing.
>
> Dress so your clothes are inconspicuous. People should remember you because of what you said, what you did, how you display your competence — *not by what you wore.* (Italics Mine)

Studies show that people form a lasting impression within the first 60 seconds of seeing you. Since clothes cover approximately 90 percent of our body generally, the advice given by Korda and Newton does make a serious point. Dr. Betty Grayson of Hofstra University, suggests that the way you dress and act enhances your chances of becoming a victim of crime. She has isolated five movements most typical of potential assault victims. "The unconscious body language", she says, "seems to act as a silent signal of vulnerability to would-be criminals." She then goes on to suggest whole new ways of walking.

Much of this advice, of course, is dross. Yet, people respond to clothes in quite real ways and the transgression of certain "rules" can carry severe penalties. John Z. DeLorean, a former $600,000 a year executive of General Motors, gives a personal account of the stringency in the top echelon of corporate life concerning "proper clothes," and the conflict of nonconformity. Although Mr. DeLorean has far more serious problems at the moment (1984) than a concern for clothes (he is on trial for allegedly dealing cocaine), the situation he describes remains valid in that it is really about power we are speaking.

61

He says, "At the time in my career when I was just one of the corporate boys spending my working and nonworking hours with General Motors people or the company suppliers, I had a tightly knit group of corporate friends, and I obeyed the corporate dictates in behavior and dress. But as I grew it dawned on me that all of us were becoming inbred. We were losing contact with America. With our customers. In addition, while I enjoyed work, I've always placed enjoying life high on my list of priorities. So I made a habit of widening my circle of friends and broadening my tastes. This awareness precipitated a seemingly endless chain of personality conflicts, the most difficult of which was with Roger M. Kyes, who was my boss while I was running Pontiac and Chevrolet divisions. He made life unbearable for me, and he was dedicated to getting me fired: he told me so many times. Fortunately, I had the protection of my ability as I ran those two divisions to fend off Kyes. But I remember vividly my conflicts with him, especially when he was irritated by my style of dress. The corporate rule was dark suits, light shirts and muted ties. I followed the rule to the letter, only I wore stylish Italian-cut suits, white-collared off-white shirts and wide ties.

> "Goddamit, John," he'd yell. "Can't you dress like a businessman? And get your hair cut, too!"

> My hair was ear-length with sideburns. I felt my clothes and hair style were contemporary but not radical, so I told him:

> "General Motor's business — selling annual styling changes — makes this a fashion business. And what the hell do you know about fashion? Most of these guys around here wear narrow-lapelled suits and baggy pants with cuffs that are four inches above their shoes!"

The fact that I had been divorced, was a health nut, and dated generally younger actresses and models didn't sit well with the corporate executives or their wives."

Clothes in the august fields of law and religion also carry a significance beyond apparel. They have a deep political implication. Florynce R. Kennedy tells of a time in court (Flo Kennedy was one of the first Black women graduates of Columbia Law School), when the matter of her clothes became an issue. She says, "When I practiced law and a judge remarked I wasn't dressed properly because I wore pants, and he's sitting there in a long black dress gathered at the yoke," I said, "Judge, if you won't talk about what I'm wearing, I won't talk about what you're wearing. It's interesting," she comments, "to speculate how it developed, that in two of the most antifeminist institutions, the church and the law courts, the men are wearing dresses."

Clothes have a social and cultural significance as well. The Beatles, the rock group popular in the 60s, galvanized an entire generation of youth into longer hair styles, jeans, T-shirts and sneakers which became symbolic of their anti-establishment posture. True political issues such as Vietnam, and other elements like "mind expanding drugs", literally stimulated a revolution which has caused a permanent change in society. The irony is that each new change becomes its own limiting regimen and ostracizes those who don't conform to either its dress code or mores. Consequently, if one didn't wear the longer hair style, T-shirts, jeans and sneakers in the 60s, one was considered establishment, "old", "square", "not with it", etc. It was not the person in the clothes but the clothes themselves that determine the person.

Many religions make this same demand: certain Jewish sects can be identified by their black formal suits, hats, and long beards; Indian women by their veils; Africans by their dashikis. The rules are very stringent and can bring punishment if violated within the group.

In the totally different world of the criminal, clothes also play an extremely important part. Willie Sutton, the famous bank robber, in "Where The Money Is", tells us that disguise was always more important than any other element. By assuming the dress and pose of a mailman, chauffeur, utility worker, priest, or wealthy patron, he invariably went unquestioned into the crucially, most guarded areas, allowing him to pull off many of his thefts.

Most people will discount much of what they hear, but they will often believe what they see. We have become so conditioned to the fact that people wear uniforms to denote who they are that we take it for granted that that is what they are. There is not a day we don't see nurses, policemen, firemen, construction workers, ad infinitum, in uniform. It is so common, most people don't even pay attention to it anymore. Our response has become automatic and stereotyped. A bullshitter knows this instinctively. He knows that the more appropriately he dresses for the situation he is promoting, the more successful he can exercise his BS. That is why many operators create an "expensive" front. They are aware most people want something for nothing, and if you look like you're successful, the "marks" are more likely to believe it and come into your net. In contrast, a "seedy", casual look may be more accurate and effective in the literary and art worlds. What ever the look, the "costume and pose" is the disguise, and the disguise is a major portion of the overall deception. The operator knows we don't see past his clothes because we see in stereotypes; consequently, he knows if his costume is right, his chances for success go up immeasurably.

PRINCIPLE NINE

THE IMAGE YOU CREATE IN A BS SITUATION IS MORE IMPORTANT THAN WHAT YOU ARE IN TERMS OF ACTUAL ACCOMPLISHMENT.

Image is what you seem to be to others rather than what you are, and quite often has little or nothing to do with actual accomplishment. It is a person refracted through "credibility," created by publicity, celebrity or fame, and it is utilized in BS as part of the deception.

Image is the perception one has of a person, company or country that is not based, for the most part, on actual fact or accomplishment. It is a deception utilizing status symbols, clothes as costume, publicity (high visibility among one's peers and the public), to create "credibility" or celebrity. Some say that "Beauty is in the eye of the beholder." Image as impression functions in this same manner.

Unbeknownst to me at a very young age, I had formed an "image" that I presented to my mother who ruled the family with a great deal of love and an iron fist. Although she was only 4'9" tall, she dominated everyone including my father and any misbehavior or opposition could release a terrifying force that threatened life and limb. As a consequence, my behavior at home was exemplary. I worked diligently and thoroughly in the family grocery store. I made sure the windows sparkled clean, arranged the fruit and vegetables until they were a picture to behold, and attended customers with a solicitude that was exceptional. I was obedient, responsible and respectful to all elders. That, of course, was at the store and inside the home. Outside the enclave, I was a hellion. I swore, played dice, shoplifted a little, fought, smoked and was quite disrespectful. When I was caught at these crimes and brought home by the ear, my mother found reports of my misbehavior unbelievable. It was impossible, she thought; this was not her son they were describing. When proof was incontestable, she always blamed my companions for leading me astray. One could say it was a typical mother's response for a son, but there was a genuine confusion. I was two different people. Fortunately for me, my "good" image held up and probably saved me from a lot of punishment which I richly deserved. On the other hand, my brothers and sisters who had set a different image were punished when not guilty.

In another instance, my mother and I had come toe to toe in a battle concerning lack of church attendance. She was a lion on this subject and her will was extremely strong. I had independently, through a great deal of reading and analysis, come to the conclusion that church and religion had very little to do with being a moral person. I had seen a lot of contradictions and hypocrisy in religion which had further discouraged me. In addition, I found it difficult to awaken on Sunday to attend church, as I was a professional musician and played engagements which lasted into early morning. Though I stood my ground, my mother's will was becoming more difficult to handle. One day I saw a possible solution to the problem and plunged ahead. A neighbor familiar to both of us was crossing the street. I said to my mother:

"Ma, isn't that Sam crossing the street?"

"Yes," she replied.

"He goes to church every Sunday, doesn't he ma?" I continued.

"That's right — that's exactly what I tell you to do," she said brightly making her point.

"Tell me, ma, do you think Sam is a good man?" I pressed on.

My mother got a little suspicious at this point and said hesitantly, "No — he's not a very good man."

"And me," I said, "even though I don't go to church — am I a bad person?"

My mother knew as I did that Sam beat his wife and children, gambled away the family's food and rent money, lied and cheated, despite being a "religious" person. On the other hand, I was industrious, had all the virtues she had taught me and was a person of ethics. I could have enumerated each of my virtues to her prior to setting Sam as the example, but I knew it would have fallen on deaf ears because that was what she had taught me and that was what she expected of me. Therefore, the argument was made much more effective by pointing out the discrepancy between Sam's "image" and his deeds.

My older brother Ben, a successful businessman, presented "image" to me as a working philosophy. He was 15 years older than I, had been out in the world, and was quite experienced. He was forever trying to convince me that a "front" was essential to success. He would advise me on what clothes to wear, what jewelry to display, and what car was most impressive. He literally preached that the way people perceive you is the way they treat you. If you looked and acted successful, people wanted to be with you, do business with you, invite you into their confidence. I did so poorly, however, he finally gave up trying to educate me. I could never resolve the dishonesty of projecting values that were not me. I could not be hypocritical. I argued that accomplishment and the substance of one's character were sufficient and would speak clearly and loudly. I was probably an anachronism then; today I know I am obsolete.

I know a woman who speaks with big words that are somewhat archaic. Her speech is rather formal and unspontaneous and she over-enunciates. She wants to appear educated and intellectual. She is able to fool a number of people with this pretense. And as long as she doesn't spend too much time with any one person, she is able to camouflage her shallowness. She is convinced the mannerisms are necessary and that the affectation works for her, even though her friends are critical of it. She is, of course, not alone. Others make an attempt at status and creating a successful image by buying an impressive home address, automobile (a foreign sports car is preferable), a designer's clothing label, a well-known university or private school, a Cartier or Tiffany watch, and Vuitton luggage. I'm not saying these aren't beautifully designed or engineered products, but that they are bought more for their status than other values.

The need for status is overwhelming for many people; it is like a moth attracted to light. The jean manufacturers, discovering the allure for "designer's" jeans, have found riches far beyond their imagination. The allure has also attracted producers even more corrupt—the counterfeiters who attach a well known designer's name and insignia to the watch, the bottle, the garment with hardly anyone knowing the difference. The duplications are often so good, it has taken the original manufacturer's close examination to discover the difference. It is all in the name: that is what confers the status for those who believe it. To be important, to have status, extends so far today that a garbage collector is now a "sanitation engineer," a cleaning lady a "household technician," a pimp a "singles referral service," and a prostitute a "physical therapist." I don't mean to pick on just these people. The same pretense can be found on any level. Is being a vice-president, when there are numerous vice-presidents in a company, any less pretentious?

Lynn Rosellini of the New York Times, in describing the Reagans' Washington, points up another aspect of status; being "in," a lemming-like action.

> "When Nancy Reagan's California hairdresser announced plans not long ago to open a salon here, 50 Washington "hair groupies" telephoned for appointments . . . being "in" these days means not only having one's hair styled by Julius Bengtsson, the First Lady's hairdresser, but also having flowers arranged by David Ellsworth, a former Californian who is her "floral director" . . . California wines, Californian flowers . . . food and celebrities (Frank Sinatra) appear at Georgetown dinners.
>
> Washingtonians . . . often look to whoever occupies the White House for clues on how to dress, how to act and who to like. And everytime a new President moves in, the nation's capital outfits itself in borrowed style . . . but one thing is certain; as soon as the Reagans leave town, his style too, will be traded for another."

If one thinks this is an exaggeration one could have viewed the disco, Studio 54, in its hey-day and seen numerous people desperately trying to gain admittance to be with the "stars" and the "beautiful people." The more they were rejected—usually in an arrogant and arbitrary manner—the more they were determined to get in. Celebrities attended Studio 54 and in return Studio 54 reinforced that celebrity. The media, of course, widely reported every little detail of who got in, what they were wearing, how they behaved.

This is one of the essential factors to the interaction which allows celebrity to expand. Publicity is the tool: media the instrument. Together they create celebrity, which is the appearance of importance based upon the image formed and by publicizing the subject widely. Whatever the subject, if it is widely publicized, it is implied to be "important." The result is a larger than life impression.

Alexander Walker in "Stardom" describes the early discovery of publicity by Carl Laemmle, the film producer, who publicized Florence Lawrence into a star. "Publicity of a belligerent, inflationary and ubiquitous kind was probably the first radical break with the old theatrical conventions that had shaped so much of the early movies; and it was linked with the aggressive selling of a performer who at one stroke had her private identity revealed and made over to a publicity machine that got to work to make it public property. Instead of an advertisement in the local paper and bills posted outside the theater where she was appearing, the new film publicity multiplied the presence of a player ten thousand times, wherever mechanical reproduction purveyed her film image, and created a public interest in her personality, earning power, likes and dislikes — things that might have nothing to do with her art . . . henceforth, a screen player was to be marketed for her admirers as a personality, an image, and to an increasingly sinister extent, an object." As one Hollywood star put it, "The fans don't really like us: they like the idea they have of us."

Once the publicity machinery had been set up and its technique perfected, anything and everything became fodder for its hunger — fabrication, minutiae, distortions, personal sexual proclivities including perversions, marriages, divorces, births. It is said if stars had not existed, it would have been necessary to invent them. But that is only to understate the truth. Where stars did not exist, with the publicity machine, they were now invented.

The transformation created by combining publicity with motion pictures was astounding. "The truth is," Walker continues, "that Hollywood life often did 'ape' art. What looks in retrospect like a fantasy existence was more often than not simply the economic and social fact of stardom at this time in Hollywood. 'In those days,' Gloria Swanson later recalled, 'the public wanted us to live like kings and queens. So we did — and why not? We were in love with life. We were making more money than we dreamed existed and there was no reason to believe it would ever stop' . . . Life did not stop at aping art — it transfused it, so that it was hard to tell what was fantasy and what was fact. The most characteristic attribute of stardom in the 1920s was the belief, held by millions in a far more passionate way than in any following decade, that the stars were in real life the same exotic creatures that they appeared to be on the screen."

As publicity was transforming the public, it was also affecting the private preserve — "Society." It was unheard of at the time to have a reporter attend a Society function, and inexecusably bad taste for anyone to write about it. A woman of old New York Society, in "The Age Of Innocence," the mother of the bride who decides against showing her daughter's wedding presents at the reception remarks: "I should so turn the reporters loose in my house."

"Not so long after this time," comments Joseph Epstein, "no society wedding, or other event of any social magnitude would be considered complete without the publicity given to it by reporters. Like caterers and florists and servants, the press became an auxiliary, for in time the arm came to resemble something more like a vital organ. Without the press's confirmation — in the form of Society pages, gossip columns, and the rest — Society could not always recognize who was part of it."

Society became as Hedda Hopper once said, "People who would rather go to hell than not to see their names in print." Not only had the tradition changed but the composition of Society itself. When Truman Capote gave his party for Katherine Graham at the Plaza Hotel in 1966 — the great social bash of the 1960s — Charlotte Curtis, who wrote about it and also published the guest list in "The New York Times," was herself invited not as a reporter but as a guest and figure of social standing in her own right. It is assumed her comment that many of Mr. Capote's guests were "disposable celebrities" presupposes her an exception, but what emerges from such zany juxtapositions is a new social amalgam composed of actors and academics, writers and singers, Jews and Blacks. Society itself, the "enviable people," does not seem only less trivial under the glare of publicity, but more disposable.

Publicity has become ubiquitous. Corporations have separate public relations departments, the military a public relations office, and independent public relations and publicity firms flourish. Even individuals (not just showbusiness personalities) have private representation. Ironically, a few of these people who were made celebrities by virtue of publicity, now employ publicists to keep their names and pictures out of the media! And when success in our society has to be ratified by publicity, its power to confer importance and status is undeniable.

It seems whoever holds the key to the publicity vault holds an inordinate amount of power. That is why in most big corporations, the public relations department is usually under the thumb of the selected few at the top. It carries a serious danger as DeLorean points out as concern with the press can easily become pathological; He says, ". . . criticism from the outside is generally viewed as ill-formed. General Motors management thinks what it is doing is right, because it is GM that is doing it, and that the outside world is wrong. It is always "they" versus "us." The press is viewed in a Nixonian sense as constantly carrying out a vendetta against the corporation." It was this same attitude which, when Ralph Nadar was about to publicly expose the fact that the Corvair automobile, a GM product was "Unsafe At Any Speed" (it killed a number of people), GM tried to stop it by employing private detectives and wire taps to find something unsavory to blackmail him with. Nadar later brought a suit against GM on this matter and won a $400,000 settlement out of court.

The quest for "image" has substantially modified the modes of making it in our society. Lasch says:

> . . . The latest success manuals differ from earlier ones—even surpassing the cynicism of Dale Carnegie and Peale—in their frank acceptance of the need to exploit and intimidate others, in their lack of interest in the substance of success, and in the candor with which they insist that appearances—"winning images"—count for more than performances, ascription for more than achievement. One author seems to imply that the self consists of little more than its "image reflected in the other's eyes" . . . today men seek the kind of approval that applauds not their actions but their personal attributes. They wish to be not so much esteemed as admired. They crave not fame but the glamour and excitement of celebrity. They want to be envied rather than respected. Pride and acquisitiveness, the sins of an ascendant capitalism, have given way to vanity. Most Americans would still define success as riches, fame, and power, but their actions show they have little interest in the substance of this attainment. What a man does matters less than the fact that he has "made it." Whereas fame depends on performance of notable deed acclaimed in biography, works of history, celebrity—the reward of those who project a vivid or pleasing exterior or have otherwise attracted attention to themselves—is acclaimed in the news media, in gossip columns, on talk shows, in magazines devoted to "personalities."

But perhaps William Hazlitt put it best when he said, "Fortune (success) smiles upon those who are thought wise rather than upon those who are truly wise, for it is for the most part only necessary to seem wise. It smiles upon those who are qualified for certain things, for nothing else. And the way to secure success is to be more anxious about obtaining it than deserving it. To have too high a standard of refinement, to have too great a respect for the republic, to have a simplicity of manner, to have no pretensions, to have taste and wide interests, to have delicacy, to have sincerety and straight-forwardness, to have a higher regard for realities than for appearances — to have any of these qualities is to be assured of being held back from success."

It is not only the "high and mighty" who seek attention. Today, it is also the rank and file who, viewing the success of fourth-and-fifth-rate people — gossip columnists, false aristocrats, corporate dopes, political nincompoops — and reading the self-help and self-interest books that preach strategy, tactics, "winning images," complete the corruption by extending it along the base of the pyramid. It is not just the corruption of designer's labels, the right address and university, or the flimsiness of celebrity that is the only concern; the more serious concern is whether this is the groundwork that has led to the sick and pitiable attempts at fame and notoriety — "to be somebody" — that may be responsible for the assassination of Dr. Martin Luther King, John and Robert Kennedy, and the recent attempt on President Reagan's life. The violence can be passed off as mental illness or sick political bias, but it just may be the symbol of dichotomy between shadow and substance, fact and fantasy, the illusion of success rather than the reality of accomplishment — of the image game.

CHAPTER IV

TYPES OF BULLSHIT

HOLLYWOOD

In these days of motion picture costs soaring from 5 to 45 million dollars, with the lucky films among them grossing from 100 to 200 million dollars, the fantasyland of Hollywood has worn its mantle of bullshit like a diamond tiara throughout history. The association of BS with Hollywood and its populace has become a stereotype.

Pauline Kael, in New York Magazine, explains how BS creates so many bad movies. She gets right to the heart of the matter of the new, contemporary Kings, Queens, Princes, and the Court in her description of ILLUSION—HOLLYWOOD STYLE.

> There is a pecking order in filmmaking, and the director is at the top—he's the authority figure. A man who was never particularly attractive to women now finds that he's the padrone; everyone is waiting on his word, and women are his for the nod. The constant, unlimited opportunities for sex can be insidious; so is the limitless flattery of college students who turn directors into gurus. Directors are easily seduced: They mainline admiration.

While this is a description of the successful director whose film has grossed the millions of dollars mentioned above, it is also true of Hollywood stars. The "factory" system of making films and stars no longer exists as in the old days; consequently stars and directors, are a rare breed today. But their power is also supreme and they reign as the new kings and queens. Kael describes the effect this has had.

. . . There has always been a megalomaniac potential in movie making, and in this period of stupor, when values have been so thoroughly undermined that even the finest directors and the ones with the most freedom aren't sure what they want to do, they often become obsessive and grandiloquent — like mad royalty . . . Megalomania and art become the same thing to them. But the disorder isn't just in their heads, and a lot of people around them are deeply impressed by megalomania.

This shift in power toward the directors and the stars has come at the expense of the heads of studios. The power in old Hollywood rested so firmly in the likes of Louis B. Mayer, Adolph Zuker, the Warner Brothers and Harry Cohn that they were virtually tyrants. What emanated from these potentates came as sheer, naked orders — almost without pretense. All that has changed as the old system has gone and the new has arrived. Kael says:

. . . Everybody in the movie business has the power to say no, and least secure executives protect themselves by saying no to just about everything that comes their way. Only those at the very top can say yes, and they protect themselves, too . . . they postpone decisions because they don't mind keeping someone dangling while his creative excitement dries up and all the motor drive goes out of his proposal. *They don't mind keeping people waiting, because it makes them feel powerful* . . . But most of the ones who could say yes don't; they consider it and string you along (Hollywood is the only place where you can die of encouragement). For the supplicant, it's a matter of weeks, months, years waiting for meetings at which he can *beg permission* to do what he was, at the start, eager to do. And even when he's got a meeting, he has to catch the executives attention and try to keep it; in general, the higher the executive the more cruelly short his attention span . . . In this atmosphere of *bureaucratic indifference or contempt*, things aren't really decided — they just happen, along bureaucratic lines. (Italics mine)

Ironically, as the recession has grown, with inflation and energy shortages rampant, Hollywood is facing what the auto industry and a number of other industries have come to know — the public is beginning to resist the arrogance, the disrespect, the attitude that says "we can shove anything we want down your collective throats." People are buying smaller, more fuel efficient foreign cars, causing havoc in the auto industry: they are turning more to TV for their entertainment where it is "free of charge," and are becoming more selective toward the films they pay for. As a consequence, a film is either a big hit or a dismal failure, and the motion picture audience which has been declining for years continues to do so.

Television, to a great extent, is beating Hollywood at its own game. In a recent incident, it even pulled ahead in the bullshit game. As reported by all media (with glee I might add), ABC Television's president, Fred Pierce, went so far as to hire a psychic to determine which new TV shows were going to be hits! (I don't want to put down psychics, per se, but it seems to me this is a lot like the "Ultimate Bullshitter" — the person who deceives himself.)

THE COME ON

Essentially, the person perpetrating this form of BS functions on the basis of having a "front." A front consists of having an assortment of symbols to which people respond in a stereotypical way.

In the case of the woman film producer previously mentioned, her big diamond rings (I learned later even these were not real but Zircon), expensive clothes, Rolls Royce, well-furnished home and apartment, combined with the casual name-dropping of well-known people allowed her to "operate" in showbusiness and high society, as well as the more mundane world of real estate people, stock brokers, and businessmen who pursued start-up capital for "glamour" companies in technology and science.

Her procedure was to set up a social situation (her party or someone elses), quietly but ostentatiously display herself in a peacock manner, and then lay out the other bait of being an "innocent" in the world of business, all the while maintaining an air of having an interest in the other person and their work. In other words, she let it be known she was a "plum ready for plucking." The set of impressions she created were:

1. She was rich.
2. She was naive.
3. She was interested.
4. She was ready to be taken.

Having spread her web, she was now ready to consume her prey. And they came in droves, particularly since this process was repeated over and over again at other social functions such as charity balls, political fund raising benefits, and ceremonial events. There were those who had film and theater projects which needed financing: those whose present businesses needed capital influx for further progress; those attempting to unload failing businesses; and those who wanted to capture the woman herself (she was very attractive and sexually desirable), despite the fact that she was already married. Their thinking being that if they captured the person, they automatically secured the money. Each of these people, in their greed or calumny, was trying to gain from her.

She had by now completed two steps of the process: one, she displayed the bait; two, they bit. One of her first victims was a young, talented composer who was seeking a producer for a Broadway musical he had written. His strategy was to personally seduce her and, in the process, secure her money for the production of his show. They met in private where she fed him supper and wine. He regaled her with stories of showbusiness, and entertained her with his piano selections. Since her ideas of morality and her feelings of fidelity were (to put it euphemistically) "modern," all that remained to be decided was when — that night, next week, next month — she would sleep with him. As her husband would be returning from out of town the next day, she decided this night would be the night. All that remained to consummate the affair was to create an impression for the composer that he had charmed her, that he was irresistible, and that she was probably being a little foolish but . . . Triumphantly, our young composer took the bait and performed his duty with a vigor and zest that made the evening exciting and memorable.

From this point on, when business aspects of the relationship cropped up, the producer would refer the matter to her lawyer who had a way (prearranged) of *always* giving her the advantage, never coming forth with any capital, always committing the young composer's assets, and never committing his client's (except on an "If" basis). As she was very shrewd, she also kept a good distance between them, other than when it suited her, thus allowing her to choose the time and place, and to conduct other relationships. Consequently, she was able to function for as long as she wished, always with the upper hand, always pursued. Eventually, as the victims woke up to the fact that they had been duped, it was too late. She had won!

BE NICE TO ME – AND I'LL MAKE YOU A STAR!

Every profession, business, or organized structure has a pecking order. Many of the people involved believe that the road to success is paved by sucking ass, or by fucking someone higher up the ladder. However sad or funny these stories might be, they demonstrate BS in primitive form.

Our story is once again set in Hollywood where many special talents are needed to make a motion picture. They include electricians, carpenters, cameramen, art directors, make-up people, assistant directors, producers and many others. It should be noted that to make a feature motion picture today, the *average* cost is approximately 8–10 million dollars. Some films like Michael Cimino's "Heaven's Gate" cost over 35 million dollars, and when it was yanked from exhibition after only one week (the New York critics were very harsh), a lot of heads rolled in the executive suite of United Artists. This points up that no director or producer, no matter how high his position, is without anxiety or fear of losing his job; so when it comes to satisfying a personal pleasure as against making a professional determination on matters of production, the reality, most often, is that the decision will be made on a professional basis.

There is a well-known story about a woman named Cynthia, a young, beautiful, curvaceous blonde who was intent on becoming a star in films. She was as naive as she was beautiful and desirable. Chances are, if Cynthia didn't start with believing sex was the road to stardom, it was inculcated through hearsay and reinforced by media – gossip columns, movies, novels, television (sex is now openly dealt with on daytime soap operas!) She might even have known a friend who utilized sex for a promotion in some company, or for some other gain. Cynthia herself, somewhere along the line, may even have had a specific offer. In someway though, Cynthia bought the myth, particularly the myth fostered by Hollywood that overnight stardom was possible, with the underlying implication conveyed by the Hedy Lamars, Lana Turners, Marilyn Monroes and others that sex was the primary reason. Consequently, there was a blurring of reality with the myth predominating for many. This then is the story of Cynthia who believed she was functioning on "reality." But as we shall see, sex goes only so far in promoting careers, if it is effective at all.

One evening at a party, Cynthia met an electrician who was going to be working on a film that was recently mentioned in the newspapers. Cynthia mentally recalled the article which gave the electrician some credibility when he made a pass at her.

> "Cynthia, while I'm not the most important person on this film, if you're nice to me I will introduce you to the carpenter who is close to the make-up man."

True to her desire for success, Cynthia "performed" to the best of her ability and gave the electrician great pleasure. True to his word, the electrician introduced her to the carpenter. To set the scene a little more precisely, you must remember that Hollywood is a stringent hierarchy and that the electrician and the carpenter are on the low end, while the director and the producer are on the high end.

Cynthia, meeting the carpenter, who promised to introduce her to the make-up man, once again gave her all. In quick succession and, in the following order, she pleasured the make-up man, the cameraman, the assistant director and the director — finally arriving at the producer.

That night she put on her most alluring dress, had her hair especially done, wore her most expensive perfume, and prepared her mind for an Academy Award performance. Since our producer was cultivated (is this a contradiction?), charming, quite handsome and rich, Cynthia had all the motivation she would ever need.

That night when the act was consummated, and the producer was gushing forth words of praise, Cynthia felt the time was right for the big question. However, not wanting to take any unnecessary chances, she decided to lead up to it with some preliminary questions.

> "Did you like my perfume?", she asked.
>
> "I loved your perfume," he replied.
>
> "Was my hair soft on your body?", she asked.
>
> "You hair was like angel dust," he replied.
>
> "Did you like my kisses?", she asked.
>
> "Your kisses were like fire," he replied.
>
> "Did my loving take you around the world?", she asked tremulously.
>
> "It took me to another planet," he replied joyously.
>
> "I'm so happy you're happy," she said, and taking a deep breath, she popped the final question. "And now can I be a star?"

True to everyone's word—their word being but a minute part of the truth—each man came through on his promise. She, too, gave excellent service as part of her contract. And without anyone being totally dishonest, the BS went down to the last moment when reality had to prevail. Was it going to be necessary to have intercourse with everyone in the public to assure her stardom! The sad reality of the situation was that even though Cynthia had performed sex with the producer, he most likely would not have given her the role unless she *was* talented and charismatic. In other words, qualified, which in itself might have obviated the need for sex. It is almost certain that the producer would not have given her the starring role, or any role for that matter, if it would have placed him in any kind of jeopardy, even for a moment. He would sooner be accused of welching on his promise or of lying, and go on to the next situation.

It is interesting to observe that when William Agee, President, Chairman, and Chief Executive at Bendix Corporation had to deal with his board and the public's impression of his relationship with Mary Cunningham, she left the company. While I believe this was immensely unjustified and unfair, it nonetheless points up that even the most powerful of men have a limit to their power.

For many victims, the conditioning which prepares them to be "taken", is a result of years of hypocrisy, distorted value systems, and a double moral standard. However, if the "hook" (greed, which may manifest itself in "something for nothing," or the attitude of taking a shortcut to something) were not present in the victim, the gulling would not be so easy. But with greed so blatant, the temptation for the perpetrator becomes almost impossible to resist.

LET IT ALL HANG OUT—OR, THE BEST DEFENSE IS AN OFFENSE

This is the story of a film commissioner, who was a part of a panel of motion picture producers assembled to discuss the film business on a local talk show. A film commissioner's main function is to generate business dollars for the city by encouraging a film production in his city. Since his position is political, he may or may not be qualified. To this particular man's credit, he was qualified.

The host, at one point in the show, alluded to the possibility of favoritism on the part of the commissioner. The film commissioner, retaining his composure, responded quite aggressively. Instead of defending his impartiality, as would have been proper, he admitted his "favoritism," — his special efforts on behalf of these producers — and said there wasn't a thing wrong with it. Further, he told his host and audience, he was as skilled as the next person at beguilement but he considered it a waste of time. The argument that he put forth for his "honesty" contained a great deal of validity when placed within a pragmatic context — the job had to get done, and without too many hassles or the producers would simply go to another state.

Since it appeared that he was not trying to hide anything, and he gave fairly reasonable answers for his actions, the overall impression was that he was a direct, "honest" man who was effective in his job. However, if one knew anything about film production, the film commission, and the nature of business relationships, one would then have to know the following:

1. The film commissioner was a very ambitious person whose $30,000 a year salary would in no way be satisfactory, particularly when films made millions of dollars profit.

2. He therefore had secured this job precisely because it would put him in a position of power with film producers and film studios.

3. By exercising his power favorably — giving certain producers community assistance (more than their share) — things like extra policemen, cutting a lot of red tape, or special dispensations such as stopping the public from using an access highway while they shot the film, he was building up future favors for himself. In this case, he later turned producer, and a studio he had previously helped cooperated with the financing of his film project. Now he was in direct position to make his own millions.

4. Overall, by publicizing the great job he was doing for the city, thereby giving credit to the administration that had hired him, he was creating brownie points for

everyone, and still selling his particular city as the great place to make films.

One can ask, since almost everyone was benefiting, what was so wrong? Nothing, of course, except that other productions which were also entitled to fair pay were neglected; some were even punished by him for some small transgression (dare I say lack of bribery); and at a later time, some producer who may have been struggling for years would have one less opportunity for financing because he wasn't "connected." In the case of the film commissioner, how many other producers decided not to use his city for their productions because of the favoritism? How much of the public's interest was neglected in order to satisfy a "favor?" For example, the tramway in New York City was appropriated for a Sylvester Stallone film, totally inconveniencing the residents of Roosevelt Island who critically depended on this mode of transportation. (The tramway is the only short way from Roosevelt Island to New York City.) Shortly after the filming it broke down causing a further inconvenience.

When the example of the political appointee is extended to civil service employees who, upon leaving their jobs go right to work for one of their old vendors, their previously made decisions become suspect. In the case of FCC, FTC, or other government agency personnel, how many decisions regarding rate increases or product safety were rendered under this kind of aegis? This type of practice grew to be so extensive, that the Carter administration saw fit to enact a law which sets severe restrictions on this kind of behavior.

"Let It All hang Out — Or, The Best Defense Is An Offense" is the technique of deception utilized to gain personal opportunity and material advantage. These practitioners lead the public to believe their interests are being served while in reality their pockets are being picked. These practitioners are particularly insidious and dangerous because they not only undermine public trust and confidence, they actually may endanger our safety.

OPPORTUNITY ONLY KNOCKS ONCE — SO, GRAB IT (ME) WHILE YOU CAN

These are the middle men — the show biz agent, the salesman, the lawyer, the real estate broker, critics, executive managers — THE INTERPOSER between you and the product, the opportunity, the other person.

Quite often, this type is a leech, imposing himself on others. He is often talentless, does not produce anything himself, and if he couldn't work off of your efforts he would flounder. This is not to say that all INTERPOSERS are this way — some give energy, specialized knowledge or contacts — but even these find it necessary to create deceptive appearances or distort nuances to make you believe they are indispensable and that what they are doing is more for your good than theirs.

Robert Ringer in "Winning Through Intimidation," tells of an agent who interposed himself between two partners in a construction project that was in financial difficulty. The two partners lived in different cities and their communications were poor, if not antagonistic. The working partner who was still trying to salvage the project, had talked a mortgage banker into increasing the construction loan on the project and advancing some additional funds immediately. However, certain conditions had to be met, the main one being a buy-out of the non-working partner.

The agent secured a purchase price for the buy-out from the working partner and then went to see the non-working partner. When they met, however, the agent did not relay the actual offer. He simply indicated that he was representing a possibility. He built up the obstacles and difficulties in getting the working partner to "buy," even alluding to the possibility he might be able to get him to increase the offer. Since a sale would get the non-working partner out from under the debt the project had incurred, he listened with some interest. The agent then suggested a price to the non-working partner that was ten thousand dollars below the actual price offered by the working partner. Since the two partners were hardly talking, the agent felt the difference in these figures equaled his worth in solving the problem for the working partner. The agent then asked the non-working partner to sign a simple document saying that the figure discussed was agreed upon, and that his commission would be whatever he could get beyond this price.

He next went back to the working partner and reversed the entire procedure. He told him how difficult the other partner was and how much "hell" he had gone through in making him see the light. He then quoted the working partner a figure that was $10,000 *above* the original figure and urged him to sign it before it was too late. The moment the "sale" was made, the agent produced another simple agreement that committed the working partner to this new price as well as his commission.

At the conclusion of negotiations, the agent was $20,000 ahead with the two partners separating amicably, each thinking they had come out ahead. In this situation, as in many others of this type, the service performed by the agent was "legitimate" even though BS was employed. In many other instances, however, the BS far outweighs the service.

To see the case above more clearly, this is the way it breaks down: first, the interposer picked up on the situation by overhearing a private conversation. Secondly, he had interposed himself through sheer dint of perseverance. He had to overcome being rebuffed and ignored, literally having had to sit outside the working partner's door for hours, "suffering great indignity." He succeeded by creating two sets of appearances — letting each partner think he was acting for their benefit alone, while in reality he was working for his commission. They might have worked their problems out themselves, but once the agent got in, he made them think he was indispensable. Not only did the agent benefit materially, he also reversed a power situation. While we might have some sympathy for the agent, it is wise to remember he wasn't exactly invited to begin with.

PIE-IN-THE-SKY

Albert Z. Carr in "Business As A Game" comments that perhaps the most painful of all experiences endured by executives is the discovery that the golden carrot dangled before them by the boss during years of hard work is, on close inspection, merely a shriveled slice of old parsnip. Management in some concerns is ruthless about stimulating their executive personnel with pie-in-the-sky promises . . . often promises made indirectly and implied rather than stated.

He continues, "Many a young executive has said happily to his wife, 'Things are looking up at the office. The boss put his hand on my shoulder today and said, 'Nice work — keep it up and there will be big things in store for you.' The executive who takes this kind of praise seriously, whose feelings are easily swayed by casual compliments, is often an easy victim for the boss who deliberately uses the pie-in-the-sky technique. Even when the promises mention actual sums, it is not necessarily dependable if the man at the top refuses to commit himself in specific terms. 'If we land those two accounts based on our present bid, Jim, I'll see that you get a percentage — say five percent. How does that sound?' Such passing remarks from the boss have often inspired men to put in an extra twenty hours of work per week for long stretches, to the dismay of their wives, and even to the impairment of their health."

In the case of "Jim," Carr sums up these negative results in the following dialogue: "Right Jim, I certainly did promise you five percent on these contracts. But we'll have to wait until we see what the profit is. What? You thought I was speaking of five percent of the gross? I'm afraid you misunderstood. I never had anything in mind but a percentage of the net. But I tell you what. I'll give you an advance against your percentage of the net, if you like. I'll be taking a chance—can't tell how the profit will work out—but I'll play along with you to that extent. Okay?"

Carr's recommended defense against this technique is the use of the written word. He advises that your position is strong only at the beginning of the period requiring the extra effort that the boss is trying to get out of you. You have lost your strategic advantage once you have completed the project, whatever it may be. A typical memorandum in Jim's case would have been: 'You certainly gave my morale a boost when you promised me 5% of the X and Y contracts if I succeed in bringing them in on the present bids. Just to avoid misunderstanding—am I right in assuming that we are talking about 5% of the gross?' If the boss is reluctant to clarify, be prepared to carry extra burdens without adequate rewards, or start looking for another job.

I'm sure we've all heard our own pie-in-the-sky phrases but here are a few other examples:

> "You just produce *the results we're looking for*, and there will be a big bonus for you."
>
> "If this program *works out the way I hope*, I'm going to ask the president to approve a twenty percent increase for you."
>
> "Invest in this project and *I'll guarantee* you'll make a million."
>
> "Take EST (and any other self-help course) and the world is yours."
>
> "Get a college degree and you'll have financial security, status, and you'll never have to worry about a job."
>
> "Sleep with me and I'll make you a star.'
>
> "Stick with me and you'll be set for life."

And of course, when ADVERTISING sells you a product there is always an *implied* pie-in-the-sky promise. Buy this deodorant or cosmetic and you'll find romance; buy this automobile and be powerful and free; buy this insurance and be secure for any and all emergencies. The deception is obvious. Anything that is "too good to be true," generally is and should be suspect immediately.

PYRAMID GAME

In this game, a letter is transmitted from one person to another explaining the rules, and urging that all directions be followed explicitly. Prior to this, the person was given a sales pitch on how playing the game will make him "rich." He is to make only one investment, get several other people to follow the same procedure, and money will flow back to him ten-fold.

Usually, the letter starts with a series of names. These are the names of the founders or of the newly entered. The most recent person entering the "game" must give half of the stipulated cash figure to the name at the top of the list (put it in a specially prepared envelope and mail it), and the other half to the name at the bottom of the list, which is the person who brought you into the game. Each new person entering the game must then get two other people to join. The reassurance that all is well comes from the fact that as you get your two new people, you will have your investment back. The selling person can point out to the newcomer those people who actually made a lot of money from this scheme. Generally, however, they are those who entered at or near the beginning. The overall image is that what is presented is accurate and "true" because it seems like "fact."

When the process falls apart and the chain is finally broken, as it inevitably is (each person has to do quite a sell job to appeal to the newcomer's greed), one comes to the realization one was not told the whole story—that one was deceived. Some would say that you should know better than to try to make a "quick buck" despite the constant bombardment of propaganda to the effect that it is possible. It is not surprising that people believe the Pyramid game can work for them when the sweepstakes, game shows, lottery, numbers games (legalized and run by the city or state), and the media exposure of how much the Hunt's make, sports begets, and many other things are continuously conditioning them for instant success.

Robert Abrams, Attorney General of New York, has chosen to call the Pyramid scheme a con game. He has labeled the deception a "fraud"—intentional deception to cause a person to give up property (money) or some artifice—and legally prosecuted those participating in it. The deception, however, goes beyond his definition, has the implication, and is in fact, bullshit.

As stated in Chapter One, BS creates a set of impressions for other than the apparent motivation—that is the deception. In addition, BS *does not state an untruth* which would be lying, and therefore prosecutable. In this instance, should you try to accuse those at the top of the Pyramid who benefited from the deception of lying, they would prove to you that certain people did make money. Also, they *never* said the process was perfect, nor did they *guarantee* you a profit, even though this was strongly implied. The strongest underpinning though, is that while the Pyramid game is mathematically possible, it is not probable that the scheme will work long enough for you to make a profit if you are at the late end of the game.

In this instance, there is such a fine line between fraud and BS that the law has *chosen* to classify it as illegal. If you are caught in a Pyramid scheme and prosecuted by law, and you are unable to bullshit the law by corrupting a law enforcement official with a bribe, you stand a good chance of going to jail. This could be some small consolation if you were the victim. Ironically, unless you realize that the Attorney General was creating his own "impressions"—that the law was alert and on the case, for instance—then you will have received a double dose of BS, making the situation that much more noxious. Now that the media has gone on to other events and the Pyramid Game is no longer new, so has the Attorney General gone on to other more "pressing" matters.

ME TARZAN, YOU NOTHING—OR,
THE PROFESSIONALS

Among this type are lawyers, accountants, agents, doctors, and of course, businessmen. Though each might vary their technique, they basically follow a common procedure of setting up appearances—clothes, status symbols, "star names"—to set the stage. And with the authority and status of their profession, the "front" is completed.

As previously mentioned, Michael Korda in "Success" points out that "appearances are nearly everything." He also indicated that telephones, their kind, number and color, are a limitlessly useful weapon in the struggle for success. "The more people you yourself can put and keep on hold, the more successful you will seem." The adjunct to this is the more distance you can have your secretary keep between you and other people, the more important you will seem. In "Me Tarzan, You Nothing," costume is extremely important. At bottom, appearances reinforce the perpetrator's technique. It says loud and clear, almost in trumpet tones, "I am important!"

A lawyer I know always makes his clients wait, even if it's for only a few minutes. He then has his secretary apologize for the delay. Once in his well-furnished office, he may give his secretary last minute instructions on "Frank," "Barbara," or "Robert;" and, if he is a showbusiness lawyer, you are supposed to know he is talking about Frank Sinatra, Barbara Streisand, or Robert Redford. He then glances at his wrist watch, a Cartier, as if to say "We'll have to hurry as I don't have much time." Eventually, when he gets to your business, he discusses nothing but simply gives you a solution, which you are expected to accept unquestioningly. He, too, is a celebrity along with his "star" clients, having appeared in gossip columns many times which verified his attendance at "important" affairs. You can be sure his bill will be commensurate with his status as a celebrity.

Another type of lawyer lays it on you heavy, in a totally obnoxious way, that he doesn't care whether you do business with him or not. His arrogance is almost unbelievable. He will interrupt you, turn his back on you and put down your actions. He demoralizes your person, your efforts, your accomplishments. He is the authority. He knows everything—you know nothing. He gains his power position by intimidating you directly. The main motivating factor for this type may be ego enlargement as much as material gain.

I have also seen doctors who not only intimidate their patients, but their staff and everyone around them, including their families. They seem to see themselves as God-like. What they are transmitting, however, is "Me Tarzan, You Nothing."

On the other extreme is "Big Daddy"—the professional who is benevolent and kind and has "your interest at heart." He applies the smell of honey but keeps the dessert away until you get the message that if you just turn over your money, trust and consent, you won't have to worry any more. He lets you feel he is omnipotent—stronger and more powerful than you. He seems to be firm yet gentle, persuasive and not pushy; he seems effective. It is only later when your health is gone, or your business investment has turned sour, or some other disaster has struck, that you find you've been deceived. Big Daddy might admit to bad judgement but never to the overall deception.

A superior position is established at the onset, be it a negative/positive, or hard/soft approach. In each instance, you are led to believe they are everything, you are nothing; in addition, that you need them more than they need you. The reality, however, is that without you they could not function, without you they would be nothing.

THE BULLSHIT CARESS — OR STROKING

Mayor Koch of New York city, during a particularly bad cold spell was covered by the media in his appearance at two armories which had been set up to house people who were not getting heat in their apartments due to landlord neglect. Viewing the newscasts, one could see that not too many people had availed themselves of this opportunity, yet the media pumped up the event and the mayor in most successful terms.

A day or so later, Mayor Koch, again with the media in tow, showed up at the Heat Complaint Bureau where he answered three or four of the complaints personally. He then said, "I am here to let the people of New York know I care that the bureau is effectively doing its job."

What we have in these examples is a crafty politician utilizing trumpery to "snow" the public. The verbal caresses, or stroking, are the reassuring pat on the head that all is well, even though you are obviously bleeding to death from a gun shot wound, an auto accident, or freezing to death. The caress and the purring is to draw your attention away from a more serious or dangerous condition.

The Heat Complaint Bureau received 9500 calls during the above cold spell in New York. By coincidence, the same newspapers, radio and television stations that had helped the Mayor exploit the previous situation had called attention to the fact that the City Administration, instead of increasing the number of inspectors during the cold months, had actually decreased the staff due to "lack of money in the budget." The reality of the matter was that no matter how hard they would have tried they could not have serviced the complaints promptly or effectively: consequently, landlords knew enforcement of the law was impossible and ignored the suffering they were causing. Further, because the laws were weak and the legal procedure laborious, the landlords thumbed their noses with gusto at the mayor and the courts. Many of the landlords went scot free, even though a number of deaths attributed to lack of heat in their buildings had occurred. More sadly, many who were freezing chose to ignore the armories. Some said they were afraid to leave their apartments for fear they would be robbed. Many others would not go because it was too great a blow to the little remaining dignity they had.

Mayor Koch also stroked the public when he called for the names of "johns" — those who use the services of prostitutes — to be read over the city-owned radio station. He justified the action by publicly accusing judges of failing to mete out severe-enough punishment on these cases. While real crime goes unabated, and the poor die from sickness and lack of proper attention, the New York public gets stroked with meaningless caresses as Mayor Koch spends more and more time tending to his "image" than to real work at hand.

However, he is not the only guilty party. You can be sure you are being stroked when the utilities or oil companies spend millions of dollars on advertising, telling you how much they are trying to conserve fuel and avoid foreign domination, or how much of their income goes into taxes. Call it distraction, or whatever you like, it still amounts to a BS CARESS.

HOSTAGES — OR, WHAT'S THE DEAL?

After the hostages had been released from Iran, I met with a group of people who had become acquaintances because we all had breakfast about the same time each morning. I was asked if I had seen the Inaugural on television the day before. I said that I did but that I had been more impressed with a news cutaway of President Carter's stop in Plains, Georgia on his way to Weisbaden, Germany to welcome the hostages home. President Carter before debarking from Georgia, thanked God for the hostages' safe release, seemed genuinely relieved, and, I'm sure, felt somewhat vindicated in his handling of this difficult matter. I expressed the feeling that I thought Carter was a great man in that he could have gone into Iran and attacked, and even if the hostages had been killed, he would have been forgiven by the American public: that to negotiate was the harder task; and to suffer the humiliation and jeopardize the presidential election was very extraordinary.

However, before I could turn around, I was viciously attacked by two of my breakfast companions who angrily denounced Carter as useless, weak, confused and inept for putting the United States in the humiliating position of appearing impotent in the eyes of the world. I tried to explain that Carter was practicing what we preached: that human life is our highest priority along with freedom, and, that despite the barbaric behavior of the Iranians, by negotiating peaceably, albiet under duress, the United States was again demonstrating the strength of our beliefs that made us an extraordinary country and world power.

No matter what the explanation, their anger and disdain for Carter continued unabated. More importantly, I knew these two people were not alone in their feelings, as I had seen many "street" interviews on TV and in the newspapers that demonstrated identical attitudes and responses. I could understand the general anger. However, underlying these feelings was a more deep-seated response that intensified the anger to the point where it was almost out of control.

In trying to understand the "hidden" feelings, I saw two possible clues. The first was the incredible concern they felt regarding world opinion of us, the most powerful nation in the world, brought to paralysis. The second was the attitude that we could allow 52 lives to jeopardize 220 million Americans by putting all of America in hostage. Did the world's response suggest that we did not know what we thought of ourselves, or who we really were? What had happened to our idealism that said *every* human life was our highest priority, and why had this intensified a desire for violence against Iran?

It's not too difficult to understand that humiliation will create violence, but where did disillusionment enter to contribute and intensify this feeling to where it was almost beyond control? Sure, Carter was indecisive at the beginning, but 52 lives were at stake. And wasn't Carter practicing what we preached, that life and freedom were the highest value in our society? As I thought about it further, I realized a discrepancy existed. Although we had preached this ideal from the time our country was born, the government's actions in regard to American Indians, the Blacks, and the Vietnamese had contradicted the country's philosophy. In other instances ranging from business education to law we had quite often done great damage to our ideals. As a consequence, the truth has always been difficult to face.

I then wondered if Iran, in provoking the United States, had been trying to get us to attack so that they could point up our hypocrisy. And did Carter resist out of sincere belief, or was it simply a strategic action? Whatever the reason, it reaffirmed to the world that we indeed placed human life on such a lofty plateau. As praise-worthy as this was, it did seem to cause severe confusion, not only to the Iranians, but to many Americans as well.

The reality, it seems, regardless of what we preached, and the expectation for many Americans was that the United States would go into Iran and punish them for their transgression. Should the hostages have been lost . . . well, that would have been tragic . . . but . . . . It now began to dawn on me that the anger emanating from my two friends and many others had arisen because they had felt betrayed in some way. But how?

Since BS has become so all pervasive, it also follows that we have had to adapt to it if we were to survive. Therefore, as a defense, many have taken the position of believing very little of what they hear or see, particularly when it comes from government. The totally cynical depend on believing just the opposite of what is expressed. The adjustment to both positions requires the experiencing of disillusionment after disillusionment, accompanied by much pain and costing a great deal in emotional and psychological terms. What many people felt was that regardless of what we preached, Carter should have sent in troops, bombed the Iranians, punished them severely, and maintained our image of being a powerful country. When Carter did none of these things it was looked upon as a betrayal. Worse, it invalidated the costly adjustments they had made in learning new survival techniques of comprehending "information accurately" to fight BS. The shock of going from "we do not practice what we preach," to "we do practice what we preach" created, I believe, a severe confusion, disorientation, frustration, and finally, an anger within my friends that was directed toward the person who was perceived to have caused it — Carter.

Patriotic fervor predictably rose to grand proportions during the release of the hostages. Simultaneously, Democracy also looked extremely good, as it demonstrated the orderly transfer of power at the Inaugural. I wonder now if my two friends still feel betrayed by Carter who upheld our ideals, values and priorities by practicing what the country preaches? I also wonder how they will respond to Reagan who does advocate the use of force, which might lead us to war?

THE ULTIMATE BULLSHITTER

William Shakespeare in "Hamlet" said it all when he wrote:

"This above all: to thine ownself be true."

We may be searching out and unmasking deception perpetrated by others, yet, there hides within each of us our own little monster, for there is nothing worse than deceiving oneself, a common occurrence. You may be able to see it clearly in another person, but like a horse with blinders, it becomes extremely difficult (if not impossible) to see ourselves in our own mono-vision.

The psychoanalysts describe this distortion as the ego gone awry. They've pinpointed the reason for it, i.e., the need to seem more than you are because of insecurity, and the attempt to compensate in various ways for that seeming lack, or rationalization. Whereas we are all guilty of some rationalization, we are speaking here of the extreme, and ironically, while this type of person is trying to fool and deceive someone else, all they succeed in doing is fooling themselves.

They are quite easy to spot, and I'm sure everyone in their experience can describe such a person. These are a few of mine:

"Short Stuff"

He is the physically diminutive man, approximately 5 feet tall, who may have the added burden of not being handsome, and may even be balding. The first thing he does is get platform shoes that raise his height to 5'2". He may wear a toupee or, if he has big bucks and can stand pain, may get hair transplants.

No matter what he thinks—it has to be BIG. When he dates a woman she dare not be 5'2" but must measure at least 6'. If he smokes a cigar it is not a Tiparillo but a two foot Cuban Corona. If he's out with a party of six, he has to pick up the check for everyone. And in business, no penny-ante deal will do, say 50–75 thousand dollar profit for him—it has to be millions. Above all, he has to be the center of attention, so he has to drive the biggest automobile, wear the most expensive clothes, talk the loudest, and boast about having the greatest number of women.

"Macho Man"

He is the rough, tough hombre whose loud booming voice masks a latent homosexuality or cowardice. He treats woman insultingly, discourteously, condescendingly: he bullies men, women and children—anyone he thinks is weaker than himself. He feels he has to athletically outperform all competition; he must be more sexually potent than any other man; look stronger, talk more fiercely, and never, never admit to an iota of sentiment or weakness. A really sick "macho man" may even carry a gun which he'll probably never dare use. Deep down, though, he is a frightened little child whose emotional growth was stunted a long time ago.

"The Genius"

This is the person who thinks he is the most brilliant scientist, the most accomplished painter, the most creative composer in the world. He feels that because he has not been showered with fame, fortune, adulation, and women fighting for his favors that the world is blind, insensitive, stupid, and vulgar.

Our "genius" carries an air of superiority at all times, is above any common labor, demands to be waited upon by his mother, mistress or wife, and always assumes the pose of being in the grip of inspiration. Quite often, he is talented, and does bring work to completion. This level of accomplishment, however, is not enough. It also makes his own deception even more difficult to unmask.

In his weaker moments, he desperately fights off nagging doubts of being a "hack," or a second rate talent: an anger constantly rages against not being omnipotent: he is forever frightened of being found out a fraud: to bolster himself, he must consistently denigrate everyone elses work.

"The Good Guy"

He is the good Samaritan. He is the kindest, most understanding, most generous, most helpful — the gentlest of men. If you went up to him and slapped him across the face, he'd turn the other cheek. If you are a bore, he'll listen. If you rob him, he'll find valid, excusable reasons for your behavior. He will take almost any abuse you give him and do it with a smile.

Under no circumstance will he even risk a hint of rejection; he would rather face death. His apparent strengths camouflage the fact that he is dependent upon you and is the prisoner of other people's approbation. This dependency has generated a killing anger that must be constantly suppressed. Sometimes, "Mr. Good Guy" is so good, you want to give him a slap and tell him to get mean and be human.

"Mr. Know-It-All"

He is the world's authority on anything and everything. If it's sports, he's got every record down pat. It it's politics, he's got the solution to every problem. Forget science. As this discipline is already factual, he's got a complete lock on it. In the more subjective areas of art, religion and philosophy, he still remains adamant and forceful.

He corrects his wife, his children, his parents, his friends. He will argue with anyone who opposes his position on the subject. When he is shaky or weak on the correct answer, he will go to stronger intimidation techniques like betting sums of money. Should he actually be on the verge of losing an argument, he will create his own "facts" or excuses — anything to blur the issue or confuse it. He will continue to the end, wriggling out of difficulty.

"Mr. Know-It-All" cannot and dare not lose because his image of himself that he is infallible will crumble. His inner world of doubt and insecurity, anxiously shored-up at every turn, like Humpty-Dumpty could not be put together again if he fell and broke even once.

"Mr. Irresistible"

He thinks he is good looking, so irresistible — God's chosen — that to be anything more than handsome, would be a waste of energy. He's spoiled by his parents, sought out by girls in high school and college, and unless he's an exception to the rule, he's been able to slide by on his studies with help from these women. He is given the "cushy" job, and he gets invited to the best parties. Quite often, this type of person will have athletic ability — football quarterback, tennis player, swimmer, golf pro — which helps to enhance his good looks with glamour. People feel compelled to give him things, do things for him: he is so conditioned to receiving, he believes it is his inalienable right. He is thought of as a good "catch" and will probably make a "good" (rich) marriage.

But sadly, all is not well in this fairyland. Because he is emotionally and sexually fickle, he is unable to have a true relationship in which an exchange exists ultimately leading to the breakup of his marriage, or marriages. But his biggest fear of all is that he will grow old and his looks will deteriorate. Too late, he realizes he has built nothing solid or permanent. Wistfully, he remembers when he was once young, beautiful, and irresistible.

There are many, many more such types as "The Big Spender," "Mr. Cool," "Mr. Law," "Mr. Religion," but they all exemplify the mono-visioned person who not only is deceiving himself but short-changing himself out of the richness of life's experiences.

While we may all get "taken" because of our own selfish interests, some of us even more than once, we will eventually bring our experience in line with the results and make changes. So, we are "curable." But for the "Ultimate Bullshitter," his case is far more pathological, hence his prognosis is quite dim. No common insight will do in his case; he will need the services of a very good therapist.

CHAPTER V

BULLSHIT IN BUSINESS

THE CORPORATE IMAGE TODAY

Where big business was once considered the ally of the public and the government, it is fast becoming the enemy. Where it was once looked upon as the savior of society and treated like a deity, it is now viewed as immoral and dangerous. It seems the public is no longer accepting "persuasion" unconditionally in the name of "economic progress."

Strictly on a consumer level, for example, David Ewing, an editor of the Harvard Business Review, wrote that "The public anger at corporations is beginning to well up at a frightening rate." He cites a 1977 study by a research affiliate of the Harvard Business School whose findings, he says, "sent tremors throughout the corporate world." The study revealed that about half of all consumers polled believed they were getting worse treatment in the market place than a decade earlier; three-fifths said that products had deteriorated; over half mistrusted product guarantees. Ewing quotes a worried businessman as saying, "it feels like we're sitting on a San Andreas fault." And according to John C. Beigler, an executive of Price Waterhouse, one of the giant blue-chip accounting firms, "Public confidence in the American Corporation is lower than at any time since the Great Depression. American business and the accounting profession are being called on the carpet for a kind of zero-based rejustification of just about everything we do . . . corporate performance is being measured against new and unfamiliar norms."

The American public, penetrating the wall of "symbolically mediated information," are indeed demanding a new concept of

95

the corporation. Alvin Toffler, in "The Third Wave," points out that where corporations were once criticized for underpaying workers, overcharging customers, forming cartels to fix prices, making shoddy goods, and a thousand other economic transgressions, the corporate critics today start from a totally different premise. They no longer view the corporation as just an economic institution and attack the artificial divorce of economics from politics, morality, and the other dimensions of life. They hold the corporation increasingly responsible, not merely for its economic performance, but for its side effects on everything from air pollution to executive stress. Corporations are thus assailed for asbestos poisoning, for using poor populations as guinea pigs in drug testing, for distorting the development of the nonindustrial world, for racism and sexism, for secrecy and deception, from the fascist generals in Chile to the racists in South Africa. In effect, the critics are saying corporations can no longer just make product or profit, they must contribute to the solution of extremely complex ecological, moral, political, racial, sexual, and social problems.

The expanded corporate role does not sit well with American business. Instead of trying to find genuine solutions to problems, or changing their behavior and limiting their greed for profits, they have simply increased the use of an old standby—bullshit. Business has chosen to maintain the status quo and fight its adversaries with intensified "public relations." The public, however, with the help of Ralph Nader and other consumer safeguard organizations have begun to unearth the techniques of BS used by big business and are now beginning to reverse some of their gains.

The John Manville Corporation, for example, is facing 11,000 law suits for asbestos poisoning which might cost as much as two billion dollars, and has filed for bankruptcy. Proctor and Gamble is facing similar law suits in the case of Rely Tampons which caused many deaths. Also, a drug for arthritis which had crippling and other dangerous side effects was taken off the market a short time after its release, causing the stock of its company to drop precipitously and in the case of Love Canal and others like it involving pollution and death, the responsible companies are also being exposed and prosecuted.

The effects of business bullshit go beyond individual businesses and are far more insidious regarding the foundation of society. It has transformed the very substance of our values into meaningless and dangerous instruments. Business, for example, went from "planned obsolescence" for greater profit to poor engineering. Products that were designed to wear out quickly, or malfunction, now cause death. Truth has degenerated into credibility, facts into statements that sound authoritative without conveying any authoritative information. As Daniel Boorstein has pointed out, "We live in a world of pseudo-events and quasi information, in which the air is saturated with statements that are neither true nor false but merely credible . . . the important consideration is not whether information accurately describes an objective situation but whether it sounds true." Although there is a "Truth In Advertising" requirement by the government, for example, it is a mockery because of the emotional symbolism that gets away from the necessity for any facts whatsoever. Ultimately, crossing the line of bullshit becomes so easy that it slips into outright lying. Policy of substance becomes a policy of process. The auto industry, for example, is integral to our economy. It employs millions of workers. It is absolutely necessary that it remain financially healthy. Yet, in its greed for profits, it ignored precise marketing information which stated that the consumer wanted a more gas efficient, smaller automobile; the same as those being supplied by the foreign auto makers. The U.S. auto industry arrogantly tried to shove the large cars down the American Public's throat because they made a greater profit on them. That is why the critics of corporate America are demanding a new concept of the corporation with many responsibilities beyond the economic. They want a policy of substance regarding environment, safety, health and morality. They do not want emphasis on the ends alone and are saying to corporate America that the means are equally important.

But despite the accomplishments of Nader and others to uncover bullshit in business, the techniques are so extensive and ingrained that it is as difficult as cancer to control and eliminate. BS is not only created and designed by the power structure, it is also taught to the lower echelons who are constantly conditioned to it through fear and ambition to where it ultimately becomes a stringent part of their education and philosophy.

THE CARE & FEEDING OF EXECUTIVES

Playing the Game

The transformation of substance has had reverberation everywhere within the corporation as well as external to it. Modern man does not much care that there is a job to be done—the slogan of American Capitalism at the early, more enterprising stage of its development; what interests him is that relevant audiences have to be cajoled, won over, seduced. He confuses successful completion of the task at hand with the impression he makes or hopes to make on others. He may put in long hours, go through the motions of the job, occupy time with minutiae, not for the sake of the work itself, but to show "loyalty" and pomp. He is more concerned with the trappings of power than the reality of power, knowing that appearances are taken in lieu of the actual accomplishment.

John Wareham, one of the top corporate headhunters, in getting important executives to change companies, details what motivates many. "Power cannot be measured in quantitative terms," he says, "thus executives value such outward signs and symbols as office location and furnishings because they know these are often the only way their colleagues and subordinates can assess their power with the organization . . . In an era in which the medium is the message—and bubble reputations may last no longer than fifteen minutes—the appearance of success is as crucial to many people as the reality. That is why benefits such as entry to exclusive clubs, access to chauffeur-driven limousines, use of company jets, are so keenly coveted. These things symbolize success. Whether or not the success they symbolize is real is beside the point; what matters is the reality of the illusion."

Corporate Philosophy and Hero Worship

Externally, the public also plays a part. As Robert Heller points out, "The public can't tell the difference because it lionizes the management hero by instinct; it dangles before him the front cover of "Business Week," or a knighthood, or membership of the blue chip panel of business leaders, or a life peerage. The public does this because it dearly loves a leader . . . Everybody believes that leadership is a supreme human attribute—it even gets praised in school reports. But in management terms, leadership is a greatly overrated quality . . . the Americans are blinded by their recurrent desire for a "man on horseback" and by the simple refusal to believe that anybody who has made millions, floated to the top of a large corporation, or both, can be an idiot . . ." Or worse, that he is mendacious, irresponsible, and dangerous.

While management schools do not run courses in mendacity,

they aren't needed — executives are to the manor born. Not the deliberate lie; that is reserved for occasional denials of financial deals or other forlorn suppressions of the truth. Not, usually, deception on the criminal scale like that of the convicted electrical or plumbing price fixers and others of a similar ilk. No, the kind of untruth that is endemic in management and potentially fatal — is bullshit. Corporate heads are fond of phrases such as, "It is our able and dedicated employees who continue to be the company's most valuable resource." Yet, often they are less important than physical assets. Companies sometimes move entire operations to new towns, leaving their labor forces in the lurch. Nearly the entire New England textile industry has shifted to the more pliable South: but its executives took care not to forget the up-to-date machines. Even if people can't be replaced collectively, they are always disposable individually. Against this background, few businesses pay the labor force much attention until trouble actually breaks out.

Executives state they exist to sell automobiles or peas, build power stations, market lingerie, or whatever, but insensibly they slide into serving none of these ends. Instead, they serve only the corporation, because inherent to the corporation is the principle that it exists only to sustain and perpetuate itself. In other words, it exists to exist. As a result, morality is violated, crimes are committed, and human rules of conduct are distorted.

Sissela Bok says, "Recent studies indicate that businessmen regard unethical practices as very widespread, and pressures to conform as strong. These pressures can be communicated directly from the top management, with an immediate effect on lower level managers. Three quarters of those surveyed agree that like the junior members of Nixon's reelection committee, young executives automatically go along with superiors to show loyalty. *Very often, however, there is no such communication from the management; the pressures are conveyed indirectly.* For example, a company may set high goals for production on sales. When economic conditions become adverse, it may be next to impossible to meet these targets without moral compromises. If the incentive for achieving the goals — retaining one's job, most importantly, but also promotions, bonuses, or salary increases — are felt to be too compelling, the temptation to lie and cheat can grow intolerable." (Italics Mine)

Quite often, however, management is explicit and obvious. One chief executive of a sales organization implemented what he termed "planned insecurity." Each month a listing in order of individual sales results was placed on the bulletin board, and the fellow whose name appeared last was automatically fired. An insurance organization created pressure in another manner; the sales competition winner was awarded the down payment on a Mercedes which was delivered to his home replete with a big red ribbon. Unfortunately, to keep the car, along with the esteem of his wife and neighbors, he had to pay installments out of his subsequent commission earnings. To do so, he ultimately felt he was expected to bend a few rules if it was necessary to meet the new quota that would allow him to retain the Mercedes.

BS in Business Schools

The inclination to stretch permissible bounds was set a long time ago, many years prior to the actual situation. Students at leadership-training institutions are constantly put in ferociously competitive situations, and thus get by implication the message that life is a contest and that satisfaction in it is to be obtained by clannishness, massiveness, ferocity, unscrupulousness tenacity of purpose, politics, and deception.

Does any Harvard Business School professional or management consultant rise to tell students and practitioners of business that what counts in the boardroom is "How you played the game?" Indeed not. What counts is winning or losing, and no bones made. "Ethics" is encouraged by the more elevated of these arbiters of business conduct, but never generosity, unselfishness, gallantry—the qualities that make up the much-dishonored but still much-promulgated ideal of "sportsmanship." No credit accrues to one who habitually applies those qualities in business dealings; rather, he is apt to be patronized as a romantic fool, and handed a pink slip on Friday afternoon. Even a sense of "social responsibility"—the appropriateness of which in a corporate leader is the subject of sharp debate among business theorists, is usually defended not for its own value but on pragmatic ground of its long term service to increased profit. In sum, in the business world, predatory invidiousness is universally accorded the highest value, while there is no code, not even a dishonored one, to embody the values of honesty or humaness.

Fortune magazine in April, 1980, treated its readers to sketches of those it had selected as the ten "toughest" corporate bosses in the country. One of them, the magazine reported, is known to his subordinates as "Idi" (after the whimsically murderous Uganda dictator Idi Amin), and likes to dress down his peers as well as his subordinates in public. Of another: "Doesn't listen well, so he is frustrating to work for; most glaring trait is his lack of feelings for people." Of another: "Accomplished at belittling people in front of others." Yet another "becomes enamored of someone, but that wears off." And another "demolishes anyone who blows smoke at him." A final entry is described as keeping his subordinates under surveillance so that "they won't go to the bathroom without his permission." In blunter language, the qualities that distinguish these men are arrogance, gratuitousness, cruelty, self-centeredness, lack of consideration of others, pettiness, fickleness, and schoolyard bullying. Yet they are high among the leaders and role models for youth entering business and other corporate executives!

Corporate Isolation

Michael Maccoby in *The Gamesman* adds two other qualities that pervade the corporate structure. "The most malignant reason why the heart does not develop (in the corporate world) is because the individual hardens his heart or, as in myths and dreams, replaces it with stone. The heart becomes perverted as the will is directed toward power . . . The process of bending one's will to corporate goals and moving up the hierarchy leads to meanness, emotional stinginess . . . and fear . . . Some are frightened that they will fail to perform well; they will lose a sale, miss a deadline, come up with the wrong answer. Someone above them will decide they don't measure up and "zap" them . . . they fear becoming losers, left behind in the dead-end jobs that satisfy neither their needs for craftsmanship nor their desire for respect . . . Careerism results not only in constant anxiety, but also in an underdeveloped heart. Overly concerned with adapting himself to others, to marketing himself, the careerist constantly betrays himself, since he must ignore idealistic, compassionate, and courageous impulses that might jeopardize his career. As a result, he never develops an inner center, a strong, independent sense of self, and eventually loses touch with his deepest strivings."

When the fear is coupled with artificial isolation, as it so often is in corporations, the end result is an individual totally alienated from himself, his corporation, and the public. Maccoby describes the isolation thus: "Corporate managers do not hear cries because they have created protected enclaves, those isolated villages that grow up wherever there are large corporations. Indeed, corporations move out to the suburbs in order to build enclaves. Many companies that set up shop in other countries house their employees in enclaves where they are either totally isolated from the locals or live with native managers who are also protecting themselves from their poor compatriots. These little villages express spatially the psychic attitudes of the corporate managers who detach themselves from what goes on in the rest of the world . . . The enclave is more than the protected village or house in the country. It is a state of mind, the psychic shell that isolates and protects the heart . . . The enclave protects a person from himself and the world. Many an American manager has moved from the city to suburb to leave violence and decay, taking no responsibility for improving the city. Because he lives in an enclave, he continues fearful of those outside the walls who may be envious of him. Isolated from the poor, he lacks understanding (not to speak of compassion) about why they are poor and how the corporate system isolates them and insures their continued poverty . . . Many managers—probably the majority—would be just as happy if all the unneeded people disappeared." The bluntest of them sounds like a middle manager in charge of a computer development who said, "we take enough Negroes into the company to keep them from burning down the cities, but we won't change our standard operating practice anymore than we have to. I don't care about those guys. It'll be better in the long run. They'll be out of the world economy." If Maccoby had added that they not only have a cold heart but contempt for others as well as themselves, the profile would be absolutely complete.

Corporate Disillusionment

These executives are only a few of the players. There are others. Dr. Fredenberger in *Burn Out* sketches some of them. He says, "It would be nice to think that all the things they taught us when we were young are true and that the people at the top got there because they were outstanding in some way. Unhappily, since incompetence rises, then the opposite is true in more cases than not. The imaginative individual who is overflowing with original ideas and abundant energy is often considered a maverick, too difficult to handle, too difficult to pigeonhole. If he doesn't fit a particular niche on the organizational charts, no one knows where to place him, and he's passed over when promotions come due until eventually he becomes disillusioned and ceases to be effective.

Meanwhile, colorless, politically oriented hacks who make no waves and offer no criticism (no innovations, either) climb the ladder, creating a dual dilemma for their capable underlings. For one thing, there's the unanswerable question, "Why him instead of me?" For another, there's the necessity to resign oneself to working under one's inferior. Executives who rise despite a lack of intrinsic merit make unsatisfactory bosses. Because they are so nervous, they are wishy-washy about making decisions, always looking to see which way the wind is blowing before they commit themselves. They are so busy preserving the status quo, they can't be relied on to back up their staff or go to bat for controversial viewpoints . . . In general, the system is not set up for the independent spirit or the talented noncomformist. Its basis is toward the staid, compliant type who doesn't rock the boat, and the people who survive and flourish within its confines are, with few exceptions, not dedicated to high achievement. Men and women who are committed to accomplishment are usually forthright and outspoken. They don't play the political game well; in fact, they don't play it at all. When they have a gripe against a colleague, they tell him face to face. It never occurs to them that many of the people they're surrounded by are not so straightforward and might be sabotaging them behind their backs . . . When a person who plays fair is responsible to, or surrounded by, people who fight foul, his Burn-out becomes almost inevitable. So many emotions surge up inside him all at once, he has to wrestle with his feelings of being taken advantage of, he even works harder at his job in an attempt to repudiate the ugliness. Should all of these fail, he may turn to a false cure for relief . . .

. . . The larger the organization becomes the more layers it seems to acquire, with every layer needing to justify its existence. In such a structure, the emphasis shifts from the work itself to the outward signs of work . . . and it disturbs people in business to find themselves spending time on everything but what they were hired to do . . .

. . . Since every office has its share of insecure people (not to mention incompetent ones), much of the memo writing originates so that someone can prove to someone else he did something that day. Department heads encourage their subordinates to hold multiple meetings and circulate the minutes in the hope their departments will look productive and busy. In many organizations the process degenerates into that oft-joked-about syndrome known as PYA (Protect Your Ass), but to someone who is neither incompetent nor insecure, it isn't amusing. In such a structure, the competent individual finds himself in a no-win situation. If he ignores the system and spends his time quietly doing his work, he exposes himself to two dangers; being considered uncooperative, and not having a record of his activities when he comes up for review. If, on the other hand, he goes along with what's expected of him, he's apt to lose his relatedness to his work . . ."

Social Transformation of BS

On other levels, Christopher Lasch points out that, "When jobs consist of little more than meaningless motions, and when social routines, formerly dignified as ritual, degenerate into role play, the worker—whether he toils on an assembly line or holds down a high-paying job in a large bureaucracy—seeks to escape from the resulting sense of inauthenticity by creating an ironic distance from his daily routine. He attempts to transform role playing into a symbolic elevation of daily life. He takes refuge in jokes, mockery, and cynicism. If he is asked to perform a disagreeable task, he makes it clear that he doesn't believe in the organization's objectives of increased efficiency and greater output. If he goes to a party, he shows by his actions that it's all a game—false, artificial, insincere; a gross travesty of sociability. In this way he attempts to make himself invulnerable to the pressures of the situation. By refusing to take seriously the routines he has to perform, he denies their capacity to injure him. Although he assumes that it is impossible to alter iron limits imposed on him by society, a detached awareness of those limits seems to make them matter less. By demystifying daily life, he conveys to himself and others the impression that he has risen beyond it, even as he goes through the motions and does what is expected of him . . ."

In turn, it engenders a deep determination to manipulate the feelings of others to his own advantage. It is for this reason that sociability now functions as an extension of work by other means. Personal life too, no longer is a refuge from deprivations suffered at work. It has become anarchical, as warlike and as full of stress as the marketplace itself. The cocktail party reduces sociability to social combat. Experts write tactical manuals in the art of social survival, advising the status-seeking party-goer to take up commanding positions in the room, surround himself with a loyal band of retainers, and avoid turning his back on the field of battle.

Where task orientation and task mastery were once the criteria in work, the shift is now to "winning images" and other players' moves. Thomas Szasz notes that success depends on "information" about the personality of other players. "The better the corporate executive or bureaucrat understands the personal characteristics of his subordinates, the better he can exploit their mistakes in order to control them and to reassure his own supremacy. If he knows that his subordinates lie to him, the lie communicates the important information that they fear and wish to please him. By accepting the bribe, as it were, of flattery, cajolery, or sheer subservience implicit in being lied to, the recipient of the lie states, in effect, that he is willing to barter these items for the truth." On the other hand, acceptance of the lie reassures the liar he will not be punished, while reminding him of his dependence and subordination. In this way, both parties gain a measure of security.

In Joseph Heller's novel "Something Happened" the protagonist's boss makes it clear that what he wants from his subordinates is not "good work" but "spastic colitis and nervous exhaustion."

> "God dammit, I want the people working for me to be worse off than I am, not better. That's the reason I pay you so well. I want to see you right on the verge. I want it right out in the open. I want to be able to hear it in a stuttering, flustered, tongue-tied voice . . . Don't trust me. I don't trust flattery, loyalty, and sociability. I don't trust deference, respect, and cooperation. I trust fear."

Is it any wonder then that the business world is characterized as a "jungle" and life as "a rat race." The greedy pursuit for more and more profit, and more and more power, has bred an irresponsible, insensitive, uncaring, cruel, unkind individual who is not only alienated from the public but from himself. He is so fearful, so insecure, so self-centered, his entire concern is narcissistic and the rest of the world be damned. For him, the ends justify the means.

Although these executives learn how to control and manipulate the media, they basically keep a low profile. They seem, like the corporations they work for, to be faceless. The corporation has the appearance of being run by ghosts, except in the rare instance of a Lee Ioccoca who takes center stage in TV commercials for Chrysler automobiles. Is there a significant reason for the camouflage?

The New Ruling Class

Christopher Lasch points out that "American Capitalism, ostensibly antiauthoritarian and with a belief in equality, rejected priestly and monarchial dominance only to replace it with dominance of the business corporation, the managerial and professional classes who operate the corporate system, and the corporate state. A new ruling class of administrators, bureaucrats, technicians, and experts appeared . . . *What unifies the managers and professionals of the corporate capitalist system is that they derive most of the benefits.* The needs of the system shape policy and set the permissible limits of public debate. Most of us can see the system but not the class that administers it and monopolizes the wealth it creates." (Italics Mine)

And when one views the enormous salaries of the executives in the monopolies and the rest of the business world who live on fringe benefits—jets, yachts, limousines, country clubs, expensive dinners—better than most kings, it is no wonder that one executive commented, "I'm not that interested in owning stock in this company. That is not where the power is. Frankly, I live better than the majority of my stockholders, and I have more control over my situation and the company being in the position I am!" And most managers get it in writing because they know enough not to trust their own peers. They make sure their salaries and perks are guaranteed. They are no longer even afraid of failure. *The New York Times* reported the "executives in the $500,000 to $1,000,000 a year category are hired on contract— then fired in as little as six months. These same people then go on to equally important and well-paying jobs in other companies. No longer is this considered failure."

While many of the public may not be able to identify them, you can be sure they are well known to each other. The point is they keep a low profile with the public intentionally so as to remain faceless and avoid any public wrath falling on them. A good illusionist shows you the "magic" not the mechanics of the illusion. A good con man relieves you of your money without you even being aware that it is gone. The corporate managers do that and much more serious damage without your being able to specifically identify them individually.

Business not only tries to hide its motives, but frequently will lie about them, even to themselves. In the days when British scientific brains were coming across the Atlantic in flood proportions, the deserters never admitted that doubling, tripling or even quadrupling their living standards was a prime reason for going west. No, the confessed lure was always the wider scope, the richer research and development budgets, the more scientific equipment. And right after World War II, U.S. business quietly smuggled in hundreds of Nazi scientists and other high level brains, with the help of the government. It was kept so quiet that much of the public never became aware of it until "60 Minutes" exposed it in 1981.

Those disinterested scientists who would have emigrated to the U.S. for unchanged standards of living could have been comfortably hijacked in one small executive jet. But Western society considers it shameful to admit doing anything (even something respectable) just for the loot. How often does a multimillionaire allow that making still more millions is his dearest hobby and most pressing motive? That he simply loves to roll around in the green stuff? On the contrary, the money, he says, is just "figures on a piece of paper." The man, of course, clings to those pieces of paper like a starving octopus. Greed is a great motivator, in all its forms, and you can't disentangle greed, for money or anything else, from nonfinancial motives of equal force, such as ambition or power.

"60 Minutes" ran a profile on Malcom Forbes, of "Forbes Magazine," a multimillionaire who deals with the executives of big business by providing lunches on his yacht, a private wine cellar at his offices where chefs prepare gourmet food, and a host of other perks which are all tax deductible. On the issue of unemployment and poverty, Mr. Forbes' callous attitude is that things must get worse before they get better. His life style, like many other executives, is so far removed from reality that he is not aware of the pain of poor and disadvantaged people and could not identify with them if he tried. In justification of Reagonomics, they say that if business is allowed to retain more of its earnings, they will put it back into more plants and more jobs, which will help unemployment and the economy. They never say it will increase their profits even more! I have momentarily digressed, but it has been for the purpose of emphasizing the primary motive and reason for much of the scam, and to put a face on the faceless corporation. The actions of big business do not happen accidently; they happen by design of individuals who are "hiding." The larger danger, however, is that BS in business has become institutionalized and is on its way to becoming ossified.

In the "Third Wave" Toffler shows that the educational and social systems trained and conditioned workers to meet the demands of the industrial revolution. The workers were technically, psychologically and socially conditioned to accept the discipline of dirty factories and uninteresting work. Galbraith adds that they were also psychologically conditioned to want more material things which kept them motivated to their jobs. In the same manner, colleges are turning out MBAs by the thousands, who embody and will perpetuate these same BS values, practices and morality. Whether the system or the individual will have to change first is difficult to answer, but it will be explored in later chapters, particularly in "Bullshit Morality Or The Morality of Bullshit."

BUSINESS SCAMS

Nader's Raiders and news shows featuring consumer advocates like Betty Furness on WNBC in New York have done a lot in creating accurate appraisals of product performance as well as uncovering a number of illegal schemes. Yet, much of the larger chicanery goes undetected because the companies involved are extremely well-known, integral elements of the establishment that operate "legally."

For example, Robert Ringer describes the legitimate scam of using your money interest free. He says, "The security deposits on rental property is an old favorite. Another is the non-interest bearing checking account where, in fact, banks usually make you pay a "service charge" for allowing them to have free use of your money. The big corporations, of course, are the best players of this game (The Cash Flow Game), which is one of the reasons they were able to get so big in the first place—and remain big. They are also most adept at camouflaging how they pull it off. The idea is to use just a few dollars from thousands, or preferably millions of customers. This is not too noticeable to the individual, particularly when disguised as something like a "deposit," but to a giant corporation it can mean the interest-free use of millions of dollars . . . (But) the American Express Company is one of the few that talks about it openly; that's because it's virtually their whole business. They bluntly refer to it as the "float." Here's how it works: American Express sells travelers checks to you, knowing that an average of sixty-five days will elapse between the time you give them your money and the time you cash the travelers checks. During that 65–day period, a large percentage of the cash is invested in, among other things, tax-exempt municipal bonds."

There are other "scams" we shall come to know, but before we examine them there are business myths that throw a broad shadow which serves to conceal the depth and breadth of these deceptions and makes them more difficult to bring to light. One of the largest myths is that business serves the consumer: that without your good will and purchase they would be out of business. Business controls and virtually owns the consumer. This is accomplished by advertising that develops a need in the consumer for products that are not essential. It develops a psychic as well as a material hunger in the consumer that is as addictive as any narcotic. The addiction permits business to charge you what it wants, when it wants. Whatever freedom of choice you think you may have is an illusion. Therefore, if we begin by understanding we are victims of business more than beneficiaries, we can start demystifying the deceptions.

"We're Stealing From You For Your Own Good"

A deception that is particularly difficult to overcome is the utility monopolies which have a stranglehold on the consumer because one cannot go to a competitor. The Monopoly myth says that they unify and standardize service, produce product and service at the lowest possible cost, and control growth that makes research and innovation possible. It must be noted here that what makes BS so difficult to combat is that although it may be a deception it need not be illegal; secondly, it may also contain verifiable facts and some "truth."

For example, results attained by the monopolies in their early years proved their claims: our telephone system is superb. Today, however, costs are rising beyond the consumer's means, the consumer's discontent is not being heard nor rectified, and in the case of energy utilities, there is the scandal of nuclear energy plants. The reality is now beginning to dawn: the monopolies are not serving the public, the public is serving them. More accurately, the monopolies are not serving the public, the public is serving *its private investors and its management*. It is becoming more and more evident that the public is secondary to the profit motive.

This, however, should not come as a surprise. Utility companies have always been *private* businesses "regulated" by government. Like any private company, they have stockholders who have invested capital and expect to make a profit. AT&T made over three billion dollars net profit for just one quarter in 1981, setting a new record for any type of business anywhere in the world! Ironically, they still continue to receive rate increases by the government watchdog-agency that is supposed to be protecting the consumer!

As a result, the cost of telephone, gas and electric service in New York as well as other parts of the country has risen beyond the means of most people. Yet, the consumer can do little or nothing to oppose the increases; the only alternative being to cancel the service, and since these services are more necessity than luxury, the alternative is an illusion.

Unfortunately, AT&T does not have to deal directly with the public, even a powerless public, but only with a government agency that seems to be ineffective. How AT&T bullshits the government will be dealt with later, but for now it is imperative to understand how and why they bullshit the consumer. Although AT&T stockholders number in the millions, the consumers who use their services outnumber stockholders by the tens of millions. Theoretically, the consumer can apply pressure to the government watchdog-agency to insure its wishes are carried out regarding AT&T. Therefore, AT&T must continually try to keep the masses "calm." Consequently, they try to persuade the public that the 3 billion dollar net profit for the quarter in 1981 was due to efficiency, good management, productive employees, and new technology!

On the other hand, they tell the government regulatory agency there is a necessity for continuous rate increases because of high wages and operating costs; that they need the increased rates for more research and development. Of course, it all sounds plausible and it is "substantiated" with loads of paper work. When AT&T adds that in order to attract new capital from the money market it must pay competitive profit percentages on capital, their request is almost guaranteed.

What AT&T is saying is that if an investor can secure 14% on his investment from other sources, then AT&T must pay the same or more; consequently, the rate must be increased to meet the competition for investment money. But there is a flaw in this logic: AT&T investors are "secured," that is, they are *guaranteed* their profit because the consumer, *must* purchase the service from them at the cost set by the government. The investor in other businesses must speculate; that is, they can make a good profit, or they can lose their investment; there is no guarantee in other businesses. Therefore, it would seem logical to me then, that a *lesser* percentage should be paid on a *guaranteed* investment than on a speculative investment.

Another point of contention is the millions of dollars the monopolies spend in advertising their services when one cannot get it from any other source. About the only competition AT&T has had in the past was in the long distance area. The point, however, is not the savings which might have accrued to the consumer but that advertising and public relations are powerful instruments that influence and/or oppose government regulations. It is a weapon that helps AT&T keep the public and government in control. It keeps the power on AT&T's side of the court.

The bottom line is that rate increase after rate increase does not necessarily get you better service or new innovations; what it does is pay for the advertising, legal fees and profit percentages to the stockholders. In many instances like the recent court case which brought AT&T to divestiture, you paid AT&T's costs to fight the government which is you and I! When you consider the nuclear danger created by the electric utilities, the nuclear pollution, the mismanagement and the increased costs of energy, and the fact that we may have to pay for these irresponsible actions, is it any wonder that we must penetrate their bullshit so that we might hold the management and their profit-making stockholders to accountability?

"Guaranteeing Success at Your Expense"

For years the government has "regulated" the operations of airlines, trains, trucking and shipping. In the case of the airlines, the government permitted fixed-pricing and other controls. This meant you had to accept poor service, bad scheduling, fares arbitrarily fixed at a higher level than free competition would allow, and all the other discomforts which go along with "protected" airlines.

Of course, the airlines at that time let the public know what a nuisance government was and that it was government which was responsible for any shortcomings, not them. So, it is interesting to note that when deregulation occurred, creating competition, many of the airlines found themselves in bankruptcy or on the verge of bankruptcy. Of course, the airlines blamed high fuel

111

prices, the increased costs of planes, the recession and cost of competition but no one blamed poor management.

Ironically, when the rich talk about welfare, aid-to-dependents, unemployment compensation, or social security they call it socialism. However, when the government supports the aerospace industry, and military manufacturers produce on a cost-plus-profit basis (a method that produces billions of dollars of waste and a lot of corruption), it is described in any number of ways but never as socialism. Too, when bullshit emanates from the top down it is called truth: when it emanates from the bottom up, it is called distortion. I guess it's all a matter of perspective—or is it?

"Growing Rich Growing Nothing"

The government has given price support to the farmers for years, driving up the prices of food which has strongly contributed to inflation and caused terrible waste. In the past, government subsidy to farmers may have had a valid reason. But in 1981, the government owned so much cheese, for example, it didn't know what to do with it before it rotted. They made a laughable effort to give some of it away to poor people, but this only pointed up the inanity of the system, so they stopped.

The government, it seems, must buy all of the cheese the farmers produce beyond what they can sell on the free market, and at a higher price than the free market. As a result, instead of farmers cutting their production, they have increased it because they have a guaranteed market. Consequently, those farmers who were producing a lot of cheese and making a lot of money—many were already millionaires—only grew richer. The government, in the meantime, was fast running out of storage space. The predicament was thorny; if the cheese was exported at a lower price than the American public was able to buy it, there would be an outcry. On the other hand, if the government gave it away to poor Americans, those that paid for the cheese would cry foul and accuse the government of socialism. An alternative that has been tried with many other farm products is that farmers are paid not to grow them! So, while rich farmers increase their wealth growing nothing, the poor of the country starve despite the fact that it is said we can grow enough food to feed the world!

"How Civil Servants Become the Civilian's Master"

The postal system is one of the largest employers in the United States. At one time it was a marvel of perfection. For a few pennies your mail got to where you wanted it to go with dispatch. However, in the last five to six years, the price of first class mail has risen from ten to twenty-two cents, and the service has gone from poor to horrible. While wages have gone up (the average postal worker earns approximately $25,000 per year) productivity has diminished.

Postal workers cite management; management cites obsolete technology and the rigidity of civil service. Management says workers' demands for increased wages and benefits are strangling the system: workers say management is incompetent. While all this BS is getting slung, private enterprise has shown that it can do the job better. Although United Parcel Service delivers as many or more packages than the post office at a lower cost, it is denied permission to deliver first class mail. A young lady in Pittsburgh showed she could deliver first class mail overnight and could deliver it cheaper, but the government put her out of business immediately. When a private competitor showed a television commercial that asked a man who was waiting to be served while two postal employees were discussing benefits, "With what you've got riding on this letter—would you trust it to the post office?", civil service got its dander up and demanded the message be removed from the airwaves. It was. Who continues to lose? The consumer. Who continues to win? The civil servants and the management. Who really serves who?

"Trust In Me"

The Securities Exchange Commission—SEC—is a government agency that was established as a watchdog over the sale and purchase of stock. It was originated to curb and control the rapacious behavior of robber barons during the 1920s and 30s, and to a great extent, compared to other government agencies has been relatively successful. It has a reputation as the scourge of stock and corporate manipulators. Yet, it is limited in what it can do to curb stock prices inflated through publicity or "creative" accounting by the CPAs of the industry. Many stock speculators are "big boys" who can take care of themselves and, being gamblers by nature, know full well the meaning of buyer beware. But there are the "innocents"—the small investor who has bought the myth of American business—who is not as sophisticated.

113

They rely heavily on the effectiveness of the SEC. If untrue claims are intentionally *stated* the SEC can prosecute the manipulators. However, if impressions of success are created through publicity and investors take the bait, prosecution is not possible. It is extremely difficult, if not impossible, to prosecute BS in court; that is one reason BS is so widespread.

Robert Heller in "The Great Executive Dream" describes a company in the late 1960s which, for a while, took in not only the innocent but the big boys as well. He says, "The public relations directed from the Litton office in Beverly Hills (a former movie palazzo, furnished with low technology antiques) cost plenty, but it worked wonders. Of all the postwar companies in the U.S., Litton was one of the most glamorous, flattered, and followed. Its emphasis on converting space-age technology into commercial products summed up the ethos of the moon age; and its specialty of "systems" introduced a new magical phrase into the salesman's sample bag.

Litton raised the pursuit of higher earnings per share, with the aid of heavy debt gearing, to an art form, starting off a nationwide chase that only ended with the 1969/70 market crash . . . The whole Litton legend was built around the constant rise of the share price, though Ash (one of Litton's chief executive officers) said predictably, in a 1968 interview, 'It is not an essential or even an important part of our growth for the price of the stock to go on rising.' *In fact, the bounden duty of the publicity machine was self-evidently to keep a high head of steam behind the stock price.* Litton's sheer growth in sales volume, half at least coming through acquisition, was formidable, but its profitability (the name of the real game) was never up to much."

Litton had gone on living its myth. Interviewed at the end of 1969, Ash said, "I regard what happened as a stumbling in the search for growth." The stumble lasted so long that it qualifies better as a crawl. In 1970, earnings after pooling of interest were only 20 percent higher than in 1964 (on doubled sales). Would Litton's management have operated any more successfully over this period if the myth had not been believed, internally and externally? If Ash and Thornton had not persuaded themselves (presumably) and the public (certainly) that there was some meaningful connection between ships and making portable typewriters? The bottom line was that investors were led to believe by appearance that something was there that wasn't. Figures are not supposed to lie but they sure can be manipulated to give various impressions. However, it was publicity that glamorized Litton making it look more desirable than it actually was. As a result, Litton investors took a bath. Even in 1971, with the Dow Jones index pushing up to the magic 1,000, Litton shares dragged along the ocean floor at only a quarter of their one time glory.

It is not my intention to single out the government as the scapegoat. Business and government have always had a symbiotic relationship. The main point is that until you can understand the appearance of government *opposing* business is an illusion, you won't be able to break through the myths. It is an illusion because of two factors: the first is that when we say "government" the presumption is that the weight and resource of the entire government is behind the action taken; in reality, it is only a department of government which, in terms of sheer power does not match the power of such larger corporations as AT&T and IBM. These companies are so big they are larger and more powerful than a number of foreign countries. Secondly, one department of government may clash with another over the same issue — the administrative with the legislative or executive, weakening the entire opposition.

Although AT&T was made to divest its local companies in the "loss" of its case with the government, it was allowed to enter the previously denied area of data communications with potential profits far superior than what was lost. Too, with its incredible financial resources, it has the strength to knock its competition right out of the box.

IBM & AT&T with their enormous financial resources go into court against any adversary including the government knowing they can legally pervert the legal system so that they obfuscate issues, make them obsolete, and simply outlast opponents to win, even when they have supposedly "lost." BS in Law has the same ability as BS anywhere to create appearances of adversaries in combat while in reality they are more or less bed partners.

For example, an editorial in the "Daily News" regarding the Manville Corporation, points out a new wrinkle of business, government, and law interacting to screw the public. Note, that while the editorial seems to be offering a constructive solution, it is but a diversionary tactic utilized in business' favor. The editorial says:

> Even in an era when thousands of companies are going bankrupt, the sight of an industrial giant like the Manville Corporation heading for Chapter 11 is a shocker. But this is a special case, one that

says a lot more about the nation's legal mess than about its economic woes.

To put it bluntly, Manville filed for bankruptcy as a device to protect itself from being swamped by lawsuits from people claiming to be victims of asbestos poisoning. The company is staring at $2 billion in claims—maybe more.

Actually, Manville is the second asbestos outfit to use Chapter 11 as a legal screen. Unless Congress steps in very quickly, there's a good chance other firms will follow suit.

Undoubtedly, some of these law suits are valid: thousands of Americans have suffered health damage because of asbestos, many of them workers during World War II who helped install fire-retardant material in the nation's warships.

Nevertheless, there's something deeply disturbing about the prospect of an entire industry being run out of business by multimillion dollar litigation. And the really upsetting part is that most of the money isn't going to the victims—it's ending up in the hands of their lawyers!

There's a plan before Congress that offers a way out of the situation. The idea is to create a pool of funds for settling claims, drawn partly from the industry and partly from the federal government because of its role in promoting the use of asbestos.

We're not crazy about such a bailout. Still, Congress should give the idea careful thought. It could be a way to short circuit those lawsuits, get the money directly to the victims, not their attorneys, and prevent an industry from being wiped out because of health hazards that weren't even recognized a few years ago.

Once again, the editorial is suggesting that the government — you and I — take over Manville's responsibility. Why should we have to foot the bill? We never made any of the profits. And why should lawyers have to take a bad rap? What about all the money industry spent with lawyers who defended them against us in government cases? As long as *we* paid *their* legal bills (Tax Deductions), lawyers were great, part of the wonderful legal system in this country.

Now that the Manville Corporation might have to pay the victim's lawyers, lawyers are vultures. I have no great love of lawyers but this is definitely a bad rap.

It seems the same value system and the same bullshit that prevailed in the early symbiotic business/government relationship is still alive and kicking. The difference this time is that "public relations" is not solving the problem, nor will the problem just disappear. It also appears that when victims start to avail themselves of the legal system in an effective way, rules may quickly change. So, not only may we have to pay for the Manville Corporation's irresponsibility without ever having shared the profits, we may once again have to face the fact that equal justice is an illusion, too.

PHILANTHROPIES

So much of business is built on a foundation of deceiving or being deceived that it is a wonder products are produced as well as they are, or that anything gets done. It seems business cannot deal with anything unless it conceals its motive, and that it cannot touch anything or anyone without corrupting it. Corporate philanthropy is a case in point.

When the Texas magnate H. Ross Perot had first made many millions, indeed momentarily a billion or two, out of installing and programming computer systems for state welfare programs, he announced that he would take no deductions on his numerous charitable contributions because he did not want to take tax revenue away from a government that was ineffably dear to him. Other philanthropists, while protesting their affection for the government, nevertheless concluded that Perot was mad. And it does appear that he soon changed his mind and began taking his deductions along with the other angels. It took this relatively naive East Texan little time to recognize formally, the moral fudge inherent in tax-deductible philanthropy, and, if briefly, to act on his recognition. His initial generosity showed clearly that the original charitable motive for sharing what one had acquired had not been entirely eroded by the onward march of industrial specialization.

"What has been most seriously eroded," according to John Brooks, "is the ability of the giver to feel, deep down, that he is or should be really acting charitably at all. This is most conspicuous in corporate philanthropy — giving for the general good not by individuals or philanthropic foundations but by corporations nominally devoted only to accumulating money. Small groups of churlish stockholders resent this imperious distribution to community projects, cultural TV programs and the like, of money that they consider to be properly theirs. The corporations, living as they do in a legalistic atmosphere, have to defend themselves on practical rather than on moral grounds. They argue that their philanthropy is necessary for the promotion of good public,

117

community, and government relations. If, say, an oil company did not sponsor exhibitions of avant-garde art, the public might come to loathe it so much that the government would be forced to crack down on its pollution or its profits. (But does the public really love avant-garde art that much? No evidence exists that it does. There sometimes seems to be a lack of communication between corporate philanthropists and their constituency.) The corporate giving department becomes, often literally, part of the public-relations department. Charity is at last reduced the ultimate step, to the status of a form of institutional advertising."

Not only does corporate philanthropy transform and distort the intent of philanthropy, but in the process attempts to corrupt the receiver. Brooks says, "Partly out of old habit, partly out of emulation of his new peers, he finds himself acting in certain ways less like the Platonic ideas of a philanthropist than like a commonplace man of affairs. Simply approving a grant request and sending a check to the applicant is not, he learns, the way things are done in his office. Such conduct is apparently too far out of the American corporate mainstream. There has to be a dicker, a tradeoff, of one sort or another. When a promising application is received, there is a conference of the department, or a series of conferences, at which the application is discussed and ways proposed by which it can be remolded to serve better the goals of society as perceived by the pooled brains of the corporate giving department. The applicant is summoned, and asked to resubmit the proposal with changes to conform to the various whims and notions of the corporate givers, (or, perhaps, the 'vicarious consumers without qualification.') The applicant, idealistic or foolishly stubborn, may balk. Now the corporate philanthropist must go carefully, because the applicant has the great public prestige and is so successful that he does not really need the grant. Not really needing the grant is, of course, a prime qualification or getting one; such a position gives an application status as a highly desirable grantee whose association with the department would be a feather in its cap."

If one can picture in his mind John D. Rockefeller giving away dimes to change his image—he was excoriated for his vicious monopolistic practice—you will have a key not only to the Rockefeller Foundation, one of the largest in the world, but to almost all other philanthropies. The philanthropies may do some good—even a lot of good—but that was never their primary objective. The primary objective was to whitewash the giver, relieve guilt feelings, to build false monuments to the source. It was all bullshit to begin with.

Is it any wonder then that critics of corporate America are demanding a new concept of the corporation, one with many responsibilities beyond the economic, and a policy of substance regarding environment, safety, health and morality? It is one thing to state that the means are as important as the ends: it is another to reverse the deeply ingrained and widespread corruption of bullshit in business that has so extensively contributed to the deterioration of society. But until we can deal with BS accurately, and accept individual responsibility for our share of it, we will not be able to change things permanently in business nor in the world.

CHAPTER VI

KIDS & PARENTS

THE CLIMATE

In general we presume that love is synonomous with honesty. If this is true, why would members of a family, or those intimate with each other, employ deception rather than direct, truthful communications? Although Freud pinpointed sex, Ernest Becker the denial of death, and others religion or collective conscious as the prime determinant of the human personality, I believe the most significant clue emerges from Professor Alfred Adler, who stated that it is POWER.

Certainly, my examination has shown that power underlies the #1 principle of BS which states that every BS situation is a power transaction in which the perpetrator maintains or gains power at the expense of the victim. In this regard, families and other interpersonal relations are no exception.

Power is both subjective — as an aspect of human experience — and objective — a fact in society. Like love it can be intensely personal, or it can be vastly and diffusively inclusive. It is a universal human experience. Few individuals at some time in their lives have not had and exercised some of it, if only in microscopic degree. A mother with her children, a father with a family, an elder in a group of juniors have held it in appreciable measure. Certainly, no one has failed to be subject to one or another form of power during most of the waking hours of his life.

Most people seem to be quite ambivalent toward power (controlling). Drs. Miller, Wackman, Nunnally and Saline point out in "Straight Talk" that most are actually uncomfortable with controlling because it has such a negative social image. They say the general attitude is, "We do not want to be controlled by others because that suggests we're spineless pushovers with no opinions of our own and no gumption to support them. But if we try to avoid being controlled we face the accusation that we're cold or remote, withdrawn or withholding."

On the other hand, the intense need of others to have control of their lives has spawned a host of best sellers, from Michael Korda's "Power," to "How I Found Freedom In An Unfree World," "Winning Through Intimidation," and "Looking Out For Number One"—all preaching the cant of self-power. I don't mean to denigrate any of these books, but simply to indicate the intense, widespread concern with power (or powerlessness), both in our private as well as public lives.

The reality of power starts with the newborn infant who is totally dependent on its parents for survival and growth. Yet, for a limited period in the child's life he/she actually feels all powerful. The child learns quickly that crying brings food or cuddling and that thrashing and screaming mobilize his mother to meet his needs. Gradually, however, as the parents begin to restrict his demands—no sucking of the thumb, no touching of the penis, no picking of the nose—the infant learns the traumatic truth that he is powerless; that civilization is cold and cruel. Instead of a soft breast, it offers a hard cup; instead of instant relief and warm diapers, it offers a cold pot and the demand for self-restraint. What is true for this infant was also true for his parents and their parents before them. Consequently, throughout our lives, we struggle constantly for some sense of power and control over our lives.

If a child is fortunate to have parents who understand the need for power, the child will consistently challenge the parents and win a fair share of battles as a normal part of his upbringing. Unfortunately, a majority of children will simply be rendered virtually powerless, taking a passive position for the rest of their lives. To their parents, power is coercing someone to accept an idea or adopt certain behavior on the sheer implication of force, if necessary. The parents who allow their children to win enough battles to build up their self-confidence will generally *maintain control with authority* which is getting someone to accept values or behavior because of respect for the figure of authority. Regardless of which procedure, the struggle for power is ever constant. And when a youngster reaches his or her adolescence, the conflict increases because it is a natural part of the process of developing independence. For many parents, this gradual change from unquestioning obedience to grudging defiance is troublesome.

By the time the child reaches adolescence it becomes clear that the impact of parental power is waning. A parent can coerce, threaten, withhold privileges, deliver ultimatums, or other punishments, but seldom can *make* a child do something. Those who utilize the approach of communicating *fear* rather than a respect of authority, generally have the most difficulty in resolving conflicts. Of course, a parent must occasionally exercise power, particularly with a young child, in order to protect the youngster, but if that same parent cannot create in the youngster a genuine respect for the parent's authority without threats of punishment, the same lack of respect for authority will carry over into adult life and into society.

Dr. Saul Kapel points out that "the stability of society and its institutions depends not upon a police force and naked power, but upon a faith in this society and its institutions and a respect for authority invested in them." Herein lies the crux of the overall problem. Most institutions, in the estimation of many, are now corrupt. The state does not serve the public, the public serves the state; the labor union executives don't serve the membership, the members serve it; the educational system doesn't serve students, students are there for its continuance. Does our government really care about peace? Business? The environment? The consumer? Or, the medical profession in health more than profit? Our value system now stands naked for all to see, including young people who are not fooled. What real respect can they have for the immoral, destructive path our institutions have taken, and the new values they represent? Paradoxically, advertising, while disseminating the new values widely, also exposes their falseness quickly.

The family, of course, has been infested and weakened by this corruption. But it has also been affected in another equally destructive way. In our grandparents' era, children were raised with authority which was reinforced by society; the values within the family and society were essentially the same. Consequently, even when grandfather was in error, he acted with certainty. Even if he was wrong, he would not have been that far off the mark. Today, although parents may be right, they act with doubt. The all pervasive influence of Freud, psychoanalysis, and an infinite number of other child raising "experts" has instilled in parents the fear of costly consequences of an unhappy childhood. Parents are not only deeply concerned lest they damage their chil-

122

dren for life, they fear their own lives are out of control. However, the problem is not confined just to parents, but to many people who have flocked to one assertive training group such as EST, or the many others that are flourishing today. The outcome has been that we've become an adversary society; it's you versus someone else. We are locked in opposition to the point where it has overwhelmed us. As a result, instead of dealing with power or confrontation in a direct, honest way and making changes, we have gone to the seemingly smoother way of indirection, subterfuge, flattery, hypocrisy—deception in general and bullshit in particular.

As an example of how BS may totally infest a family, here are a series of situations within one family that might possibly have transpired during a short time-span.

Mary, John's nineteen-year-old daughter, was unhappily contemplating the thought that if she had to spend the four hundred dollars she had saved to repair her automobile, she would have to forego the wardrobe she had planned which was essential to her social life. Two days later she visited her father at his office. He became immediately defensive when he saw that particular look in her eye which meant she wanted something from him. At first she flattered him by saying she "needed his advice." This softened him up. She then told him the service manager at the auto agency had warned her that her car was unsafe to drive. She had thought of buying a new car but the cost was beyond her salary. She felt she couldn't ask him to buy it even though he was "generous" and would. But she did tell him the service manager felt if the brakes were relined and a new transmission installed, the car would be good for another two years. In addition, the service department had a "special" on transmissions for the next few days, and 20% of the cost could be "saved." But—she was short of money to pay for it, even at reduced rates. What did he think? By the time Mary finished, her father was so relieved that she was not asking him to buy her a new car, he readily agreed to pay for having her old one fixed.

Mary knew her father had trouble denying her anything. She knew it made him feel important to be consulted, and that he would be less reluctant to spend money if he felt it was his decision. She also knew he had trouble passing up a good bargain. Unfortunately, although this was a conscious manipulation, it was also a longstanding, habitual way of relating to him since childhood. John, no matter how many times he resolved not to give in to his daughter, usually ended up granting her wishes. Even though spending money caused him anxiety, the need for his daughter's approval and admiration was stronger.

Mary's brother, Steven, agonized over what to do about his mother's birthday. She had told him not to buy a present. She had said, "There's nothing I want and I wish you wouldn't spend your money. Just come over for dinner. That's enough for me." But Steven wasn't sure whether his mother's "no" really meant no. If he bought her a present she might get mad because she told him not to, but if he didn't she might get mad and accuse him of not loving her. No matter what Steven did, he was in a "double-bind" and could not possibly win. He would feel guilty regardless of which way he decided. In either case, his mother could portray herself as the victim of his inconsiderate behavior, or accuse him of being wasteful and extravagant.

A few years earlier, her husband John had seen a set of expensive golf clubs he really wanted to buy but felt he shouldn't. Whenever he found the time he would stop at the sports store to admire them. Finally, his wife said to him, "Go ahead and buy the clubs. You know you really want them. Besides, playing golf is good for your health and you need more exercise. Too, you'll look more impressive to your business clients on the golf course. And certainly by next year those clubs will be more expensive so you can actually save money by buying them now." However, once John had purchased the clubs his wife never missed an opportunity to mention the new dress, the new stove, the new vacuum cleaner or the new watch she had denied herself so that he could buy the golf clubs. She now had John in her control, which is where she kept him for a long time.

But John was no angel either; when his wife was not sexually responsive, he went out of his way to accuse her of some frivolous or wasteful action. This was, of course, far less frightening than accusing her of being frigid. More importantly, it allowed him to control her.

As John and his wife had two other children besides Mary and Steven, they also had other problems. The teenage son had dropped out of school, hung around with other teenagers his parents did not approve of, and was suspected of being on drugs. When confronted he fought back and said to his parents, "You're out of date," "You don't understand," and as a topper, that they were moral hypocrites—they came home from social affairs drunk, cheated on their income tax and were bigots hating Jews and Blacks. Of course he achieved a standoff until he decided to leave home by joining the army.

Earlier, the three year old had discovered by trial and error that "You don't love me," "I hate you," or "If you love me you would do such and such," was extremely effective in coercing her parents into satisfying her demands. As they complied she would reward them with a smile or an occasional kiss.

You might not be able to accept this as a typical family, but as will be shown, every family has some dynamics of power operating at all times, the balance of which is maintained through BS.

THE WEAPONS OF GUILT

One of the most striking and effective weapons utilized in interpersonal relationships is guilt. Guilt is a particular kind of anxiety, a desolate sensation accompanied by feelings of unworthiness and failure. It can be extremely painful. Overall, I believe that *true* guilt is absolutely essential to the moral fabric of civilization; that is, there are destructive actions against other human beings for which the person committing them should feel badly. Murder, genocide, racism, intolerance, cruelty to the sick and maimed, and lack of concern for the poor are just a few of the things justifying guilt.

Guilt is an interpersonal phenomenon. An individual develops it because other persons produce it in him; it does not spontaneously occur on its own. However, once guilt is produced in a person, it may become a persistent part of his personality. Thus, guilt which begins as an interpersonal process may become internalized, and the person will carry his guilty preoccupation into each new relationship. The person into whom guilty feelings were drummed throughout his childhood years tends to feel guilty when problems arise in his marriage, his work situation, his friendships, and other interpersonal contacts.

Not surprisingly, children too, pick up on this weapon. Their intuition and powers of observation are keen, and although they may not be conscious of how it works, their trial and error method confirms it for them. This is particularly apt to occur with children whose parents are vulnerable to guilt throwing because of emotional damage sustained during their childhood. And as previously mentioned, the onslaught of child rearing "authorities" complete the job of making parents extremely insecure and vulnerable. When anything goes wrong, from a temper tantrum of a two-year-old to the sexual promiscuity of a seventeen-year-old, a parent today usually asks himself, "What have I done wrong? How have I failed my child?" The readiness of modern parents to feel guilty about their children's problems have made children hardy adversaries.

Jim, a six-year-old, refuses to eat his peas and carrots. His mother insists that he eat them. Jimmy says, "They make my stomach hurt?" The enlightened father offers a concern: "Maybe the kid is allergic to carrots?" Jimmy picks up on this fast: "Then why do you make me eat them?"

Everytime Sammy was denied anything or prevented from having his own way by his mother or step-father, he would say, "If my real Daddy were only here, he'd let me do the things other kids do. I'm going to run away and go live with my real Daddy. He loves me." This devastates his mother who tries reasoning with him. The more she assures him he is better cared for by them, the more Sammy denies it, saying "I'm not better cared for because you won't let me do what the other kids do. When I'm older, I'll live where I want. I'll go live with my real Daddy. He knows what kids need and he won't tell me all the time, 'You can't do this, and you can't do that." By this time both mother and step-father, frustrated and angry, are under his control. They are now sufficiently guilty to give him his way.

John, sixteen, was chafing because of his parent's restriction on his social life, his allowance and his constant demand for special clothing. His demands not only put a strain on the family budget but on his parents' idea of prudence. When the haggling between them reached a high pitch, John would say to his father, "Why don't you make enough money to buy me what the other kids have?" Or, "If you can't give me the clothes I want, I'll drop out of school and earn the money myself." By this time, both parents are cowed and reluctantly give in once more.

Cynthia, a sixteen-year-old, chafing under the yoke of her parents' restrictions concerning her dating and her sexual attitudes, first escalates the entire issue of sex and then lays on the intimidation. Next comes the guilt; the damage they may be doing to her. Cynthia may or may not be into sex but underneath her confident guise the chances are she is really frightened and insecure about it. Basically, she simply wants more freedom to act on her own. This is Cynthia's attack on her mother and father:

"Everybody does it."

"You're so old fashioned. You haven't kept up with what's happening today."

"You're so hypocritical, mother. You wear skimpy bikinis, watch the hottest flicks and you read those sexy novels. And Dad, I know you read 'Playboy' magazine — they're hidden in your drawer in the bedroom!"

"When I have a nervous breakdown and I have to go to a psychiatrist what will you say then?"

"Do you want me to run away from home to have a little freedom and love?

Once Cynthia's parents come out of shock and things have cooled down, Cynthia will be allowed a little more freedom than her parents wanted to give her but much less than she demanded. However, Cynthia knows she has a weapon whenever she chooses to use it. Underneath it all she is secretly pleased she doesn't have to live up to all her outrageous statements about sex.

Because children essentially begin life powerless, they must find methods that work for them. In general, they learn by example, observation, intuition, trial and error. The tools of deception they use, while naive and relatively innocent, are nonetheless effective. They learn from adults who utilize deception much more calculatingly. Adults plan and design their deception. To a great extent they have made a choice of this method over direct, honest communication. For children, however, it may be their only weapon.

PSEUDO-GUILT

Even more destructive, however, is the pseudo-guilt that many parents instill in children; guilt predicated on false feelings, concerns, or issues, for the purpose of controlling the child for their own self-interest. For example, if the child is playing with the dog in the living room and mom wants to nap on the couch, she might say, "Why are you playing with Samson?" The child might come up with a reasonable answer: "It's fun." However, the sheer fact that mother even asks gives the child an uneasy feeling of ignorance. And should the child reply honestly, "I don't know," the mother may then escalate by saying, "Why don't you go play in your sister's room with her?" As the child gropes for a reason why he prefers playing with Samson in the living room, he is cut off with "It seems like you never want to play with your sister. She wants to play with you." Feeling guilty, he remains silent as his mother delivers the coup de grace: "If you never want to play with your sister, she won't like you and won't want to play with

127

you the next time you want to." Now, feeling ignorant *and* guilty, but also anxious about what his sister might think of his attitude, the child departs with Samson to take up his rightful station beside her.

In a situation where Mom wants to lighten her work load of picking up after the child, as well as teaching him responsibility, she might, if she were honest, simply praise the child by saying, "That's a good boy. You were very grown-up putting your toys away, and very helpful to mother." But if dishonest, "What kind of kid are you? Only naughty children don't clean up their room!" The child soon learns that "naughty" (whatever that means), applies to *him*. Whenever it is used, Mom's voice and mood tell him that something scary and unpleasant may happen to him. Mom also uses words like bad, terrible, awful, dirty, willful, unmanageable, and may even use words like wicked and evil, but they all describe the same thing: You! And what you are: small, helpless, not knowing much. And how you "should" feel: dumb, nervous, perhaps frightened, and certainly guilty. All because mother wanted to nap in the living room, or because she was tired.

While the above examples are relatively mild, many others are not, such as "You are making me sick by all the things you do." "You are destroying our marriage by all the trouble you cause between your father and me." "You will cripple your sister for life it you go on hitting her like that." "You are bad and God will punish you for the way you're making us suffer."

Quite often in later life, when the children have left home, the parents will continue to ply guilt. Laura is one of those fortunate young women who is very attractive, bright and personable. She attended a high school that emphasized secretarial skills, and having graduated with honors, was given a position in a high technology company as secretary to an executive. The job not only paid well but put her in contact with many attractive young men. Her salary allowed her to have a very nice apartment as well as a decent wardrobe. She dated a lot, was having fun and enjoying life.

During this time Laura's mother was experiencing loneliness — the empty nest syndrome — and not having found a new interest or hobby, felt adrift and out of control. On many occasions she called Laura's apartment to find she was not at home which increased her feelings of anxiety. However, her thoughts frequently focused on the possibility that Laura might be having "affairs" with some of the men she was dating. In her youth the mother's parents had severely restricted her freedom which translated itself now to Laura being "loose." To offset a secret envy and to bring Laura under her control again, she projected guilt to her in many ways. These are some of mother's comments to Laura on the phone:

> "I didn't raise you that way. Why can't you settle on one man to go out with?"
>
> "People will talk."
>
> "Your father feels the men you're dating will see you as being easy. He's afraid they'll get the wrong impression of you."
>
> "What did I do wrong? I never raised my child to lead such a wild life."

So, although Laura had her own apartment, supported herself financially, and believed herself to be an adult, she felt uneasy and guilty. After these conversations she would feel her self-confidence wane. Eventually she got married — much sooner than she would have preferred — to a man she was not totally sure she loved.

Jane and Jay also have a problem with parents. They've recently married and are ensconced in the apartment watching a favorite television show. But they have not visited Jane's parents for several weeks. Jane's mother calls again. Jane answers the phone.

> MOM: Jane, your father's not feeling too well.
>
> JANE: Gee, what's wrong?
>
> MOM: I don't know. He'd like to see you this weekend.
>
> JANE: Is it serious?
>
> MOM: You talk to him. (She turns the phone over to Dad)
>
> JANE: Dad, what's wrong?
>
> DAD: It's just my back again. I think I pulled another muscle trying to prune the trees.
>
> JANE: Thank God! The way Mom sounded I thought you were dying.
>
> DAD: It's not that bad. It's just that I'm in pain a lot of the time. When can you come over this weekend?

Jane has been through this routine before and has made up her mind not to leave the house and the comfortable privacy she feels she needs. She has also resolved not to be intimidated by the guilt

129

she knows she is about to be faced with. These are the further comments she has heard from both mother and father.

DAD: What's more important than seeing your mother?

If you don't come over for dinner, what is your mother going to do with that turkey.

Your mother is going to be very upset about this.

MOM: What have we done that would make you turn on your father like this? He's a sick man. Ever since he developed that heart murmur last year I've been worried about him. He's not going to be here forever, you know.

If you really loved us, you would want to come and see us.

You've changed since you married that Jay. I told you before you married him you would have to watch out.

Although this was a short fifteen minute conversation, the actual guilt inducing statements were even more extensive. Any other daughter, less determined, less knowledgeable, would have caved in after the first four or five guilt-producing accusations.

In contrast, the pseudo-guilt parents may produce can be clothed in very positive words and actions, and may be quite subtle. For example, John's father had always been supportive of him. He strongly encouraged him through college, was enthusiastic concerning his marriage, and gladly helped set him up in business. When John's marriage was breaking up, his father gently argued against it, citing the effect on the two children. John somehow felt a gnawing guilt even though he felt he was right in his decision. And when he told his father he was also going to sell the business and split the proceeds as part of the divorce settlement, his father once again gently objected. John's guilt intensified. He also detected a quiet kind of panic in his father, making him feel even worse. Since John had gone into therapy to deal with his wife's dominance and manipulation, he related his feelings regarding his father. John finally had to admit that his father's "concern" with his marriage and business had produced the guilt he couldn't quite identify, and was the result of his father's terrible fear that as he grew older he might not be able to continue working. John realized that he was his father's insurance policy; having accepted help with his schooling costs, marriage and business, John was now actually paying the premiums—building security for his father's old age. John had felt guilty because he had been made to feel he owed his father.

130

The pleasant camouflage — genuine appearing concern for John's life — had driven any conscious reason for the guilt into his subconscious. But it was his father's insecurity and his selfish concern for his problem that had created the guilt in John.

You, I, and most of the population are trained to be responsive to manipulative control. The psychological puppet strings parents attach to children through learned feelings of nervousness or anxiety, ignorance, and guilt control the child's assertiveness. They effectively and efficiently keep children out of real and imagined danger and make the lives of adults a lot easier. But when communication and training become perverted and transformed into pseudo-guilt, the side effects on children are usually very destructive.

Most people experience a feeling of guilt consciously and directly when they deliberately do something they consider to be wrong. When they are aware of guilt there are positive steps that can be taken to eradicate it. They can try to undo the acts that caused the feelings of guilt. They can seek to make restitution or perhaps seek forgiveness if they have wronged another person.

On the other hand, many things people do are not so obviously "wrong," and the resulting guilt is also not so obvious. The discomfort may not even be recognized as guilt making it extremely difficult to take positive steps to rectify the situation. Guilt may also result in psychosomatic complaints or be transferred to feelings of depression or to unconscious attempts at self-punishment.

But pseudo-guilt is simply the *way* deception is practiced. More importantly, is *why* it is practiced, and that is because of the ever constant struggle for control and power. This was emphatically and unforgettably demonstrated to me by my mother who had ten children to care for, plus a grocery store to operate which kept the family alive. She and my father seldom, if ever, went anywhere unless it was a dire necessity. So, when I absolutely insisted they attend school to confront a teacher I felt had wronged me, I was asking a lot. The teacher had accused me of cheating during a test and had banged my head against the back of the desk. In truth, I had only asked the student next to me for an eraser. My humiliation was intolerable so I demanded my parents attend school. I believe I was either nine or ten years of age at the time.

When the confrontation finally occurred, it not only involved the teacher and my parents, but the principal as well. I was ecstatic when the teacher admitted she could have been wrong and apologized to me in front of everyone. Just as I puffed out my chest in victory, my mother slapped me half way across the room! I was shocked. "What was that for," I asked indignantly through my tears. "So you won't forget that when you're home, I'm the boss. When you're in school, the teacher is the boss," she replied pointing her finger at me. "Don't get any ideas of stepping out of line!" she added menacingly. I got the idea alright but I also learned to be a lot more circumspect. Children, not succeeding in an honest way, will go to a variety of other ways for a modicum of power. They learn quickly that honesty is not always the best policy.

When a child tells his mother that he hates his sister, she may spank him for telling the truth. It takes just a few instances like this for the child to realize that honesty doesn't always work. So, even though he may hate his sister, he may hug and kiss her. He now knows that his behavior will not only bring approval but it may even bring hugs and kisses from his mother as well.

On his first visit to kindergarten, while mother was still with him, James, age five, looked over to the paintings on the wall and said loudly, "Who made those ugly pictures?" Mother was embarrassed. She looked at him disapprovingly and hastened to tell him, "It's not nice to call the pictures ugly when they are so pretty." James was adamant: "They're not pretty, they're ugly and rotten." Mother grabbed him by the shoulders and shook him. She then left him sobbing and departed. The teacher tried calming him down and asked why he was crying. James, still angry with his mother, rebelliously repeated his feelings. The teacher was quite understanding. She said, "You don't have to paint pretty pictures here. You can even paint mean pictures if you want. You can paint any picture you feel." James broke out in a smile and accompanied the teacher willingly to the group of other children.

If we want to teach honesty and minimize deception, then we must be willing to listen to all feelings be they positive, negative, or ambivalent, in a "non-punishable" way. By acknowledging the child's true feelings and possibly creating alternative ways to handle them, he comes to understand that he does not have to hide or distort them in any way.

However, when we establish deception we go from the child who says openly, "I hate cheese," to the pre-teen who slides the cheese into a sandwich to the dog; to the child who says freely, "I don't want to go to bed now," to the teenager who dallies over homework until bedtime passes; to the child who says directly,

"Sally is a pig. She takes my toys. I don't want to play with her anymore," to the adult who doesn't return Sally's phone calls and snubs her at parties.

Dr. Haim G. Ginott in his many insightful books on the interpersonal relationships between children and parents points out how many parents awaken in the morning with the resolve that today they will not yell, nag, or humiliate their children. Yet, in spite of their best intentions, find themselves saying things they do not mean, in an unintended tone: no parent deliberately tries to make his children fearful, shy, inconsiderate, or obnoxious, but in the process of growing up, the children acquire these undesirable characteristics no matter what our effort.

We want our children to be polite and they are rude; we want them to be neat and they are not. If one were to eavesdrop on a conversation between parent and child, one could not but observe how little each listens to the other. The conversation might sound like a series of criticism and instructions from the parent, and denials and pleadings from the child. Or it might take this form: the parent asking the child, "Where did you go?" "Out." "What did you do?" "Nothing."

The tragedy of these relationships is not that they don't love each other, but the lack of understanding that exists; an inherent characteristic which makes them adversaries, albeit "friendly" adversaries. And that is because of the child's struggle for identity and power, and the parent's need for control and the status quo of power. Although it may appear the conflict is being resolved in direct confrontation, the chances are that it is really being avoided with the use of deception. This gives rise at some point, by both parties, for a yearning of genuine, upfront exchanges. It is commonly expressed in such phrases as: "I only wish they would be straight with me," or, "Give it to me straight," or "Why can't they just tell me the truth?" Simple, yet difficult to achieve. Tragically, parents and children are both *victims*, despite the individual power each may attain. Both inherit past tradition, history, and culture, and consequently are conduits for behavior and ideas society generates to keep the flow moving orderly, and to keep control and power vested in the few as much as possible. Within this context two other instruments are brought into play.

ROLE PLAYING

Dr. Humphy Osmand, clinical professor of psychiatry at the University of Alabama says, "Roles are marvelous human inventions that enable people to get on with one another . . . We are all players in a changing drama. We cannot live without roles. But we cannot allow ourselves to be oppressed by them either."

That overbearing aspect is a principal problem for mothers, fathers, and their offspring who are trying to cope in a rapidly changing society. As a consequence, people are defining their own roles now. *But society very much likes to parade its own ideal picture of family roles, and this can cause suffering if those ideals vary greatly from the reality.* "Socially defined roles," continues Dr. Osmand, are difficult to change because each one confers rights upon, and exacts obligations from, those who play them."

An illustration of this — one familiar to virtually everyone — is the "sick role." Every society we know shows that cultures hold a special niche for the sick. The sick has individual rights: society permits the person not to function until he or she gets well.

It is the duty of the sick however, to get well by not enjoying himself too much, and by seeking medical treatment to the fullest extent. Anything less is frowned upon as malingering. The sick role also entails an appeal to the third party — the healer. The healer must perceive the patient as trying his best to get well — and the patient must perceive the doctor as sincere (i.e., the doctor must not be thought of as greedy or a quack).

The roles we play vary with each person we encounter, and roles change throughout one's life. The normal person can, at very high speed, adopt the role that others expect. Much of one's social assessment entails perceiving and judging the appropriate role and allowing other people to assume their roles with you. This means that one is able to solve a continuous equation based on constant assessment.

Some people, of course, are better at role-playing than others. The less talented actors are clumsy at adopting roles — *or are cynical about it all — they give you exactly what you want, with the full intent to deceive you.* Individual roles are strongly conditioned and reinforced by the prevailing attitude and philosophies of society. In the area of business, for instance, the attitude that "good guys finish last" shapes the perception of many young people who contemplate going into business, pressuring them to adopt such a posture. Or, the feminist movement which has not only changed women's roles, but of necessity the man's role. In this period of transition, unfortunately, changing roles leaves parties somewhat confused. To the same extent, the roles of mothers, fathers, and children have undergone more than a cosmetic change.

The danger of "role-shorthand" is that it can easily be perverted by the individual who is not sincere. But the greater danger is that it can lead to viewing people in stereotypes, which dulls perception and diminishes human sensitivity, shortchanging both parties. And roles "set" by society may be distorted simply to serve its need to control. As the roles filter down to the individual level, a further distortion may take place as it is adapted to serve that particular person's need to control.

MYTH

The second instrument that plays a significant role in determining our response to each other and society is myth. One of the most distorted and widespread myths is the glory of parenthood. This myth is reinforced by advertising which sells parenthood like so much cereal: gratification, love and happiness through Pampers, Luv diapers, Johnson and Johnson baby oil and powder and Beechnut baby food. Therefore, when the first baby is born, couples receive a severe shock with the realities of parenthood. Then, for months or even years, they may go into another kind of shock. Relationships with their spouses, friends and family change significantly, attitudes toward careers, life goals and leisure activity are altered. And parents are curiously unprepared for the emergence or intensity of these reorientations.

"People have been taken in by the myth that parenting is supposed to be easy, second-natured like eating and sleeping," says Peggy Wegman, a Boston therapist, "so they are not prepared for a real identity crisis, a total reorganization of their lives." She says another reason for the "airbrushed" views of family life is that couples with children regularly share the "glories and war stories," but are conditioned to withold their "illegal feelings."

Ellen Galinsky, in "Between Generations, The Six Stages of Parenthood," believes that fantasies play a major role in determining people's reactions to parenthood. To help prepare for a future event like childbirth, people develop and rehearse images. "Success is felt when reality becomes congruent with an image: anger and depression may result if the image, conscious or

135

unconscious, is not realized." For example, during pregnancy, parents-to-be dream up scenarios with a mystery star, their baby. Parents deeply identify with the child, frequently thinking of giving the child everything that was lacking in their own childhoods. At birth, though, "the baby tells us he is very different from us and as he grows up, we see he is a very separate individual." The process can be relatively smooth or tortuous, depending on how well the parents can adapt their images to fit the reality. For many, these constructive adjustments to reality will be impossible, so they will live a lie or in a fantasy, or they will punish the child for their disappointment.

OTHER MYTHS

Family myths build protective facades which are continually preached to each other until they become reinforced a thousandfold. For example, "In our family we are . . . 'successful in business' . . . 'good with our hands' . . . 'poor but proud' . . . 'too smart to be caught cheating' . . . 'know how to hold our liquor'." Whether these myths are positive or negative, when they clash with the contradictory messages from inside the child himself, or from school, from stories he reads or watches on television or gets from an admired playmate, from other family visits, the child feels he has been deceived—and he has.

In the same token, education of sexual matters in today's climate have gone a long way to dispel sexual myths for many young people. Yet, many more are still suffering nervous tension, breakdowns, guilt, and may even commit suicide. Fortunately, safe, sanitary, civilized abortion which is becoming more and more accepted has helped to lessen the tragedy of sexual hypocrisy, duplicity, and ignorance fostered by blinded groups who are fighting to the death to continue the deception. At this moment there are well organized groups fighting the National Planned Parenthood Association, an organization that deals with sexual information, contraceptives and abortion, and are attempting to shackle their efforts. They want to force the NPPA to reveal to parents their children's request for help. In other words, they want the information their children would have given them in the first place if they, the parents, would have been honest, open and truthful, except now, they are demanding it by law. This struggle for power goes all the way up to Congress which must determine whether funds are granted to NPPA or not. Certain minority groups such as the Right To Life, the

Moral Majority and other puritanical, punitive groups want to abridge the work of National Planned Parenthood, deny the help and knowledge to the young which they desperately need, and perpetuate the same old murderous sexual myths that have plagued us for years. They organize and proceed under the guise of "morality," but their true purpose is to exercise power.

The tragedy of bullshit between kids and parents is that not only is the virtue of honesty corrupted but that family unity and love—the foundation of the edifice—is debased. Like telling "little" lies, or being a "little" pregnant, it just doesn't leave the relationship a "little" infected—it drastically alters it. It eventually affects mutual respect, trust, cooperation, pride, and self-confidence.

The struggle for a power equilibrium between kids and parents has existed from time immemorial. It was there yesterday, it is here today, it will be there tomorrow. The old cliche that total power corrupts totally is just as true for parents as it is for tyrants. But it is also true that power shared has the reverse effect of strengthening oneself as well as the family.

Allowing your kids to gradually experience power does not mean abdicating personal authority. Parents have a definite responsibility for and toward their children, and there is no question that it should be exercised. But authority is not a synonym for coercion. The key to effective parenting is to exert authority without becoming a dictator, without blaming, shaming, belittling or bullshitting your children. That means recognizing control over your offspring is not only temporary but that you must gradually relinquish authority and replace it with influence.

If parents are lucky and recognize early on what they can and cannot control—the limits of their authority—this process evolves naturally. Tough as it may be to swallow, this means you have no authority whatsoever over your children's thoughts, feelings and wants. But parents do set the tone, the standards, the conduct for the gradual shift of power to create a balance. Personality and character flourish only when methods of child-rearing are imbued with honesty, respect and sympathy. In other words, parents set the example by which children learn moral conduct as well as other desired behavior.

My mother once said to me exasperatingly, "You have the hardest head in the world! Where did you pick that up?" I replied, "I got it from you." Of course, it doesn't always work that way, but in many cases the child will reflect the parents' example. As a result, I know that I also reflect many of my parents' wonderful qualities as well. While they exercised absolute power, it was tempered with love that allowed for legitimate negotiation. They set high standards for honesty, integrity and pride. There was little room for deception, and when flushed out, carried severe penalties. Although bullshit is more pervasive today, it also existed then, too. However, my parents *chose not* to participate in it. As a consequence, they broke the vicious cycle of dishonest ideals, distorted role images, and destructive myths.

Confrontation may be painful, negotiation tedious, patience time consuming, direct communication difficult, and sharing power frightening — but they are the honest hard work of human relations that are enduring and life enhancing. They build trust, respect, self-confidence, self-esteem, sincerety and love. They cannot be substituted nor replaced by the "smoother seeming," devious deception of bullshit.

CHAPTER VII
LOVERS & SPOUSES

THE CLIMATE

The extremely high divorce rate today points up the escalating war between men and women. Where marriage may have camouflaged the conflict at one time, the reported increase in single-member households undoubtedly reflects a trend away from marriage and a repudiation of this facade. It is also a more open acknowledgement of the conflict. The battle of the sexes has deep roots and a long history, but recently, the battle has intensified.

This may be due to the collapse of "chivalry;" the liberation of sex from many of its former constraints; the pursuit of sexual pleasure as an end in itself; the emotional overloading of personal relations; and most important of all, the irrational male response to the emergence of the liberated woman.

"The decline of paternalism," says Lasch, "and the rich public ceremonial formerly associated with it, spelled the end of gallantry. Women themselves began to perceive the connection between their debasement and their sentimental exaltation, and rejected their confining position on the pedestal of masculine adoration. Democracy and feminism have now stripped the veil of courtly convention subordinating women, revealing the sexual antagonism formerly concealed by the "feminine mystique." Denied illusions of politeness, men and women find it more difficult than before to exist as friends and lovers, let alone as equals."

The "repeal of reticence" has dispelled the aura of mystery surrounding sex and removed most of the obstacles to its public display. Institutionalized sexual segregation has given way to arrangements that promote the intermingling of the sexes at every stage of life. Efficient contraceptives, legalized abortion, and a "realistic" and "healthy" acceptance of the body have weakened the links that once tied sex to love, marriage, and procreation.

The feminist politicization of this issue combined with the increased social, cultural, and legal acceptance, have formed a battering ram against the man-made institutions that codified male power and protected them against the women who would usurp it. As more and more women came out of the "closet" and demanded "equality," the walls of these institutions, like the walls of Jericho, have started to come tumbling down. The upheaval has been tremendous. Women have dropped their sexual reserve. In the eyes of men, this makes them more accessible as sexual partners but also more threatening. Formerly, men complained about women's lack of sexual response; now they find this response intimidating and agonize about their capacity to satisfy it. "I'm sorry they ever found out they could have orgasms too," complained some frightened man. And rightly so that he should be frightened. Not merely the cult of sexual companionship but feminism itself has caused women to make new demands on men and to hate men when they fail to meet those demands. Younger women rightly reply that no one should settle for less then a combination of sex, compassion, and intelligent understanding. But the attempt to implement these demands, unfortunately, has exposed them to repeated disappointments.

Formerly, men and women acknowledged each other's shortcomings without making them the basis of a comprehensive indictment. I'm sure this was due, of course, to the fact that the overwhelming power of men left few alternatives other than for women to find as much comfort as possible in what was left, and also, partly because men and women found more satisfaction than is currently available in casual relations with their respective sexes. As a result, they did not have to raise friendship itself into a political program, or as an ideological alternative to love. But women's rage against men originates not only in erotic disappointments or the consciousness of oppression but in a perception of marriage as the ultimate trap, the ultimate routine in a routinized society, and the ultimate expression of the banality that pervades and suffocates modern life.

"The aggressive stance of the sexually liberated woman, on the other hand, has reactivated man's fear of the devouring mother of pre-Oedipal fantasy," points out Lasch, "and gives rise to a

140

generalized fear of women that has little resemblance to the sentimental adoration men once granted to women who made them sexually uncomfortable. A fear of women, closely associated with a fear of consuming desires within, reveals itself not only as impotence but as a boundless rage against the female sex. This blind and impotent rage, which seems so prevalent at the present time, only superficially represents a defensive male reaction against feminism. It is only because the recent revival of feminism stirs up such deeply rooted memories that it gives rise to such primitive emotions. Men's fear of women, moreover, exceeds the actual threat to their sexual privileges. Whereas the resentment of women against men for the most part has solid roots in the discrimination and sexual danger to which women are constantly exposed, the resentment of man against woman, when men still control most of the power and wealth in society yet feel themselves threatened on every hand—intimidated, emasculated—appears deeply irrational, and for that reason, not likely to be appeased by changes in feminist tactics designed to reassure men that liberated women threaten no one." When even Mom is a menace, there is not much that feminists can say to soften the sex war or to assure their adversaries that men and women will live happily together when it is over.

As the power equilibrium began to change, the "new warfare" brought with it "new weapons." Now, both men and women have come to approach personal relations with a heightened appreciation, not only of the battle, but of the emotional risks involved. On a private level, quiescently, both sexes have developed the sophisticated shell of manipulating the emotions of the other while protecting themselves against emotional injury. As a result, the sexes have cultivated a protective shallowness, a cynical detachment they do not altogether feel but which soon becomes habitual and in any case embitters personal relations merely through its repeated profession. At the same time, ironically, while this battle is raging, the sexes are demanding from their personal relations the richness and intensity of a religious experience. Although men and women have had to partially modify their demands on each other, especially in their inability to exact commitment of lifelong sexual fidelity, in other ways they demand more than ever!

This contemporary view of the battle of the sexes, touting its new appearance and the use of new weapons is still, however, the same continuing battle that has gone on since man and woman were created. The prize is still for power: who will dominate? In the past man seized the power and developed it to its institutional level, which in turn reinforced his original position. His power was so complete that he had little need for specific deception because he had successfully worked the big deception — men were superior in every way to women — and solidified it with actual gains of real power. As a result, he simply exercised his authority and his will was done.

Women, on the other hand, had to be very shrewd and cunning in one-on-one battles while appearing relatively harmless and innocent. Whatever power they secured had to be acquired indirectly and with deception because, for the most part, they had been disinfranchised politically, socially, culturally and economically. All that remained was what had been unique to their gender — sex, love, motherhood and the remnants of chivalry. In reality, though, while women were portrayed as the weaker sex, needing the protection of men, they were actually the stronger sex. Their strength was simply hidden; it had to be camouflaged, but as women gained the vote, as they joined the work force, as they became economically viable, as modern contraceptives became safe and acceptable, and as they became social, creative, and cultural "equals," they achieved independence and became a solid force of their own and began to change the power equilibrium. More and more, women have begun to confront men directly, using less and less deception. On the other hand, men who ruled by a powerful and rigid authority, now have found it necessary to develop their own deceptions. And to the extent that society has become inundated with bullshit as standard operating procedure, is the extent to which both *men and women* use this tool to avoid direct confrontation and to maintain present power or to increase it at the expense of the other. Since males originated bullshit and have been at it much longer (even though they have not needed it for a long time) their present need for it puts them in the forefront of its use today.

As an example, Ted works for a conglomerate as a junior executive. His salary of $30,000 a year should be enough to financially support the family; but the house in the suburb, the two automobiles, the country club membership and the general cost of keeping up with the Jones' makes his salary insufficient to cover this lifestyle. One night after supper, Jane, his wife, broached the subject of going to work, reasoning that they needed more money to make ends meet. Ted rejected the suggestion vehemently.

TED: How can you think of getting a job when the house is constantly a mess?

JANE: I could work at it harder, more efficiently, and I could do both.

TED: What kind of a job could you get? You don't have any real skills that would pay enough. And you couldn't take care of the house, the children, and work. You would have to pay someone to come in and help.

JANE: I could at least begin with some minor job and work myself up to where it pays well.

TED: What about the kids? Who is going to drive Marcie to her music lessons? What about when the kids come home from school and no one is here to take care of them? I hated my parents when they weren't home for me.

JANE: There would always be that chance, but I could ask Jennifer to look in on them. Besides, I was talking to Marge the other day and she said the kids can come to her house after school.

TED: Jesus, do they all have to know our business. Why don't you just let the whole world know we're strung out financially.

JANE: I'm just trying to help.

TED: I know, I know. But I don't want you to go to work. We'll just have to cut back on a lot of things and make do with what I earn.

This is the first of a series of conversations Jane and Ted will have. On the surface of their discussion, the intentions of both parties appear laudable. However, Ted's concern for the children and the running of the house, and Jane's concern to help out financially are not quite their true intentions.

Jane is tired of the role of mother, housewife, driver—the suburbanite. Her home has become a prison. She feels that life has more to offer and it exists in the world beyond her home and family. Too, she's detected a boredom in Ted who has been taking her for granted for sometime now. She also sees signs that his sexual interest may be drifting to other women. She has grave doubts that some of his late hours are concerned merely with business. But she is too insecure to face Ted directly. Consequently, she has utilized their financial weakness to put her deception into action.

Ted, on the other hand, does not want to upset his routine. It allows him the freedom to do his job aggressively and to go with the "boys" after work, (and sometimes with the "girls"). However, the most significant reason he does not want Jane to go to work is that it would bring remarks from his father-in-law who has constantly put him down and with whom he has never gotten along. In addition, he feels that if Jane goes to work it will affect his status with co-workers and the neighbors. So, not only will his freedom be abridged, he is afraid he will be perceived as a "failure" for not being able to support his wife and family in the "proper" manner.

What is actually happening within the deception is a power struggle. This time, however, Jane loses because she is more insecure than Ted and because Ted's "story" seems more solid. In the future, though, Jane will find a way to increase her weapons, probably guilt or some feminist philosophy, and reverse the present defeat.

If Jane, in this example, had skills and had sacrificed her desire for a career, there might be far more serious consequences. Nathaniel Branden in "The Psychology of Self-Esteem" points out that she might "feel occasional spurts of hatred for her children which would horrify her. She represses such feelings and is not aware of them again—except that sometimes she is inexplicably and uncharacteristically careless of her children's safety. Then she is horrified to discover feelings of contempt for her husband. She represses them and throws herself with renewed fervor into the role of devoted wife, except that sexual relations with her husband become empty and boring. She takes great pains to present to their friends the picture of a cheerful, 'well-adjusted' wife and mother—except that she begins to drink when she is alone." Or, in my observation, she may turn to an extra-marital affair.

Quite often, lack of honesty with one's spouse or mate—or with one's self—leaves the relationship resting on a foundation of deception which eventually crumbles. And when deception becomes everyday procedure, it soon spreads to all other relationships—children, family, friends, co-workers—to anyone and everyone and then even infiltrates simple actions.

Barbara wanted a new dress even though she already had an extensive wardrobe, the cost of which was a strong source of conflict with her husband. In order to go shopping, Barbara had to secure a babysitter. On this day, no one was available. So, Barbara gathered up the child, went to the department store and headed for Children's Toys. Here, she flattered the salesperson shamelessly and convinced her to "watch" the child who was now playing with some of the toys.

Barbara quickly rushed to the dress department, found one she liked, overspent outrageously, and returned to gather up the child who by now had become quite attached to the toys. The thought of spending any more money frightened her. Barbara sweetly kissed her daughter, removed the toys gently, and said, "No toys today, Darling. Instead, you can have an ice cream cone. What flavor do you want — vanilla, chocolate, or strawberry?"

Upon returning home, Barbara began to prepare her husband's favorite meal including dessert. When he arrived she pampered him even more. She made a point of getting the child to bed early which was a sign to him that they would be having sex. Naturally, he was delighted.

As her husband disrobed and settled into bed comfortably, Barbara took out the new dress and displayed it against herself. "Isn't it pretty?" she said. "I'm going to be a sensation at the party Saturday night." Although he was extremely angry with her spending, he was even more angry because he hated her surprises such as the Saturday night party. But he suppressed his feeling so that they could get on with sex and forget the deception for the moment.

DOUBLE BIND

Of course, the more extensive BS becomes, the more new techniques are created. Unfortunately, almost anything based on pseudo-guilt works extremely well as you can see with the following couple. Mary and John had been married for two years. It was the second marriage for both. Mary was bright and independent, while John was fifteen years older and insecure. Mary, however, had a problem of being thirty-five pounds overweight. The fact that John was a splendid gourmet cook and encouraged his wife to eat heartily did not help her problem.

In John's insecurity, he suspected that his wife might be having an extramarital affair and that he might be losing her. Neither was true, as Mary genuinely loved him and their sex life was gratifying. What would particularly set off his insecurities was the natural intellectual opposition Mary offered to his knowledge and authority. To regain control, John would needle her about her excessive weight. At times a sadistic streak would take over and he would tell her she was unattractive, a slob, or that she was sexually unappealing.

Mary decided to lose the excess weight. At first it was terribly difficult because John continued to tempt her with gourmet

145

dishes. But Mary established the will and discipline to refuse his enticements. Little by little, her figure returned, prompting many compliments from men who innocently flirted with her in front of her husband.

John's jealousy began to surface more strongly. He imagined the flirtations developing into liasons and sex. Eventually he accused her directly. She assured him she wasn't having an affair, that their sex life was excellent and that there was no need for her to go outside the marriage. John was temporarily mollified until she discussed a new wardrobe to accommodate the loss of weight. Once again he was convinced she was "flaunting her body" to attract men. When Mary replied that he wanted her to lose weight and be more attractive, it did not register.

Discouraged and worn out, Mary began to put the weight back on. In turn, John began to complain again. No matter which way Mary decided to go, there was no way she was going to be able to win. John effectively had her in a DOUBLE-BIND and, as long as she stayed in this trap, John would shift the DOUBLE-BIND from her weight problem to some other weakness and so keep her entrapped.

DIVIDE AND CONQUER

In the singles scene, Joe, a short, egotistical man had the reputation of being a rover. It was said he would try to seduce anything in sight resembling a woman, married or single, young or old.

Joe made his living directing television commercials which gave him an aura of glamour that attracted people to him. One day a "friend" visited his office bringing with him a very attractive young lady who lived in Chicago and whom he had been dating for several years. The young man had come to New York to pursue his career while his fiancee finished her degree in theater. In addition to being attractive and well-formed the young lady was also bright and ambitious. She had been left a moderate sum of money by her grandfather which had helped to pay for her education.

Joe immediately spotted a "pigeon" and invited them to supper. First, he filled the young lady's head with the great success she could have if she moved to New York. He assured her he would try to use her in commercials where she could earn a great deal of money, and he would introduce her to others important to her career. He suggested it would be important to create a successful "front"; a $1500 a month apartment furnished to the hilt, stylish clothes — and she would have to be seen with the right people. As supper was coming to a close, Joe excused himself and departed to the men's room. As he passed the waiter, he signaled for the check to be given to the young man at the table. When he returned, the bill had been paid. As the evening ended, Joe suggested Sheila come to the office the next day and he would video tape and evaluate her performance. He also suggested she be alone so as to avoid any possibility of self-consciousness.

During this session and at every other meeting between them, Joe subtly denigrated her boyfriend. Although Sheila gently defended him, Joe finally convinced her that her boyfriend was a hindrance to her career. In the meantime, Joe set up auditions with advertising agency producers who conceivably could hire her. But unbeknownst to her, many of these producers had never worked with him, and the only way they would grant an audition to her was because Joe implied they might have a "shot" with her sexually. On the other hand, Joe told *her* to anticipate their sexual advances and to gently put them off.

Gradually, Sheila accepted Joe as genuine, knowledgeable, and just what her career needed. She subsequently followed his advice. Sheila's boyfriend, however, smelled a rat. He made inquiries to others in showbusiness who were not so optimistic about her prospects. He relayed these doubts to her and suggested it might be wise to make occasional visits to New York to establish a foundation before settling permanently. As Joe now had her confidence, he persuaded her not to follow that advice. Shortly after, when Sheila's boyfriend had to go out of town on an extended trip, Joe went in for the kill. Since he was an excellent cook, he set up a gourmet-candlelight-and-champagne dinner. Exercising his considerable charm, he seduced her.

As the months passed with no actual television commercial jobs, no film or theater commitments and her money diminishing fast, Sheila began to worry. When phone calls to Joe took longer and longer to be returned, she started to become very suspicious. Accidently, in an evening out with her boyfriend and a mutual friend of Joe's, she was finally able to get to the bottom of what was happening. It seemed their mutual friend did not admire Joe very much, consequently revealing that Joe had been putting her boyfriend down to everyone and that he always tried to seduce every woman in sight. At that moment, Sheila and her boyfriend looked at each other, knowing that they knew the truth. A week

147

or two later, they split and she returned to Chicago terribly disappointed, feeling foolish and in pain . . . but infinitely wiser.

MIND READING

Another control mechanism operates when the victim is maneuvered into the position of having to read the mind of the perpetrator, anticipating his needs and responses. It is difficult enough in formal situations such as employee-employer relations to fulfill defined expectations, but in intrapersonal relationships where so much is left unsaid, the difficulty may be insurmountable. It would seem that in "loving" contexts expression would be easier, but the reality is that it is often more difficult.

In this situation people hint, imply, suggest, or subtly act as if they expect us to do something for them. They may look hurt, or angry or they may just be silent. Generally, these responses follow a conflict of some sort between the two parties. Most often, it occurs when the "injured" party feels the other has done or not done something the other person wants.

When our husbands, wives, lovers are unhappy about something we did or didn't do, they have the ability to make us feel guilty. A certain look does it, or a door closing a bit too loud announcing an hour of silence, or a frosty request to change the television program. A friend once complained to me, "I'll be damned if I know how she does it, or why I respond that way, but somehow I finish up feeling guilty, even when there's nothing to feel guilty about."

Instead of verbally stating their displeasure or their need and possibly gaining through compromise, the perpetrator attempts to make you "feel" you should have known; that you're wrong; that you have hurt them. You are made to feel that you should have *intuitively* understood they were displeased with your behavior; or, you should *automatically* understand what behavior pleases or displeases them; and last, that you should change your behavior so that you do please them.

If you allow the other person to put you in the position of having to mind read, then you are fully expected to change your behavior to suite their convenience, or to relieve their hurt or angry feelings. If you allow this kind of manipulation, you end up not only blocked from doing what you wanted to do, but doing something else to make up for wanting to do it in the first place. You are under control.

148

THE PUT DOWN

In a prior time when men were allowed the freedom of attending bars, restaurants and other public places alone, (while women had to be accompanied by a man) it was presumed that men, by having this right, "owned" the establishment as well—it was presumed they had proprietary rights. However, all that has changed. Today, women can go to almost any establishment they please. As a matter of fact, the law has struck down the last few "men only" clubs run privately. Now, women act as "equals"; they pay their own admission fee, buy their own drinks, food or whatever service they want. While they may attend the establishment for the pleasure of it, it is understood and permissible that they could be attending to meet attractive males. Conversely, with these changes men must now deal with women as "equals," even if they take the initiative. He cannot make presumptions as to her purpose for being there; consequently, he is immediately at a disadvantage. So, if he is interested in a particular woman he must genuinely try to win her by his charm, personality, intellect or looks, on a one-to-one basis. But there are men who have not caught up with the new changes. They continue to operate in the old way; they take the offensive and if flattery doesn't work, they go to the PUT DOWN.

> JIM: Hi, I'm Jim Smith. I've been watching you since you came in. I couldn't keep my eyes off of you. You're stunningly beautiful. What's your name?
>
> LAURA: I'm Laura Strong.
>
> JIM: You look pretty enough to be a movie star! Are you here alone?
>
> LAURA: No, I'm with a girlfriend of mine. She's dancing with that fellow there.
>
> JIM: (With a cursory glance in that direction) This place bores me. What do you say we go to the village. I know a terrific place there!
>
> LAURA: No thanks. I've been out most of the evening and I'm tired. Besides, this is the first time I've been here and I'd like to see what it's like.
>
> JIM: C'mon, I'll pay for the taxi. I've got plenty of bread! Believe me, they got some real goodies down there—make you feel wonderful—make your tiredness fly away!
>
> LAURA: No thanks, I don't go in for that.
>
> JIM: Look, I'm bored with this place and I'm getting bored with this conversation—do you want to come or not?

149

LAURA: Thanks, but I think I'll stay.

JIM: Did anyone ever tell you you're kinda boring.

LAURA: No. Have you ever thought you might be boring and that you're boring yourself?

Laura is a self-assured woman who has a good sense of values and much self-esteem. She has also earned the right to be independent and will not enter into a relationship unless there is mutual interest and respect. A number of women with less confidence might have been seduced with flattery, and when that didn't work, they would not have been able to withstand the assault of criticism — the put down. Too, other factors could enter this situation which would affect another woman adversely; is she lonely, is she living up to the image of being "hip" and how strong is her sense of values? Almost any vulnerability could make her a victim. Laura, however, remained in control and created a standoff.

FLATTERY

All of us have many associations in which there is a mutual unspoken proscription against saying anything to irritate the other for fear of causing dislike. With deception so widespread in the nonpersonal area, individuals have become totally wary, with a spill-over into the most personal of relationships. As a consequence, there is now a greater hunger for truth and honesty in close relationships. However, in this day and age emotional integrity comes across as a quality that seems almost obsolete. A friend of mine commenting on another, said of their relationship, "It is both a great relief and reassuring not to have to spend time guessing how the other person really feels — what they are really thinking." Another person commented, "any hint of insincerity puts me off." And still another said, "truth in a relationship is the most important quality I look for. The moment I detect otherwise, the relationship is at an end." In marriage and love it is absolutely essential if the relationship is to last.

For example, John had just been promoted in his job. Instead of being delighted, he was frightened. He knew absolutely he was going to be unable to meet the new demands. He had taken the promotion anyway because if he had not he would have been severely damaged in the eyes of his superiors. Unfortunately, he also felt he could not reveal his fear to his wife because it would have diminished him in her eyes.

On the other hand, Mary playing the role of the "good" wife, automatically praised his promotion. She went further; she over-praised him telling him it would be a snap and that someday she even expected him to become president of the company. Long ago, Mary found that praising people indiscriminately made her more well-liked, allowing her to manipulate others to her will. She found flattery and praise to be a narcotic to most people. At home it kept peace, harmony and cheerfulness. In the community it made her an attractive neighbor. Overall, it gave her control.

John, however, knowing himself, felt even more fraudulent because he didn't stop her praise immediately. The feeling grew so worrisome it began to affect him sexually. Even here, Mary chose to ignore his performance and praised his love making. John strongly felt she was playing the role of the good wife and that she did not have the least inkling of how he truly felt. He began to wonder how much of her flattery and "encouragement" was genuine. Gradually, as Mary continued to praise his poor sexual performance, he began to feel contempt for her. The more he examined her past flattery, the more he realized it was insincere. Ultimately, it affected him so completely that he not only became disenchanted but totally impotent. With the eventual failure of his promotion and his sexual performance, the marriage deteriorated completely. John and Mary later divorced.

In a recent research project, it was found that out of 20 negative qualities presented to respondents, insincerity or lying ranked in the top three as the most unattractive quality in a partner. It was also found that the above qualities along with money and sex, ranked as the most important factors in the breakup of relationships. Flattery may seem to smooth the path for many but eventually its insincerity becomes apparent and it exacts a high toll for all.

EXPECTATIONS

One of the most common breeding grounds for deception is the standard of conduct each party indicates should be followed in their relationshiup. If you abide by what you think is the established standard and then find that your child, wife, husband, lover or friend hasn't, you will feel hurt and that they have taken advantage of you.

Quite often, the problem is not one of misconduct, but rather that no attempt was made to specifically identify what each party expected from the other. In other instances, a deception will be perpetrated because we believe we will lose stature with the other person if we reveal the true situation. And the closer, more valued a relationship, the greater we feel the risk of losing it should the less-than-perfect facets of ourselves be revealed. Instead of a woman saying to her boyfriend, "I'm jealous when you're with her," she says, "You have no right to be with her," or "I haven't done that; therefore, you shouldn't."

Intimate and close relationships, if they are true and genuine (if each person truly cares for the fulfillment and happiness of the other as much or more than themselves), should lead to more freedom than less. But what happens, quite often, is that the relationship severely restricts choices and freedom of action. It becomes restrictive and possessive and leads to a double standard where one person does things that are denied to the other. It also breeds deception.

For example, it's possible that a man's work may involve regular contact with women, while his wife or lover's routine does not offer the same opportunity to be in contact with men. The woman may indicate to him that she is concerned he might find one of these females interesting and take her to bed. Therefore, even if the man is free of any transgressions, he may find it necessary to constantly give her the impression that he only occasionally meets women in his work, they do not mean much to him, or that they don't exist at all. He may even go out of his way to indicate that his business appointments are with anyone but women.

Specifically, in a reverse situation, Charlene, a married woman, came home one afternoon after discovering Ted who worked at the shopping mall bookshop. He was bright, stimulating, easy-going and charming. At supper she enthusiastically mentioned Ted to her husband who, while expressing interest, secretly felt jealous. However, he managed to mask his insecurity. But as Charlene continued to report her occasional meetings with Ted, she realized her husband had become suspicious. From that time, she refrained from saying anything else in regard to Ted. As a matter of fact, she covered up their meetings by implying Ted was pretentious, a "know-it-all," etc., consequently, relaxing her husband's suspicions and insecurities. In the meantime, Charlene continued to see Ted, even considered going to bed with him, but in the end rejected the idea, not because of her husband but because she knew she would not like herself for it.

Love, closeness, affection, family interactions can be enjoyed without having to build elaborate, restrictive structures that destroy the independence of everyone. Certainly there are no easy rules to follow but the odds are greater that with less restrictions and more freedom there will be less need for deception. Unfortunately for some, even when freedom and trust exists it will not be believed. Some people are so habituated to deception they compulsively follow this destructive course. For them nothing less than therapy can help.

THE INVISIBLE LOVER

In general, a BS situation always relies on the appearance of things rather than their substance. This can be particularly true when it comes to the war between the sexes. Interestingly, it would seem that deception would be more difficult to execute because the people involved are intimate, see each other frequently, if not each day, and consequently would detect subtle changes. Like the con game, however, it is always easier to con another con person because the greed that makes the con person good at his profession is the same quality that functions against him. In the case of lovers and spouses, trust is the key quality. When trust is put into doubt by creating other appearances, control is temporarily shifted to that person.

Ethel and Joe had been going together for several years intending to marry in the near future. Joe, however, had been taking her for granted lately. Ethel decided that something had to be done so she devised the following plan: she first indicated a disinterest in their sex life. Though they continued to have sex, she did not respond to his love-making enthusiastically. She then made favorable comments about other men in his presence, and following that, she would pick up the phone when he was in the other room and dial it, all the while keeping the phone blank. She would then hold a conversation with herself until she had hooked his curiosity. When he entered the room she would lower her voice "mysteriously." By this time, Joe was putting two and two together and concluded precisely what she wanted him to. From then on, he paid great attention to her, was particularly sensitive and caring, and immediately stopped taking her for granted. Each time Ethel determined he was slipping back into his old ways, she simply brought out her "act" and regained control.

In another instance the situation was far more serious; Sandra's husband was cheating on her. She accused him directly, threatened divorce, screamed at him and withheld sex. Sandra

would become particularly infuriated when Jimmy pleaded innocent, pointed out that she had not "caught" him in any specific
liaison, and implied she was insanely jealous. He did admit to
liking the looks of a well-formed female figure, but that's as far
as it went. Although Sandra could not prove it, she knew he was
unfaithful.

One day she took stock of the entire situation and came up
with a rather brilliant idea. She had remembered a time early in
their marriage when Jimmy seemed jealous of a rather innocent
relationship she had with the owner of a local bar. At the time,
when she realized it upset him, she went out of her way not to
give him cause for concern; she stopped all such conversations
with other men. Now, however, it was different. She knew if she
attempted to obviously talk to other men, Jimmy would immediately construe her action as an attempt to make him jealous and
he would just laugh at her. So, she began her campaign slowly.
At first, she applied men's cologne to some of her clothing. She
observed the puzzled look on his face when he realized it was not
his cologne. Still, he said nothing. Then Sandra bought a pair of
men's cufflinks which she hid. But the bill for the cuff links was
partially displayed on the dresser where he would be sure to see
it. Still, Jimmy said nothing. Sandra now placed a mono-
grammed handkerchief that did not contain his initials, as well as
a pair of socks that did not belong to him, in his dresser drawer.
When Jimmy still did not respond, she thought he simply was
missing the clues, or that he was a superb actor. But she continued. Since Jimmy called her at preset times, she made sure not to
answer the phone.

Eventually, Jimmy's suspicion was aroused. He started to
examine her more closely, but did not bring up the subject
directly. He would innocently mention her absence when he
called to which she would give an innocent explanation. Soon,
Jimmy started to hang around the house more often. As Sandra
begged off sex occasionally, Jimmy's suspicions grew more
intense until one day he accused her of infidelity which she quietly denied, challenging him to prove it. When he couldn't, he
began to wonder if he was unduly jealous. It left him so upset he
stopped doing whatever it was he was doing. Coincidentally, at
about the same time while riding in his automobile and listening
to the radio, he heard the lyrics to a popular song current then,
which asked the question, "Whose making love to your wife
while you're making love to someone else." He got the point of
the song and subsequently ended the game. Sandra never did

know whether he continued to cheat, and he was never sure if she was, so in their uneasy standoff they stayed married for another few years. Ultimately, the marriage broke up not over sex but because Jimmy was a compulsive gambler and had concealed it long enough to bring them to financial ruin.

OFFICE ROMANCES

Lovers and spouses in the home may be a lot more familiar to us than lovers and spouses at work. With more and more of the work force comprised of women, what goes on in the office is pertinent to promotion, productivity and progress. As usual, there are rules that apply unevenly between men and women. Business has always been in the forefront of BS and the bastion of men's authority. However, it now faces a severe change, if not willingly, then by law. It is a rapidly growing area that should be studied closely as it becomes more and more the new battlefield.

From an overall point of view, Dr. Robert Quinn of the State University of New York points out that office romances do not seem to enhance company morale. Increased gossip around the water cooler is the common and obvious result. "In most serious relationships," he said, "the parties are seen using each other for different rewards. The male for sexual and ego gratification and the female for power."

In another study made recently, it was found that one romantic partner was dismissed in ten percent of the cases explored, with *women* twice as likely to receive a pink slip. This confirms that business is still a bastion of male authority. Lee Colby, head of a Minneapolis consulting company specializing in male-female teamwork says, "Women are still vulnerable to the charge, 'she's sleeping her way to the top.' It's such an easy thing to say about a woman, regardless of the truth. It destroys her prestige, her credibility and, therefore, her effectiveness."

Two insurance executives, although warned by management, continued to date discreetly, but, of course, the gossip did not stop. Nothing more was said, no one was fired, but after a while the woman realized she was no longer on the fast track. She sort of got "frozen out."

Despite cautions about mixing business and pleasure, some women insist business is pleasure. Power is seductive, three piece suits are sexy, and mapping corporate strategy with a loved one is every bit as heady as dancing an exciting dance. In addition to

155

fighting off these attractions there is the constant danger that deception may develop between the two lovers.

Natalie was on her way up in an electronics firm. She found she was attracted to one particular executive. When she and Tom were in executive meetings, their vibes were so together it was like they could read each other's mind. Eventually, they were thrown together continuously by the project they were working on. The romance developed to where they were now living together. They even discussed marriage. But Natalie was a little concerned because she detected a need in Tom to always have a competitive edge in the executive sessions attended by other high level executives. But Tom was bright, attractive and a good lover. He also flattered Natalie, built up her confidence and minimized her vulnerabilities. Gradually, he assumed the dominant position in their lives. Before she knew it, she was deferring to him at meetings. Although they were on the same level, and technically competing, she became more concerned with his career than hers. She was even bringing him coffee which everyone seemed to notice.

In turn, Tom was being sought after by others in the company, and was deferred to by the staff. As the project developed, it required that Natalie travel a lot. On her return she would notice small changes: Tom was not at home as often, he was doing more things alone, and most damaging of all, she detected signs of another woman. As Natalie was direct in their relationship, she confronted Tom with her suspicions. His response was well prepared. But she could sense the deception. Although she did not want to face it and it was extremely painful, she went over their past relationship, and upon cold examination realized his flattery had been false along with most of his other behavior. She realized she had been used and was now in an awkard position. Tom, of course, reneged on marriage having found another willing victim, and was promoted over Natalie to a very important position. Humiliated, Natalie left the company, and after eight months found another job that was not quite comparable to the one she felt forced to leave.

In another example, Barbara, an executive secretary was determined to rise in the world. Her boss was an important and powerful executive in a large corporation. At first, Barbara was a model of efficiency anticipating his every need. Gradually, she began to add personal touches such as attractive flowers in his office, special soap and towels in his private bathroom, candies which he had a special fondness for, and a very special coffee which she had prepared so that when he arrived in the morning it was ready. It did not take too long before he became very dependent upon her.

Although he was older than Barbara by twenty-five years and married with three children, when he asked her out to supper, she flattered him shamelessly on what an honor it was. At supper she continued to flatter him on his youthful vigor, his business acumen, and his importance to the company. One supper led to another and these developed into liaisons and invitations to business meetings outside the city. In the meantime, Barbara ended a prior relationship with a young man her age who was in love with her and whom she liked a great deal. But she knew her boss to have an iron fist in his velvet glove and was not beyond investigating her. She could take no chances.

Eventually her boss was asking for her evaluation on other employees, and based upon what she said, they were either demoted, fired, or promoted. He was also talking about a divorce from his wife. Though Barbara could barely tolerate him physically, she repressed these feelings while focusing on the immense power she was about to acquire. They did get married and she fulfilled her ambition, but when she finally admitted to herself that it was a loveless marriage, she started to drink heavily. As the facade was too great a burden to carry on a day-to-day basis, she began to unload her pretenses one by one, to where her husband/boss could see that he had been deceived. Not without intelligence, he wisely realized he had actually deceived himself.

Legally, issues like equal pay for equal work and sexual harassment are being dealt with in court, which is helping to create more of a balance. One by one, the pillars supporting the vast foundation of BS in business will come tumbling down. But BS in business has such a long history and tradition and is so well concealed, it is doubtful that women in the near future will become the major force, or get the recognition or pay commensurate with their capabilities.

ROMANTIC MYTH

In the end, the greatest enemy outside of ourselves may be the "Romantic Myth" that has evolved since the time of chivalry. No matter how much change feminism has wrought, how much sex has been brought out into the open, or how permissive society has become regarding sex, we still remain essentially a romantic, idealistic nation. In the current mode of technology and science there seems to be a greater need than ever for romantic myth, and although they are no longer functional, they die hard. Somehow, we can't seem to face the reality that people are only human, that many are motivated by base considerations, and that we are all a little less than we would like to be.

In the face of high divorce rates, single person households, delayed marriages until out of school or until situated in careers, marriage is still considered the best and most ideal coupling. Whether one just has sex and housekeeps together, or ties the knot in holy matrimony, we insist the couple be "in love." Yet, people get married for many reasons other than to enhance a love relationship. Many times, the other motivations which are not nearly so romantic or idealistic, are the stronger motivations for the coupling. But in most instances, they will be kept well hidden or masked in someway, often for a lifetime. Consequently, many marriages start out dishonestly, with a foundation of deception. Among some of the reasons people couple or marry are:

1. To confirm that one has "won" his lover once and for all, and can now stop putting further energy to this purpose.

2. To achieve social respectability or social advancement (making a "good" marriage — marry above one's status financially — into a special circle of friends, into a more glamorous or powerful society, into more important business contacts).

3. To make sexual intercourse more easily accessible.

4. To be financially supported.

5. To avoid loneliness.

6. To have a housekeeper.

7. To get a working partner and increase income.

8. To guarantee that someone will be around in old age.

9. To escape the need to do something more challenging with one's life.

10. To build one's ego that one is desired over others; or, the feeling of power through children; or, the extension into a future generation through them.

There are some indications, however, that we may be coming to grips with reality. Seminars espousing "financial contracts" between couples living together but not married, a contract that legally divides whatever possessions they own; pre-nuptial agreements that not only assign possessions but may detail each party's responsibility in the relationship.

The establishment of individual rights of women, abortion and otherwise, including career and financial independence, while not documented between mates, has gained the force of a contract. More and more, these issues are understood prior to the coupling.

Yet, the more things seem to change, the more they stay the same. Even though there may be a more equitable distribution of power between male and female, the battle of the sexes will remain constant as to who dominates, who controls, who has the power. While the appearance of the battle may seem either more adversarial than ever to some, or more "muted," as the changes become more accepted, it is certain that both sides will use deception even more extensively, thinking it is the more efficient, smoother, less conflicting way to function. They are wrong: the figures prove it, the crumbling walls of their relationships prove it, the sheer discontent proves it. Though more difficult to accomplish, the old cliche still stands up: honesty is the best policy. Direct, straightforward, honest communication combined with a sincere concern for the other person, still makes for a more fulfilling, gratifying, happy, and longer-lasting relationship. At the least, this approach always lets you know where you stand with the other person. It eliminates doubt, confusion, guessing. Then again, that may not be exactly what you want. Every manual from Machiavelli to many contemporary tomes exhort the lesson that to have power you must use deception.

Leo Buscaglia, a lecturer, television personality, and a professor at a Southern California college, has as his main topic—love. He is so dynamic in presenting this subject on various media including a series of books, that he is not only a best selling author with two books on the best seller list, but in enormous demand personally. He says, ". . . love is trusting (and) experience seems to convince us that only fools trust, that only fools believe and accept all those things." He then cites Eric Fromm who says, "Love is an act of faith, and whoever is of little faith is also of little love," Buscaglia then adds, "The perfect love would be one that gives all and expects nothing. It would, of course, be willing and delighted to take anything it was offered, the more the better. *But it would ask for nothing, for if one expects nothing and asks nothing, he can never be deceived or disappointed.*

It is only when love demands that it brings on pain." (Italics mine)

I am, of course, delighted with Leo Buscaglia's success and popularity. I am also inspired when I hear him speak. I desperately want to believe him. I yearn for what he speaks of, and I am sure it is possible for some. But I don't believe many of us can be "saints," nor can we be totally idealistic, or love "purely"—that is, we cannot live in a vacuum, we must live together as individual human beings in all our "imperfection."

A power struggle is as much a fact of nature as love is. It cannot be eliminated. We are never equal in this regard; someone or other must always dominate and as a result we may not always be loving or sensitive or caring. We may be conniving, cruel, careless or guilty of any number of baser instincts in our relationships, including the most personal and intimate. This is one of the realities of life, just as loving with expectation is, and not to face and accept reality is setting oneself up for a great deal of disappointment, disillusionment, deception—a great deal of pain.

In accepting reality there are "ideals" which can be worked toward, that can be accomplished by the "imperfect" human beings we are. We can realistically work at honesty in love eliminating as much deception as possible that will build a realistic trust with a strength all its own. We can realistically have expectations of one another that can be compromised fairly and equitably if we are willing to face each other honestly and with the truth. We can even deal with power—creating a power equilibrium—by dealing with it honestly, with a sense of fairness, a sense of self-respect, self-esteem, mutual concerned "love" for each other, always granting the other person a sense of sovereignty.

In accepting reality it will be necessary to dissolve false or misleading ideals, romantic notions, myths, whether propagated by society, family, or loved ones. More important than "faith and trust," we must see human motivation and action as accurately and honestly as possible, so that we can eliminate its most destructive element—deception.

160

CHAPTER VIII

COUNTERBULL

Oh what a tangled web we weave
when first we practice to deceive.
— *Sir Walter Scott*
MARMION

To many people I am sure it seems there is little hope that bullshit can ever be eliminated. What chance do the innocent have if the bullshitter can, with ease, dupe the aware, the trained, the sophisticated, the prepared, the cunning? (The fact is that anyone can be fooled, and everybody can be fooled some of the time.) Once this realization hits home, the tendency for many is to go to the opposite extreme of believing almost nothing; to be forever on guard, frightened of any true interrelationship or trust, possibly becoming paranoid. Much worse are those who conclude that if the game is played that way, that's the way they'll play it too. Some even become determined to play the game better than their opponents and become a bigger bullshitter than anyone else!

It was precisely such thinking which precipitated one of the most important crises in my life and pushed me to the brink of suicide. The conflict was between the way I had been raised — the idealistic values my parents instilled in me and which they exemplified — and the reality of the totally opposite practice I found in society when I left home to take my place in the world.

I was taught the virtue of hard work, persistence, patience, honesty, loyalty, friendship; that giving my word, and certainly shaking hands on it, was tantamount to a contract; that being a man was choosing between right and wrong and accepting the responsibility of whatever choice was made. I was also taught it was better to give than to receive; that to have good neighbors and good friends one had to be one first; that a spirit of helping others was a generosity that enhanced the human condition. I could go on but I'm sure I've made my point. In essence, I was an "innocent."

Naturally, I ran into a wall of pettiness, envy, greed, vindictiveness, treachery, calumny, and a hundred other forms of human weakness and corruption. I saw so much of it, it seemed the whole world was this way. I was being eaten alive by it!

At first I could not accept the reality; I thought it might be just a few rotten apples in the barrel. Then I rationalized their behavior as the fault of the system. Finally, the truth came crashing down on me; I realized much of the world was exactly as I was seeing it and that the responsibility for it was as much the individual's as it was society's. Overall, the barrel and the apples were rotten!

My initial confusion was transformed into anger. Ironically, I was not angry with the people who were inflicting disillusionment and pain upon me, but with my parents. I wondered — how could they have allowed me to go into the world so completely unprepared for reality? How could they have handicapped me before I had even begun my life's trip? Didn't they love me? Or did they love me too much — "good intentions but bad judgement" sort of thing?

In my perplexity, confusion, and anger, I realized that no matter how I had come to this position, I still had to deal with the problem; I had to deal with "reality." I concluded that since I couldn't beat them, I would join them. However, I would be better at it than they were! In no time at all I became an unmitigated bastard. I lied, cheated, took unfair advantage — I was all the things I saw in them — and I was very good at it because I worked harder at it than they did (a carryover of the family work ethic virtue). I was not only recognized but even admired now. According to their standards — celebrity, status, money — I had become very successful. But every morning when I looked into the mirror I saw someone I hated more and more. I was miserable, unhappy; nothing was fun or interesting or worthwhile doing anymore.

I was between a rock and a hard place. If I reverted solely to the family virtues, I would be destroyed. If I retained the new cynicism, I would wind up destroying my life anyway. I did not have a solution. I was in so much pain I almost decided to resolve the problem by ending my life. Fortunately, I had a friend who was patient, experienced and wise, who worked with me constantly until I could see there was a way out where I could be what I was, and still survive. He showed me how to defend myself without resorting to the tactics and behavior I loathed, and how to win the battle without losing the war. I have come to believe that one can communicate clearly, straight-forwardly, and honestly and not be at a disadvantage. You do not have to add to the mountain of manure to survive and function well. But in order to do so, you will have to learn how to defend yourself without falling into their traps. You can not only succeed – you will feel good about yourself in the process. But first you must understand why you are so susceptible to deception, how you must change, and the technique of detection and Counterbull.

One of the main principles of bullshit is that most often it starts at the very top – where the power is situated. We must realize that the powerful have inculcated us with ideals which are observed more in the breach than in practice. They have used these ideals to control, intimidate and dominate us at every stage of our development. And when the authority finishes with us at one stage, control is passed on to the next authority so that we are always controlled by others. It is only when authority is questioned, opposed, and overcome that we are able to acquire a measure of power that allows us to control our own behavior or destiny. It is only when we are able to strip away false images and see intentions clearly that we can attack the enemy with any degree of success.

OUR CONTRIBUTIONS TO THE SUCCESS OF BS

Basically, bullshit succeeds because of the following reasons:

1. We give people, companies, institutions, governments more credit than they deserve. The obverse is that we lack self-esteem. We feel everyone is either smarter, more glamorous, more important, richer, more influential, more powerful, or more perfect than we are.

2. We have succumbed to the human weaknesses of greed, envy, and self-deception and bought the myth that by being shrewd we can get something for nothing.

3. We have allowed our desires, our needs, and our fantasies, to distort reality. We no longer separate fact from fiction, truth from credibility, illusion from reality.

4. We have abdicated our power by not accepting the responsibility for it. In return, we have settled for the

163

illusion of security, of being in "good hands" of doctors, teachers, lawyers, psychiatrists, the government, or even the insurance company.

All through childhood we had to accept the dictates of parents, teachers, scout master — any adult or authority. We had to accept on faith that what was presented, taught, or preached was the gospel truth. That is, until one's independent thinking, or life's experience showed us differently. However, in most instances, one could not contradict authority without fear of actual punishment for doing so. Punishment could be physical but much more painful was ostracism or the withdrawal of approbation and "love." Consequently, we went "underground." We noticed the discrepancies, kept quiet about them, but continued to observe the difference between what was preached and what was practiced. It was but a short step from this to our practicing deception. Either we saw adults using deception, or we came to know it by trial and error. We came to know that it was a method that could work with our lack of real power, and that if we were caught at it, it brought the least amount of problems. Although we occasionally lied too, we stayed away from it as much as possible because we were aware that lying brought the harshest penalty.

Thus was formed a generation of youngsters, who upon leaving childhood and school and entering the world of business and government, continued to use deception, particularly BS, as an everyday tool. What started as a need to avoid punishment for contradicting authority, gradually developed into a tool to wrest personal advantage, and that in turn became a life style and philosophy. This type of person believes he has an accurate fix on reality (and to a great extent he does because he sees the greed, envy, jealousy — the baser instincts of people); he feels superior to others because he utilizes their weaknesses and quite often gains the advantage. In the secret recesses of his person, however, he lacks self-esteem. His method masks the question-mark of his true ability, his true identity, his true values. He struggles constantly to escape those vague but consistent feelings of self-contempt.

Those of us who are most likely to be victims, however, responded quite differently to authority in childhood. Basically, we were unquestioning, or when we found discrepancies, we suppressed our knowledge of it because we would not jeopardize approbation, acceptance, and love. Our fear was so intimidating, we not only drove the knowledge of discrepancies into our sub-conscious, but we transformed the instigators of our fear into idealized forms. In other words, we placed our parents, teachers, and other authority figures on a pedestal, making them the fount and dispenser of all knowledge and all good things including security and love. Anything that threatened this balance was put aside, forgotten or hidden. The result, of course, was an idealistic but distorted image of reality, and a *predisposition* to being deceived.

Interestingly, this type of person is psychologically similar to the deceiver in that both lack self-esteem. He feels that other people, organizations, institutions, government are more important and of more value than he can ever be.

So, in order to attack this problem, we must, like in any good rehabilitation program that deals with changing one's behavior and psyche, first acknowledge and admit our susceptability, and that we are viewing life through a distortion. More precisely, we are not seeing reality. Reality is not the way you *wish* things to be, nor the way they *appear* to be, but the way they *actually* are.

The most difficult problem people have with reality is that they tend to confuse it with likes and dislikes. Unfortunately, one's personal feelings regarding a given reality are not relevant to the reality itself. It is very easy to fall into the trap of allowing your desires and emotions to play tricks on you, creating illusions intended to pass for reality. Distinguishing, for example, between what "should be" as opposed to what "is", is the difference between being deceived and being a realist who cuts the possibility of deception at its source.

A realist is simply a person who believes in basing his life on facts and who dislikes anything that seems imaginary, impractical, theoretical, or utopian.

There are those who argue that reality is not an absolute, that it is different things to different people. The premise being that each of us perceives situations differently and, therefore, that reality changes from person to person. As Robert Ringer points out, those who make this argument are partially right in their words, but completely wrong in their conclusion. Ringer says, "Each person does perceive reality differently, but reality is fact. What reality is not in all cases is a *known*. And that's where perception of reality comes in. Reality is the given; perception of the reality is the variable . . . It's tough to comprehend ideas and circumstances we are accustomed to hearing and seeing within invisible perimeters that surround our lives. Yet, common sense tells us that all we have learned and understood certainly does not comprise all the knowledge that exists on earth, let alone throughout the universe . . . (therefore) the antidote to the restrictions of our "own world" is to reject custom and tradition as a basis for fact, and in its place, put the acceptance of logic and reason."

But first we must recognize the "variable" — those factors that bend, distort, and falsify our perception of reality — that cloud and hide our ability to determine actual reality — the given. Of the variables, one of the most prevalent distorters is egotism.

EGOTISM

Egotism is self-conceit. And conceit is having an exaggerated opinion of oneself, one's merit. It is telling yourself that you are more beautiful, smarter, stronger, quicker, shrewder, more talented, more important than the next person. Self-conceit is synonomous with self-deceit. When your opinion of yourself is not based on fact, it is you fooling yourself.

I have personally seen this quality destroy hundreds of personal relationships, business partnerships — relationships in every type of organization — causing extensive waste of time, money and effort. It has shipwrecked many a hope and dream, leaving a residue of intense pain.

Self-conceit is an over-compensation for the lack of self-esteem, the feeling of being worthwhile, of value. Self-conceit is like a balloon filled with hot air that eventually bursts into shreds from over inflation. Or, when the hot air is exhausted slowly, the balloon shriveling up into an unattractive piece of material. It is a distortion lens which prevents you from seeing reality accurately. When one comprehends reality and deals with it properly, self-confidence grows. Unlike a lack of self-esteem or self-conceit, self-confidence is the fact that you have seen clearly and accurately and brought about an effective resolution to the matter.

Like the cliche, charity begins at home — so does honesty begin at home — it must begin with you. It must begin by asking questions: Am I deceiving myself so that it is obvious to everyone I can be fooled with almost no additional effort because I have already fooled myself? Am I over-exaggerating my qualities?

FANTASY

Fantasy is a series of mental images more-or-less-connected, as in a day dream, usually involving some unfulfilled desire. At one time or another, we have all fantasized about being extraordinarily beautiful, rich, brilliant, all powerful, and all knowing. Fantasizing in general, is both a harmless as well as healthy way to diminish frustration, disappointment, and the actual lack of power. But fantasy carried too far becomes a permanent and dangerous distortion of reality. Initially, the trip into fantasy and back to reality gets more and more difficult until one isn't aware of whether one is coming or going. The line of demarcation becomes blurred if not eliminated. Secondly, the intensity of our desires develops into a yearning, a hunger for the desired condition. The yearning and hunger becomes so extreme, so "real," that reality is rejected. At this point, one is literally incapable of recognizing reality.

At the moment of "unreality," the yearning and hunger is so intense, it is flagrantly projected to the deceiver. He can see that you are already so self-deceived that if he plays to your desire, even in a blatant manner, you will fall hook, line, and sinker for his deception.

The antidote to this problem is not so simple because it may have progressed to a level requiring therapy. Barring that, the important questions you must ask are: What is the extent of my desire? Are they extreme; would it require a "miracle," or such a fantastic stroke of luck to make them possible? If the answer is "yes," pay attention and try to change. Better yet, find a friend who will shake you to attention repeatedly.

Should therapy or self-discipline not be possible, another method which is effective is to shift the focus from yourself to the other person. Ask yourself, what is the other person implying, suggesting, offering? Is it too good to be true? If it seems so, then even in your fantastic state of mind there is still a corner of sanity. Use it!

GREED

Greed is wanting, craving, or taking all that one can get with no thought of others' needs. Being greedy implies an insatiable desire to possess or acquire something in an amount inordinately beyond what one needs or deserves. Two facets of greed are avariciousness, stressing greed for money or riches, which often connotes miserliness: and gluttony, having too strong a desire for food or drink.

Greed (like fantasy) indicates a compulsion, the inability to reasonably control one's behavior. It creates a monomania that blinds one to other elements of life. It distorts logic, the reasoning process which allows one to see reality clearly and in a balanced way. Some horse bettors, for example, will risk their rent money and car payment in the hopes of striking it rich with the following reasoning: "If I bet two dollars on the number six horse at two to one, I'll win four dollars. But if I bet on the number three horse, I'll win over a hundred. I really want the hundred dollars (who wouldn't), so I'll bet number three. And since a fool and his money are soon parted, so is our bettor a loser. Although a bettor occasionally wins a long shot (rarely wins is more accurate), the reality is that because the odds are not assigned randomly, he has the least chance of winning.

Not only is the greedy person's perception of reality warped, but his greed is the perfect ally of manipulators and con artists. The number of successful scams, swindles, and cons that have been perpetrated on the greedy is legendary. Greed is typified by "the something for nothing" attitude which becomes the perfect "hook" the deceiver utilizes almost everytime. Most of these schemes are so blatant and laughable, except for the tragedy they cause, that one would have to be blind—or insane—not to see them. As far back as 1642, Thomas Browne commented that "avarice seems not so much a vice, as a deplorable piece of madness."

If you told them they were greedy, they would think *you* were insane. They would point out, for example, that they believe in maxims such as "You get what you pay for," or, "If you want the best, you have to be willing to pay for it." Yet those same people will spend hours and hours trying to get more than they pay for—to get a bargain or, better yet, to get something for nothing. A shrewd merchant will either overprice merchandise so people will think they are getting a bargain, or may give away an expensive looking item for "free" which is compensated for in the sale price.

What can one do? Again, depending on the extent of the affliction, therapy may be the only solution. However, as a general approach to minimizing this problem, one should constantly ask oneself the following questions: Is the proposition or situation too good to be true? Does it seem like a "once in a lifetime opportunity?" Is there pressure to act now or will you lose the

168

opportunity? If the answer is "yes" — be suspicious and stay away from it. If your greed is too strong, get a friend to arrange preconceived signals between you, and who will lock you into a room until it is over. Someone said concerning exercise, "Everytime I think of exercising, I lay down until it goes away." You may not be able to lie down until your greed goes away, but you can acknowledge the greed to yourself and try to set up as many obstacles as you can to make it harder for you to participate.

ENVY

Envy is another distorter like greed. It is generally a distorted perception of reality that causes feelings which are difficult to control. It is feeling hateful, ill-willed and discontent because of another's advantages or possessions. The envious person keenly desires for himself something the other person owns or has achieved. He either begrudges or covets ardently and wrongfully something belonging to another.

Someone commented dryly, "Envy is a pain of mind that successful men cause their neighbors." Many envious people would be content to get along with less than they have if it would insure that none of their neighbors had more. Envious people may also limit their own opportunities: they have the philosophy, "cut off your nose to spite your face." A real-estate broker commented, "I never cease to be amazed at how many people will turn down a good buy because they find out somebody else is making a profit." One of the problems with envy is that it causes people to spend time and energy attempting to keep others down, which could be better spent in trying to improve their own situation.

What has envy to do with deception? Other than blocking your ability to see reality clearly, it creates a host of other conditions that make you vulnerable to it. "Keeping up with the Joneses," one-upmanship, or the put down places you in an offensive position which is difficult to disguise, thus leaving you open to retaliation. Keeping up with the Joneses has financially broken many a person. Envy is a negative activity. The more you are involved in it and its related facets, the less time you are spending on constructive actions of your own to benefit you. The only solution I know for conquering envy is to concentrate more time and energy towards your own efforts to make money or achieve whatever else is important to you rather than prevent the success of others. The reward is the pride which results from your own accomplishments.

However, since we are talking about the necessity of being realistic, we must face the fact that most people are too weak, too lazy, or too far gone to establish the discipline within themselves that is necessary to prevent deception. What hope is there for them? Fortunately, there is always more than one way to solve a problem. For a majority of people then, the simplest solution will be to shift the focus away from themselves and onto the deceiver. By reducing deception to its most basic mechanism, and with the help of a few general rules, you can unclothe and screen out most bullshit situations in their budding stage. The remaining situations will require a certain amount of energy, effort, and a firm determination not to be taken.

GENERAL RULE

For every good magician to succeed in his tricks and illusions, he must always create an action that directs the attention of the audience away from the main action so that something can be put in place or taken away. In other words, the key to the magician's performance rests on how he can *misdirect* the audience's focus.

In the same token, all deception is built on a distortion of a perceived reality. The deceiver always leads you to believe one thing while he does something else. Formally, a bullshitter lays down a set of impressions for other than the apparent motivation. In other words, he masks his true intentions; he misdirects you away from them by creating a misperception, while he separates you from your money or your power.

Before we get to the first specific COUNTERBULL action, common sense should tell us that it is necessary to be constantly skeptical. American culture has always placed an emphasis on generosity of spirit which is why charity flourishes in America. We pride ourselves on the law which says innocent until proven guilty. We overtly promote a sense of fair play. We do not want to see ourselves as mean, petty, grasping — small in any away. So, it is not exactly normal, natural, or comfortable for us to doubt and question easily. But if you want to win — to protect yourself well — it will be essential to start with the premise that you don't trust anyone until he or she has proven themselves trustworthy. "Trustworthy" has to be earned. Innocent until proven guilty is okay for the criminal courts: what works best in everyday life is that nobody is trustworthy until they prove themselves so.

BEING AWARE OF INTENTIONS

The motivation of the perpetrator is the one quality that is masked or hidden in all instances of deception. The deceiver will always try to divert your attention away from his true intentions. The high success rate of the deceiver attests to the exceptional skills they possess, making it extremely difficult to pinpoint their intentions. It is of such difficulty that Milton Fisher advocates the use of intuition to determine intention. He says, "The intuitive system brings holistic awareness to the fore and sees things that are missed or overlooked by conventional awareness, the trapping of wealth, fame, good looks, position, or status. It picks up signals that are not apparent and integrates them with others from the conscious system into a more realistic assessment of a person. Your intuitive sense is an invaluable "bullshit detector" . . . the intuitive is priceless because it is able to see behind the insincere smile, the surface charm, the superficial attractiveness. It sloughs aside the outside trappings and deals with the essence of the person. Guile, cunning, and duplicity are all functions of the reasoning mind, the left brain. Intuition can no more initiate guile or cunning than can your eyesight or hearing."

I heartily agree with Mr. Fisher, but with the reservation that while intuition is a valid tool, it requires a lot of time to establish this discipline, and many people do not have the time, even if they had the desire. A modified version that would require almost no time is to look to the many clues other people inevitably give off as to their true intentions and feelings. No matter how clever or skilled a person may be in hiding their intentions, if you are aware, they will give themselves away each time with various and sundry subconscious "slips" that they cannot control.

But the COUNTERBULL method that has the most to recommend it, is to automatically go to the opposite assumption of what is being presented. If someone is presenting themselves as kind, presume they are cruel; if rich that they are indigent; if an authority on some specialized subject, that their attitude is narrow and restrictive, maybe intolerant; if honest they are dishonest, etc. You may feel this is unfair and restrictive—that it will eliminate the good potential along with the bad. Overall, this is not true because of two reasons: one, the law of percentages is on your side. I know an executive who summed up his job as being a "rejector," that is, he rejected 98% of the new projects that came across his desk. He pointed out that contrary to the common image people held of most executives that they "promoted" new ideas, the reality was exactly the opposite, and that was because most new ideas failed, therefore, he was automatically on the winning side in rejecting them. The one or two that got away he simply rationalized by saying, "You can't be right all the time."

With my recommended method, however, you can succeed almost 100% of the time! That is because the assumption you make about another person is kept "silent," that is, it remains in your awareness, not the other person's. As far as the other person is concerned, you are accepting what he is presenting. He is the one making the wrong assumption. Of course, if his actions continue to be positive — conform to what he is presenting — he gradually begins to earn your trust and becomes trustworthy to the point where you permit his presentation to stand as essentially honest and true. I say "essentially" only to indicate you should never let your guard down, that you should be constantly aware of changing signs. Nothing ever stays the same!

ADDITIONAL COUNTERBULL TOOLS

1. After you have made an automatic assumption concerning the other person, you can fortify yourself by asking a few simple questions that will either strengthen your first conclusion, or change its balance:

a. WHAT is this person really saying?
b. HOW is he or she saying it to me?
c. WHY is he or she saying it to me?
d. WHERE is it leading to?
e. HOW is it making him or her feel?
f. HOW is it making me feel?

These questions are important because they begin a two-way process that hopefully will not only allow you to see the other person more clearly, but will start an insightful trip into your own responses, possibly creating an awareness of your own weaknesses.

2. Do not trust any piece of information that cannot easily be verified, and preferably from two sources. Once you have gone beyond all the mental and emotional calculations, there is no substitute for energy and effort. Most people, including myself, find investigation distasteful. In addition, I am simply lazy! I do not like writing inquiries, or phoning strangers. On the other

hand, out of sheer curiosity or malice (I haven't decided yet), I will talk to "friends" about other acquaintances. I am curious about their prospects, problems, vices, sex life, conflicts, accomplishments, and a host of other things. You might construe my curiosity as being a gossiper and I wouldn't argue with that either. However, I choose to interpret my curiosity or "gossiping" as being interested in personal history. I also know that it is very helpful to me in knowing where some people are coming from, which allows me to see them more clearly as well as telling me what I should do and how I can possibly defend myself.

Whether you like it or not, you have been documented and checked out all your life, starting with your birth certificate, school records, medical records, military service records, credit records, and business employment. There is so much public information on you that there is really no way for you to hide or prevent others from knowing about you. And I am not talking about securing information surreptitiously, although that is an extensive practice too. I am saying that securing information is an accepted formal process — standard operating procedure — and that we do not even question it anymore. We "willingly" give out information to others so they can check out and verify our honesty. Since we grant this permission ourselves, we shouldn't give it a second thought when and if we do it. We have the same right to protect ourselves. And, you will be amazed at the number of people who want to talk about others. It gives them a sense of power knowing that what they say might determine the outcome of someone else's life!

If the other person should learn that you are investigating them, they may not like it, but they will start developing a healthy respect for you. At the least, they will quickly surmise you are not a complete fool, easily deceived, and that they better be on their toes or go elsewhere if deception is on their minds. A fierce looking, loudly-barking dog is more often than not respected. He really may be a gentle soul underneath his exterior, but anyone approaching him will first look for friendly signs before advancing; secondly, everyone will stay on their best behavior for fear he may revert to less friendly actions.

3. *Follow the payoff.* People deceive others for a reason. As I have previously shown, the greatest difficulty was in being able to determine the intangible payoff — power — as against the obvious payoff, material possessions or money. But money is synonomous with power; it is just a more visible manifestation of it, and its path easier to follow.

173

It is universally acknowledged that money is the great motivater, the root of all things. I wouldn't go this far, but I certainly agree with many great men that money is central to our existence and responsible for good and bad.

Horace proclaimed, "Money is the foremost thing to seek; cash first and virtue afterwards."

Cicero warned that, "Of evils current upon the earth, the worst is money."

Alexander Hamilton called money, "an essential ingredient to happiness."

Tolstoy regarded money as "a new form of slavery."

Heinrich Heine claimed, "Money is the god of our time."

George Bernard Shaw called money the "most important thing in the world."

Sophocles observed, "For money you would sell your soul."

In "Money Madness," Herb Goldberg and Robert T. Lewis comment that, "People often give each other double messages in regard to money. They claim it is 'good' to strive to obtain money but 'bad' to admit that one wants a lot of it. Money is viewed as the most important commodity in the world, but social etiquette demands that it be spoken of as having no value. People give lip service to the democratic ideal that everyone is equal but give differential treatment to those who have money and those who do not. Hypocrisy about money is therefore inevitable. In fact, hypocrisy becomes the norm. People who deviate either by openly avowing their desire for money or by not devoting most of their time and energy working to acquire it are looked upon as peculiar."

Goldberg and Lewis also point up the dichotomy and ambivalence in institutions as well as individuals: great religions of the world that preach poverty and denial have leaders or representatives who live lavishly; or church leaders who stress the value of sacrifice and penury but build churches, cathedrals and temples that are architectural masterpieces richly adorned with gold and silver and housing some of the most valuable art collections in the world.

Pablo Picasso accumulated more wealth in his lifetime than any other artist, yet, for many years he was an ardent supporter of communism, an economic system which advocates equal distribution of wealth. During the sixties, many rock singers such as

Bob Dylan, became rich by writing and singing protest songs which berated the establishment for its concern about money and materialism rather than human rights and social reform. Later, Dylan built an ultraposh home overlooking the Pacific Ocean in Malibu at a cost of $2 million.

All this talk about money is to make the point that if you presume money is the reason for the majority of cases of deception, you would not be far off at all. If you also presumed that some form of power was the reason for the majority of deception, you would also be correct. There are other motives for deception such as pleasure in sex, but so much of sex is also a power situation that it would be difficult to separate the two. Therefore, if we immediately ask — "What is the motivation for the seeming deception?" and "What is the payoff for the deception?" and we assign money or power as the reason — we would be almost automatically right. So, if we keep our eye on the payoff and follow its path, we will be able to see how the deception is being accomplished: we will be literally x-raying the scheme or pretense because we are able to get underneath the mask at once!

With these few general rules and simple tools, you should now be able to remove the many MASKS that hide the true intention of the deceiver. It should enable you to get to the deception sooner, stop it quicker, stop it better. In order to facilitate the process, and in order for you to identify quickly some of the many other masks that exist, we shall now examine their appearance.

MASKS

Experts

If we viewed experts as people with informed opinions in their respective disciplines rather than as authorities who are infallible, experts would not be in such disrepute. The responsibility for this condition is not solely the experts; if we did not inflate their importance in our own minds, accept their opinions unconditionally, they would not be able to promote the image of a "know-it-all," or of seeming God-like, nor would their membership have increased rapidly.

With knowledge proliferating at an ever increasing speed, more and more specialization has occured among professionals. In medicine you have everything from penis specialists to brain specialists. In accounting, everything from personnel and corporate tax specialists to systems design and installation specialists. In law, from corporate, to criminal, to maritime law.

Ernest Becker, in the "Denial of Death" makes the statement that there is too much truth. This statement is apt to take one aback until Becker describes how white light is refracted into the many colors of the spectrum when shown through a prism. If you are viewing refracted light from one position and you see the color red, and another person from a different position sees the color blue, and still another yellow or green, they would all be right—they each see the color they describe. Yet, they are all wrong. The prime color before it was refracted was white. It contains all of the other colors. So, like the "truth" viewed thusly, there are too many specialists who see a part but not the whole. Just because their view is narrower does not make it more accurate or the "truth." Experts can also be wrong. They once thought the world was flat, or the Titanic could not sink; doctors misdiagnose illnesses and remove wrong organs in surgery; engineers miscalculate stresses and buildings fall down, bridges collapse, and hundreds of people die. If you think these are exceptions to the rule, or that they don't happen frequently, you should read "The Peter Principle," which explains how we all rise to our level of incompetence if we are not careful—and experts probably faster than all others.

And experts disagree among themselves. In a court of law where the case of a murderer was being pleaded on the basis of insanity, two psychiatrists for the prosecution said he was sane, two psychiatrists for the defense said he was insane. Result, the jury was more confused than ever. One expert says eggs increase cholesterol which is bad for the heart; another says it doesn't have much effect at all. One expert says jogging is good for you; another says it is the worst exercise possible. As a matter of fact, it is quite often difficult to get two experts to agree on anything. As a general rule, for every expert who expresses an opinion, there is another expert who will have a different opinion on identically the same subject and evidence.

In other areas, the consultant has become commonplace during the last five to ten years, particularly in business. Since most forms of consultancy require no official licensing of any sort, the field provides rich opportunities to mountebanks. Some psychological consultants or counselors have degrees of one sort or another, but many do not. The sole prerequisite to becoming a consultant seems to be simply hanging out a sign and saying that you are so. Quite often, consultancy is simply an attractive front for some people who are temporarily or permanently out of work. John Brooks in "Showing Off In America," notes that, "the appetite of *consulters for consultants* is apparently voracious to the point of insatiability. Let the slightest thing seem amiss in a corporation, foundation, cultural institution, bureau of government, or personal life, and the all but reflexive response, in many cases, is to call in a consultant . . . The outcome of this response has been to call into being a huge industry — one with an emergent literature of its own, designed to provide expertise on the expertise business." There is also another practice that has grown to grand proportions; experts sending you to other experts! In this way, they support and encourage each other at *your* expense. (Italics mine)

COUNTERBULL: Remember, experts take their pants or pantyhose off one leg at a time, just as we do. At best he is expressing an informed opinion; at worst he is nothing more than an ordinary guy from out of town who doesn't know his ass from a hole in the ground. Many of them will quickly tell you all the reasons you can't do something. Personally, I prefer to determine for myself what I can or cannot do, and I hate paying high prices for what will turn out to be simple common sense anyway. The biggest discouragement for any expert is to tell him you are going to get a second, if not third opinion. It lets him know immediately you have not bought his recommendations unqualifiedly, and that you are not a pushover for experts.

Credentials

An expert with a piece of paper that "certifies" he is an expert, is an expert with credentials. He has a license from a school, the government or the Mafia, or any other gang that allows him to practice without too much interference. Credentials imply that he knows all the answers and/or has the experience to deal with a certain area of expertise. Credentials also say he has paid the price to the authorities, or head of the gang, which is a little like buying "protection" you might not need; some would call it extortion.

But credentials — diplomas, licenses, awards, and experience — are not necessarily synonomous with knowledge of the facts or wisdom. I've known some people, new to a field of endeavor, who instinctively knew more than others who had been in it for years. Seniority was irrelevant; talent, ability or knowledge was not. History shows hundreds of self-taught people without even a high school education who created the most brilliant of inventions, great art, or succeeded incredibly in business. As a matter of fact, schools which are greatly responsible for many of the credentials, are also responsible for producing illiterates and incompetents, as well as giving illusions of grandeur to many youth who will have to face painful reality later. Karl Hess, an important speech writer for Barry Goldwater, and who dropped out of school at fifteen, commented, "I loved education which is why I spent as little time as possible in school . . . the only thing you have to do to get kids educated is abolish the school system."

Credentials can be killers. A college education can easily cost parents forty thousand dollars per child which puts an enormous financial strain on them. But these high costs are necessary to set the limits of the "select circle" which keeps out the mass of other competition that would develop if not for credentials. A number of years ago, I developed a program after much study and research, that I thought would solve the problems of the school system and produce truly educated students in the most efficient manner. As a lay educator, my knowledge wasn't revolutionary but I knew it was effective. To make a long story short I contacted foundations, business, and the government to no avail. I did succeed in getting a visit from an official of the Department of Health, Education and Welfare, who proceeded to tell me honestly (or is this a contradiction), that I couldn't or wouldn't get to first base because I didn't have the credentials. He stated that educators with degrees would be looking at this program and would tear it apart on that one point alone. They would be absolutely, unforgivably resentful of my attempt and would do everything in their power to prevent it. Although I resisted his cynicism momentarily, feeling people couldn't be so petty, I instinctively knew he was right, so I went on to other ventures where I did not need credentials. I was not crushed but I did feel a sense of sad disappointment which was somewhat mitigated because I knew that the great Admiral Rickover, the father of the nuclear submarine, had experienced a similar situation with professional educators. While he wrote a book about his experience, I was effectively blocked because I did not want to make a crusade out of mine.

Ironically, the value of credentials has plummeted in the last few years. For one, the recession has put hundreds of Ph.D.s out of work, and with the prior over-production of doctorate degrees, the market was glutted anyway. In addition, like counterfeit Cartier watches, Gucci bags, and designer jeans, one can actually buy a college diploma without ever having had to attend classes or test for it. One can just as easily become a minister of his own church and be exempted from paying taxes by simply paying the fee and sending away for the official document. In the same manner, someone, somewhere, will sell you a piece of paper for anything you want to be. Sadly, the counterfeits fool many of the authorities, as well as the majority of people who have made official looking credentials their requisite. They have bought the BS that credentials certify both knowledge and experience. But long before phony papers came along, official credentials were so over-inflated their true value as criteria were quite questionable.

COUNTERBULL: I suggest you visualize diplomas, licenses, or any other paper credential as toilet paper. This will initially put things in perspective. Secondly, if someone presents their credentials to you at first instant to show their authority, legitimacy or knowledge, get suspicious fast! Since checking the source of credentials may be ineffective because the source itself may be phony, check out the associates surrounding the presenter—birds of a feather flock together. But most of all, use your common sense and intuition to evaluate what the person is saying, and how he is saying it. Quite often a pretentious person is synonomous with the lack of real substance and "truth" in a situation.

Track Record

Track record does not refer to running races on the track field. "Track record" is an expression most often used in business to refer to the previous successes a person has had in their field of endeavor. Track records are used as a herald in securing future opportunities. It is based on the premise that if one succeeded before, the *chances* of succeeding again are greater for him than for someone who does not have a track record.

Track record is very much like "expert," and "credentials." The difference is that track record does not need to be based on diplomas or other credentials, but on actual success. For this reason, it is more difficult to separate what may have been pure luck from design, knowledge and execution. In Hollywood, as in other industries, executives are paid hundreds of thousands of dollars to literally *guess* what the public will pay to see. In many cases they don't even bother to guess, they imitate. In 1969–1970,

179

the entire Hollywood film industry almost went bankrupt (cumulatively, they had lost some 600 million dollars in less than two years) because they tried to imitate the incredible success of the musical, "The Sound of Music." Instead of making at least "educated" guesses of other subject matter that might have appealed to audiences, they just made other musicals in the 20 to 30 million dollar range, all of which failed miserably!

However, because executives generally get sufficient opportunities to be proved right or wrong in their guesses, the odds are they will get lucky and win sometimes. On the other hand, if one cannot even get up to bat, one will not be able to hit the ball under any circumstances. However, even a rank amateur can get lucky if the ball is thrown to him to be hit. Consequently, whether one has true ability and knowledge or not is rather academic if one doesn't get the opportunity to be proved right or wrong.

I remember going into shock one day when a phonograph record producer with a reputation as a "genius" told me that if he succeeded as much as two percent of the time, he was doing fantastic! That meant if only two of a hundred records he produced were commercially successful, his reputation as a genius remained intact. And when you recall that Ford Motors, with the best brains—people with top track records—and millions and millions of dollars to back them up, produced the historic failure, the Edsel automobile, that should put things into perspective. But it really won't because most executives are insecure and desperately need the reassurance given to them by this token symbol. In addition, track records are used by executives as a defensive tool to protect their flanks. In most instances, executives must answer to someone for failure; the vice-president to the president, the president to the board of directors, the board of directors to the stockholders, the stockholders to their wives and families, and family to friends! As a consequence, when a failure occurs, if that person can point to the people hired and say, "Well, I hired the 'best,' what can you do?" He shifts the onus of the failure on to "track records," which in most cases is enough of a shift to save his job.

COUNTERBULL: Don't let other people's successes blind you. Just as the grass is always greener on someone else's side of the field, you will never quite know all of the specific reasons behind someone else's success. It may have been pure luck, a combination of other circumstances the person was in no way responsible for, etc. In making a decision to hire a lawyer, accountant, contractor, plumber, doctor — anyone — listen closely to the solution they are offering to your problem. Evaluate how he is presenting it to you. Is he pretentious, arrogant, boastful, arbitrary, overpowering, or impatient? If he is, then seek out some younger, "less-experienced-hungry-for-opportunity" person, and let him convince you of what he is offering. This procedure is a lot more work than just buying someone's track record, but it can save you money, time, and pain in the long run. In addition, it will yield the pleasure that comes from discovering, encouraging, and supporting new talent.

The Intellect

The ultimate weapon of the credentials-wielding expert is vocabulary or the way he expresses himself. If he can't "snow" you with his reputation, diplomas, or his brilliance, he will try to overcome you with a dazzling array of incomprehensible words. He will try to talk "over your head." If the words are not "high falutin," they will be so technical that only another technician could understand them. When that doesn't work, they go to the "jargon" of their professions — specialized idioms used in a particular field — sort of a shorthand. Add to this the taking of a relatively simple idea and making it so complex you can't begin to follow what he is saying, and you now have the arsenal and technique of the "intellectual."

His purpose is to make you feel so uninformed, so helpless, that you will gladly open your arms to him as your savior. In my experience, so-called intellectuals are formally overeducated. I stress formal because it is really impossible to be overeducated in the true sense. But one can get so involved in academic, technical, and sometimes hypothetical matters, one can lose sight of the subject of living. They can't see the logic for the words.

COUNTERBULL: When a person is talking "over your head" it may well be that his points are not strong enough to stand on their own when stated in simple, straightforward language. Esoteric terms are often a smoke screen for an irrational or weak argument. So, the objective is to get the "intellectual" to express his ideas on your level of understanding. What consistently works for me is that I admit to being ignorant! I say, "I'm sorry but I don't know your field of endeavor, but I sincerely would like to understand. Would you try explaining it a little more simply for me?" I will then keep at him persistently until he either drops his pretentiousness or he throws up his hands in frustration. Since I have been warm, congenial, and interested, if he hasn't communicated his message or idea to me, it's his failure, not mine. If he doesn't succeed, he will realize he didn't or couldn't "snow" me under.

The "Big" Person

In a literal sense, the physical stature of an individual is of real significance to others. There are so many hang-ups concerning height, for example, that a tall, imposing person may be reluctant to date a short person, or vice-versa. It is a well-known fact that most people who have to look up to a "big" person are in some way intimidated. A big person knows this from experience and will try to either emphasize it or diminish it to his advantage.

Small men, in particular, seem to be most intimidated; to counteract this feeling, they fall prey to the "big" syndrome. They develop Napoleonic complexes—they try to raise their height with platform shoes, smoke big cigars, make big gestures like picking up the check at restaurants, date very tall women. But "big" is as much psychological as physical. It is also synonomous with strong and powerful. In reality, unless it is a matter involving physical strength, the big person has no more advantage than anyone else. So, "strong and powerful" are mental and emotional images ascribed to big people because of their size when there may be no basis for it in reality.

There are additional ways we equate big with other qualities. In the case of wealthy people, an otherwise inept person is granted extraordinary powers of being brilliant, talented, and an expert—many things they may not be at all. Henry Ford, founder of Ford Motors, did so many asinine things and made so many ridiculous pronouncements on subjects he knew nothing about, he became laughable. But initially because of his success and wealth from the auto industry, he was given rapt attention. Some even listened and acted on his words.

The underlying strength of "big," however, comes from the posture a person assumes and projects in a situation. A woman I know invariably projects a sense of warmth but an equal sense of being somewhat aloof. She projects a propriety stance and a reserve that lets people know she is not to be approached lightly, familiarly, or in any way less than befitting a lady. Her attention is much sought after and her reputation is sparkling. Yet, in no way is she a brilliant conversationalist, nor of high social standing, or is she wealthy or beautiful. But she has firmly established her posture that keeps people at a proper distance, and men from coming on too strong, romantically, or in a physical way.

Otto Preminger, the great film director, when being interviewed on a television talk show, was asked why he always acted cruelly and tyrannically toward the people he worked with. He replied simply, "Familiarity breeds contempt. If I acted more in accordance with my true nature which, believe it or not, is to be kind, I would be treated like a fool. I know this is a fact because it has happened to me a number of times. Now my reputation precedes me and I am treated respectfully and my orders are obeyed without too much opposition."

Almost every person presents a posture whether they realize it or not. They may come off as weak, strong, dull, flamboyant, rustic, macho, or sinister. Many, however, assume different postures by design, postures intended to intimidate in some way. They may emphasize physical size, wealth, status, brilliance — anything that says "powerful." Although a person can control and/or assume a posture that is not true to themselves, it poses several dangers. First is the danger of being totally discounted immediately because the "pretension" is so obvious it is transparently not true. Secondly, someone might feel you are bluffing and simply call the bluff. Overall, I feel it is best to base your posture on actual accomplishment, knowledge or fact.

COUNTERBULL: Though your posture may be weak, equalizing the posture of others can be implemented by these rules: the first is psychological; you must realize your own vast power. *You* control the decision as to whether to join the game or not. A person may have more financial strength than you, but he can't *make* you play marbles with him if you refuse to do so. Secondly, don't ever be at the mercy of any one person. One may need clients, but not any particular client. One may need a job, but not one particular job. One may need the companionship of a man or woman, but not any one particular man or woman. Do not get suckered into playing the other person's game. You have that choice.

But the more effective and probably more difficult way to de-bull a person is not to want or need whatever they think is their strength. If it is a beautiful woman who uses her beauty to intimidate or dominate — well, there are hundreds and thousands who are more compatible and reasonable. If a person is using his wealth to intimidate or dominate — well, there are other ways to make a buck or accomplish something. If a person is using intellect or talent to intimidate, stimulation can be found in a thousand books or theaters. The point is, you can satisfy your needs in many ways, with many different people. The sooner you can convey this message to Mr. Big, the sooner he will abandon his pose. If not, good riddance.

Mr. Inaccessible

There are many people who go to great lengths to convey to you how important they are, how much in demand they are, how little time they have, how superior they are to you by not being available to you. They are called The Inaccessibles. They make it almost impossible for you to talk to them face to face, or any other way. They place between you and them a host of obstacles.

Ostensibly, the innovation of the telephone was intended to increase convenience. While it has done precisely that for millions of people, its true purpose for Mr. Inaccessible has been to minimize his vulnerability and increase his power. John Brooks dates this perversion with the introduction and use of the extension telephone. One of the first to utilize the extension phone was the industrialist, E.H. Harriman, who had approximately one hundred of them installed in his country mansion, including the bathroom. Brooks says, "The multiple-extension user gains the advantage of being able to place calls at anytime from wherever he happens to be, and thus not only to place calls more conveniently but also to place more of them. Meanwhile he is protected from receiving unwanted calls by a necessary component of such a system, one or more servants who screen incoming calls and pass on to the user the only calls that are appropriate and acceptable."

The modern counterpart to the servant is the secretary who intervenes. She has been trained to take the message to determine its importance, and then to give the caller some excuse that the person they are trying to reach is indisposed, out-of-town, in an important meeting, etc. Quite often, the secretary, taking the cue from her employer, will blatantly or arrogantly act as if you committed a crime in calling. Secretaries will also place the caller on "hold," that is, make the caller wait an inordinately long time, and then give him an excuse. This is not only rude, but if you are calling from a pay phone and you are out of change, maddening as well.

Next came the unlisted phone number which screens out all

who do not know the number, and supplanted the extension phone. The implication, of course, is that Mr. Inaccessible is obliged to keep the masses away or go mad. This status symbol, however, has become so over-used that even secretaries, clerks, and the man-on-the-street, have unlisted numbers.

Today, the over-use of unlisted numbers has all but given way to the telephone answering machine. Mr. Inaccessible, as the new and chic thing to do, wants to give the impression of being open, direct, gracious, so he has a telephone answering machine. But the impression is false. The answering machine still gives him total control over who he talks to. He may not choose to return the call if he has been out, or he can interrupt the machine and talk to the party if he is in. The caller in the latter instance, realizes the machine is being used for call screening but is momentarily flattered at being among the select. On second thought, the caller also remembers when the machine was not interrupted, nor the call returned, and realizes that he may have been blacklisted.

Interestingly, technology brought us the Picture Phone years ago for which there were high hopes of widespread use. But it failed miserably. It seems that though people spoke openly of wanting it, secretly they had no intentions of ever using it. Most people do not want face to face contact; it would make them too readily accessible, it would take away secrecy, it would eliminate the games people play with telephones.

But the telephone is not the only obstacle. Mr. Inaccessible rides a limousine or private jet, goes to private clubs, eats at exclusive restaurants, has homes on remote islands, or if in New York, an apartment with such heavy security it is impossible to penetrate. Of course, all of these things are status symbols which serve the double purpose of impressing Mr. Inaccessible's peer group who are playing the same game. Frequently, they are easier to be duped by this game than the man-on-the-street.

Playing Mr. Inaccessible, however, can backfire sometime. An unpretentious founder of a very large company had the idiosyncrasy of showing up in places where least expected, and of doing unorthodox things to keep track of his organization. One day he called a key executive in his company but gave a false name. The secretary played Mr. Inaccessible and was rather brusque and haughty with him. He then called another executive with a different secretary and received the same treatment. Later that week he called a meeting with those executives and asked that they bring their secretaries. The executives were puzzled but complied. At the meeting the founder explained what he had done. He fired the secretaries on the spot, and told the executives that if they did not convey the importance of courtesy, and did not talk to callers no matter who they were, they would also be fired. He then had them make up a memo on the matter which was circulated throughout the company. From then on, callers were treated respectfully.

In the case of unlisted telephone numbers, a nurse was caring for a man with a heart condition. She had to go to court on a personal matter and left the man's house in a rush to be on time. A couple of hours later, while looking in her pockets, she discovered she had his medicine which was crucial to his health. She panicked. She did not have her address book with his telephone number, and she couldn't remember it. She called a few close friends of his to get it but they were out. She then called the telephone company and explained the situation to the operator who refused to give her the number. The operator suggested that the nurse have the man's doctor call her. The nurse desperately asked for the operator's supervisor to whom she repeated the story, but to no avail. The nurse quickly left the courthouse, grabbed a cab and returned to the house. When there was no response to the bell, her own heart beat fiercely. She broke a window, entered the house, and ran to his room where she discovered he was dead. Now, he really was inaccessible!

On the other hand, a small appliance retailer called the president of a company that manufactured appliances to complain of mistreatment by the distributor. When the president came on the line, the retailer was shocked. He fully believed the president would not talk to him and that he was simply going through the motions. The retailer explained how surprised he was to be speaking to him. The president replied, "If it's important enough for you to spend your dime to call me, it's important enough for me to call you back." The president later visited the retailer on a cross-country tour he had set up to solve a problem he was having with the competition. Of course, the retailer came through with flying colors for him.

While these examples may seem extreme, in actuality, they are not. They do point up that Mr. Inaccessible does not function without some danger. At the least, Mr. Inaccessible is building up a big cheering section, hoping if not praying, for his downfall. Until then, however, to equalize Mr. Inaccessible this is what you might do.

COUNTERBULL: If a secretary puts you on hold, hang up and call back and let her know your time is limited and important. If she is also haughty, remind her that she is an employee and you are an important person. In other words, remind her that her position is lower than yours. You may have to be blunt. If you still cannot get through to the executive or the person you are calling, write him and let him know that you know the game. Let him know he is being discourteous and rude, and that if he continues to be so, you will let the truly important people in the company know of his rudeness, and if that isn't enough, you will take out an ad in the local newspaper and tell the world. This may not make him conducive to giving you a job or an order, or correcting some error, but it will get his attention, and maybe his respect. There are times when finesse will not, cannot de-bull a person. Then you must be outrageous, more outrageous than they are. Very few can stand the embarrassment of this kind of exposure.

Flattery

Though "Pride Goest Before The Fall" is quite true, I've seen many more cases where "Flattery Goest Before The Fall" might be a more accurate description of the situation. I've seen people so blinded by false flattery and their perspectives so distorted, they couldn't even see the roof caving in on them.

The flatterer is absolutely deadly because he attacks where you are must vulnerable; in your need to be complimented, and in your need to be told how great you are. And with the music of sirens he fills your ears to overflowing, dulling if not obliterating logic or common sense. Many a fortune, battle, or life has been lost while the flattered was thusly occupied. It takes the greatest will to withstand such sweet music as praise. It takes the ubiquitous Otto Preminger, the film director, for example, who was viewing a roughly edited version of the ten million dollar film he was making, to ask an important film executive of a major studio who had just viewed the film with him, what he thought. The film executive gushed on about how great the film was, and how great Otto was as a film maker. "You've done it again Otto," he said brightly. With a scowl on his face, Otto Preminger turned to the rest of the group and said, referring to the flatterer, "Either he has no taste, or he is a terrible liar!" Then turning abruptly to his editor said, "We must tear this film apart and start again."

Flattery has a long history as one of the most effective tools of deception. Machiavelli, in the early 1500s, was so accurate in his advice to the Prince regarding flattery, that he should be quoted verbatim. "The Prince," of course, has long been the one standard tome indispensable to any politician, head of state, or business executive, who wishes to know the place and function of deception in the scheme of things. Here then is Machiavelli's advice on how to handle and counteract flattery. He says, "I must not omit an important subject, and mention of a mistake which princes can with difficulty avoid, if they are not very prudent, or if they do not make a good choice. And this is with regard to flatterers, of which courts are full, because men take pleasure in their own things and deceive themselves about them that they can with difficulty guard against this plague; and by wishing to guard against it they run the risk of becoming contemptible. Because there is no other way of guarding one's self against flattery than by letting men understand that they will not offend you by speaking the truth; but when everyone can tell you the truth, you lose their respect. A prudent prince must therefore take a third course, by choosing for his council wise men, and giving these alone full liberty to speak the truth to him, but only of those things that he asks and of nothing else; but he must ask them about everything and hear their opinion, and afterwards deliberate by himself in his own way, and in these councils and with each of these men comport himself so that everyone may see that the more freely he speaks, the more he will be acceptable. Beyond these he should listen to no one, go about the matter deliberately, and be determined in his decisions. Whoever acts otherwise either cuts precipitately through flattery or else changes often through the variety of opinions, from which it follows that he will be little esteemed . . . A prince, therefore, ought always to take counsel, but only when he wishes, not when others wish; on the contrary he ought to discourage absolutely attempts to advise him unless he asks it, but he ought to be a great asker, and a patient hearer of the truth about those things of which he has inquired; indeed, if he finds that anyone has scruples in telling him the truth he should be angry."

COUNTERBULL: Know thyself. Know your true qualities and accomplishments. Ban anyone who falsely exaggerates them to you. He is your enemy.

Snobbery

A snob is a person who attaches great importance to wealth, social position, status symbols, and has contempt for those he considers his inferiors. He admires and seeks to associate with those who he considers his superiors. A snob feels and acts smugly superior about his particular tastes or interests. In other words, a snob sets up his own criteria that cannot be objectively evaluated. It is almost as bad as if he took the color black and said it was white. In the same manner, critics will attempt to shove down your throat abstract painting if you like representational painting. They will tell you what is "artistic" in movies, literature, sculpture, architecture. They will tell you what is "in" and where it is in.

Then there are the social snobs, the wealthy with new or old money, the jet set commonly known as the "beautiful people," and the academicians, the bookish, university group. All set themselves up as being better or superior than anyone else and they establish symbols and criteria by which they exclude others. But you don't even have to look that far today because snobbery is now common practice among the general public. They buy designer jeans, drink Perrier water, carry Louis Vuitton bags, and wear Gucci shoes.

In reality, snobs know they don't have the "real goods," which is based on solid accomplishments and an interior sense of self-esteem that doesn't have to be artificially reinforced by other artificial people. The contempt the snob feels for "inferiors" is really a self-contempt they project outwardly. They really are contemptuous of themselves because deep down, no matter how much they hide from it, they feel an emptiness and an alienation from the solid values and emotions that count the most.

COUNTERBULL: Ignore them. Do not play their game. They hunger for our acknowledgement. If they attend "in" places, patronize another establishment. If they try to foist their taste on you which is purely subjective, or criticize you, do not argue. Simply say, "I don't criticize your taste because I don't like it — please give me the same courtesy, or leave. Snobbery has no place in my life. I believe in individual expression and tolerance." This should let the snob know immediately that you know his game and you are not impressed nor "snowed."

The Discouragement Fraternity

In the guise of giving you good advice, there are those who discourage you from doing anything. Because the advice may come from your family or loved ones, or from an expert in the field, or a professional such as a lawyer, accountant, or consultant, the implication is that they are advising you out of "love," experience, or knowledge.

In reality, giving advice may be motivated out of fear, insecurity, or sheer malevolence. Your parents and spouses, in fearing for you, may be really fearing for themselves. If you fail they may be hurt, so they would rather you play it safe. The professionals may be saying, "how dare you succeed in this business when you have no experience in it — no license, diploma, awards, or track record. They want you to pay your dues but won't even let you get started. The experts may simply be trying to prevent you from getting out of the starting gate, thus avoiding the obstacle of yet another player with whom they are not equipped to compete. The Discouragement Fraternity can be deadly because their mask is one of good will. In addition, you may have gone to them for the advice, and quite often, they don't seem to have any axes to grind. Too, you may be fighting your own doubts and insecurities during this time. What then?

COUNTERBULL: Whether it is a decision as to which line of work to go into, how to handle a specific financial problem, or which school to go to, the first step should always be to secure as much knowledge as possible on *your* own, so that you will have some basic reference for your ultimate decision. The second step is to consider the source of the advice you are getting. In other words, try to determine the true intention of the giver, as well as the quality of the advice. You must also be a little cynical; no one is really interested in helping you and many will go out of their way to harm you. On the other hand none of these people owe you anything. Therefore, you must "discover" yourself or it might not happen; you must do it yourself or it might not get done. The third step is to combine all of the advice you've been given with the knowledge you've come up with, and take a consensus. That is, see where the advice converges or diverges most, then measure it against your own knowledge and feelings. Once you've determined the pro and con, act. If your feelings are strong but you still have doubt, you must have the courage to go ahead and try. Failure is not the worst thing that could happen to you. Even if you fail, you may still feel strongly and want to try again. The lessons learned will hold you in good stead.

Going Great

This is the person who is always willing to tell you, whether you want to know it or not, how great things are going for him/her. As a matter of fact, some will corner you and insist on telling you. Have you heard the following:

"I've really got my act together now!"

"My business is making so much money I don't know what to do with it. I'm always talking to tax specialists about one tax shelter or another!"

"Our marriage is absolutely terrific! We never argue and he's a terrific lover. I don't see how it could be better!"

"The kids are terrific! They're so good and all. I know I'm blessed!"

COUNTERBULL: This one is easy. Simply translate what the person is saying to its opposite and you'll come extremely close to what the actual situation is really like. For example, "I've got my act together now," becomes, "I'm so screwed up I don't know what the hell I'm going to do next. It's so bad I feel like ending it all now."

"My business is making so much money, I don't know what to do with it, I'm always talking to tax specialists about one tax shelter or another." This becomes, "The IRS is one step behind me which might mean ten years in prison, and my Mercedes is going to be repossessed in two weeks, so unless a miracle happens soon, I'll either be going to jail or bankrupt. I don't know which is worse!"

"Our marriage is absolutely terrific! We never argue and he's such a good lover. I don't see how it could be better?" Translated: "Argue? We don't even talk. And I'm sure we haven't made love for the last two months because he's screwing his secretary. I'm going to hire a private detective and hit him with everything I've got in the divorce!"

"The kids are terrific! They're so good and all. I know I'm blessed." Translation: "I wonder if Jimmy is on any other drugs than the pot I found in his room. Come to think of it, the $100 that disappeared may have gone into drugs! Maybe he's really hooked? And Gina has been acting strange. God, I hope she's not pregnant. With that Planned Parenthood literature—she

191

couldn't be thinking—of an abortion! What did I do wrong? Why am I being punished?"

The translations may seem a little extreme but in many instances they are just that. You might make little adjustments for those who are a little more low key, but always beware of those who either boast too much or protest too much—they are guilty of something they are trying to hide while trying to make you envious.

When Opportunity Knocks—Beware

I had to get "stung" three times in my youth before I learned that no matter how terrific a piece of merchandise looked from a peddler on the street, or how terrific a "bargain" it was, do not buy it! First I bought a set of "cashmere" sweaters from a man selling out of a truck. The sweaters looked soft, warm, and beautiful. The price was ridiculously low. But, the moment someone dropped a cigarette ash on one of the sweaters it burst into flames. The second sweater just shrunk to a frazzle when washed. My "Cartier" watch I bought for thirty dollars stopped running two days later and, when I took it to get repaired, was told it was junk. The third purchase was a "diamond" ring that was pure fake.

Since that time, it seems I have encountered every fantastic "get-rich-quick-scheme," or "sure-thing" invention, or "can't-miss" opportunity in the world. The usual characteristic of these deals are that they are always presented in an exhilarated manner, as if the presenter were on a "high," or driven by a vision. Secondly, the payoff is always incredible. You are not only going to be successful, but hugely successful. Third, it has a "can't-miss" tag. It looks like an absolutely sure thing. These three elements are so enticing I would venture to say they have separated more people from their money than any other single action, and this is because Americans have overwhelmingly bought the myth of being your own boss and becoming an instant millionaire. It is in the American tradition to "invest" and this tradition is reinforced by the constant success stories in all media. Very seldom does one hear of the failures, implying that failure is rare.

Another aspect to the myth is that if you build a better mouse trap, the world will beat a path to your door. The implication is that if you have a good idea or product someone is just waiting to invest in it. You will be told about "Arab money," "Indian money," "Latin American money," conjuring up images of a turbaned, berobed exotic, adding to the unreality. This money may exist but I have never seen it, nor has any other person I know seen it. If it does exist it exchanges hands on a much higher level than most of us function.

If, on the other hand, we are not inclined to the foreign, we then proceed logically to American big business. Unfortunately, I am afraid you will find it just as difficult, if not impossible to secure money from this source. In addition, you really have to be careful of your idea or product because it just might get stolen. The television show, "60 Minutes," did a segment on just this subject, confirming that it is a frequent occurrence. I don't mean to say that some don't get through and succeed, but that it is a total long shot and that the odds against you are astronomical.

COUNTERBULL: If it is not in your area of specialization, forget it. Most of the successes I know of or have read about, stress one significant fact: the successful person is single-minded and places his entire focus and energy on his objective. The second significant fact is that it sometimes takes years of constant work and effort to break through. It is never an overnight success story. By simply rejecting most of the "opportunities" that come across your desk you will achieve almost 100% chance of not failing. However, if there is something that has the resemblance of reality and you are truly interested, then make it your business to get some expertise before you jump into it. Go to others in the same area, question them. Get the best books possible on the subject. Check out the people involved. I don't mean a cursory check, but one that might involve lawyers, accountants, even police. The more time and energy you spend in learning and checking before your decision to commit, the greater your chances of not being taken, and the greater your chance of success.

The Law

Legal systems are arbitrary rules society has adopted to provide negative consequences for behavior that society wishes to suppress. Laws have nothing to do with absolute "right" and "wrong." Systems of right and wrong are used to psychologically manipulate people's feelings and behavior. In addition, as Flo Kennedy, lawyer and Feminist, is fond of saying, "I stopped practicing law when I found out it had very little to do with justice." It not only has very little to do with justice, but it is also very expensive which makes it a very effective tool of the rich.

193

Should you be poor and idealistically motivated by principle, you would be in a world of difficulty in our court system.

This makes it quite easy for wealthy people to hide behind lawyers and law, as some executives hide behind their secretaries. In many cases it is the same person. One doesn't have to be right or wrong when it comes to law, one just has to be able to afford the luxury of good representation. That's why you see the Mafia, big business, wealthy individuals, and the government taking up more time in the courts than the common criminal.

I'm not saying one doesn't fight an injustice in court, but that you must choose stringently what you fight, and on what basis you fight it. I believe litigation is one instance where you have to mothball principle and morality, and approach the problem pragmatically. Other than criminal law, the courts seem to be materially oriented: they want to know what material (money) damages you sustained; not the potential, but actual damages. Therefore, that must be your practical guide as well. However, there are those who can easily afford proper representation in the courts who will present their law mask to you to try and intimidate you into conceding or withdrawing from your position. What should you do?

COUNTERBULL: Under no circumstances, unless you can't help it, should you be drawn into the legal system. A characteristic of systems including the legal system is that they inexorably grind you to pieces. Don't be taken in by that symbol of justice where the figure is supposedly holding balanced scales. In reality, the odds are mostly against you.

Secondly, if someone is threatening to sue you, give every indication to that person he will actually have to take you to court. Do not let him bluff you. Chances are, he too, knows what court costs, and he will try to make some compromise. But if he still insists, let him take the initial action, which will put you in the defensive position—the best position to be in: he must prove you are wrong. The burden is on him. At this point, get a lawyer. Don't ever go into court, not even small claims court, without a lawyer who knows the custom, the language, the formal procedures. Many cases are lost for technical reasons rather than substantive ones. If you do not have much money try the Legal Aid Society or an inexpensive legal clinic.

Overall, I would venture to say there are probably 100,000 threats of going to court for every one that actually materializes. If you threaten someone or are threatened with court, unless it is

194

strictly a bluff, beware of getting involved in the legal system. Even if you win, it will leave you drained and beat up.

CONFORMING

Morals are arbitrary rules people adopt to use in judging their own and other people's behavior. Of course, there will always be those who place themselves in the position of authority and who will try to set the rules for you. The moralist will be supported by organizations such as the church, social groups, clubs, and many others. Basically, they want to control how you think, as well as your behavior. Their techniques are many.

Shame

The moralist is quick to shame you into line. Shame on you if you're an atheist. Shame on you if you're not patriotic. Shame on you if you're liberal in politics. Shame on you if you enjoy sex. No matter what you are, if it's not what the moralist is, you are wrong. In fact, every single moralist is intolerant. He can't stand that you are different in any way, for any reason. If you don't function by his criteria you are wrong.

Line Drawing

When the Moralist wishes to disguise his intolerance, he will say he is not against what you are doing so much as the degree to which you are doing it, and someone must draw the line. This is identically the same approach used by any crusader, bureaucrat, and would-be dictator who is intent on limiting your choices and freedom. Unfortunately, since it is more than evident that most people find it difficult to agree on anything, they can easily become prey to line drawing.

Custom and Tradition

Moralists are also intent on maintaining custom and tradition. They are the bed partners of the conservatives. Custom and tradition are not necessarily bad, but they must be kept under surveillance at all times and they must be made to stand the test of changing circumstances. Otherwise, protecting the cherished "good old ways" is simply the facade to maintain the status quo which in turn controls the way you are suppose to behave according to the moralist.

195

Fictitious Entities

The moralist, to back his position, will create fictitious entities out of large numbers of individuals. For example, they will talk about "government," "the people," and "society," as if these abstract terms were specific and had real meaning. Anyone who tells you he "likes people" is a total fraud or a saint. When you finally pin him down, he will admit that he likes some people better than others, and some not at all.

"The Moral Majority," a stringent group to the extreme right, is a prime example of creating a fictitious entity. One just has to examine its name. For one, it would be impossible to determine what constitutes a majority on morality, or what the morality is that the majority holds. Certainly, on the basis of the approximate number of people who feel like the Moral Majority, their actual numbers constitute only a *minority*, not a majority. Yet, they would have you believe they speak for almost everyone. And should you say, "I'm not one of the Moral Majority," the implication would be that you are in the minority and not moral.

Conformity

The purpose, of course, is to have you conform to the moralist's beliefs. The moralist knows that you are basically a creature of conformity. When you join in a new fad that has gained wide acceptance, you are conforming. When the Beatles became prominent in the sixties, and the long hair, sneakers and T-shirts were the "in" symbol of the "now" generation, those that joined to show they were "with it," were conforming. When street gangs set up their rules and costumes that set them apart, those that join them are simply conforming. Whenever you do anything just for the reason everybody else is doing it, you are being intimidated into action motivated by the fear of standing apart from the herd. And fear, not love, is the moralist's tool. He tries to frighten you into believing you are in the minority if you do not join and obey, and that he is in someway, the power structure. He indicates God, "the government," or "the majority" is on his side.

COUNTERBULL: The initial sign of intolerance is the biggest tipoff to the moralist. You must immediately recognize any mask that is based on someone trying to "persuade" or force their beliefs on you, and who imply that what they believe is more right and superior to your beliefs. The second sign is the feeling a moralist will try to instill in you: shame, dirtiness, embarrassment, guilt, and fear. All the moralist wants to do, in essence, is run your life. Their whole stance is not based on logic but emotion. If you make any attempt at reasonable thought or logic, you will be wasting your time with the moralist and you will fail. There is only one thing which can frustrate him into leaving you alone, and that is to be firm in your beliefs and walk away from him. You will not change him. Just get away from his grasp without antagonizing him. He is a dangerous person. In extreme cases, he may feel morally obliged to kill you in order to "save" you from your disbelief!

There are many more masks than demonstrated above which you personally may be able to add to, or which you can discern with the help of the few general rules I have espoused. The main thrust, however, is to see through the masks to the true intention of the deceiver. If you keep in mind that intimidation, control, and dominance are the pathways to the main payoff of either a material advantage such as money, or your power, and you keep focused on the payoff, you will be able to effectively counterbull the bullshitter.

PART 2

CHAPTER IX

THE PSYCHOLOGY OF BULLSHIT

In the exploration that is to follow, we shall see that the key to the psychology of bullshit lays with the factor of self-esteem in both the victim as well as the perpetrator.

If you recall, one of the equation factors in the foundation principle—every bullshit situation is a power transaction—was that the perpetrator enlarged his ego at the expense of the victim whose self-esteem was diminished in the process.

Nathanial Branden, the psychologist, points out that from the time he began the practice of psychotherapy, some twenty five years ago, he was struck by the fact that regardless of the particular problem for which a client or patient sought help, there was always one common denominator: a deficiency of self-esteem at the base of the individual's symptoms. There was intellectual self-doubt, moral self-doubt, feelings of inadequacy, helplessness and guilt.

Self-esteem entails a sense of personal efficacy and a sense of personal worth. It is the integrated sum of self-confidence and self-respect. It is the conviction that one is *competent* to live and *worthy* of living.

The effort of the individual to defend himself against this self-esteem deficiency—and to avoid the fact of the deficiency—is clearly central to his motivation and behavior. And to the extent that men lack self-esteem, they feel driven to *fake* it, to create the *illusion* of it—condemning themselves to chronic psychological fraud—moved by the desperate sense that to face the universe without self-esteem is to stand naked, disarmed, delivered to destruction.

Unfortunately, man has not only been moved to the desperate sense of facing the universe with psychological fraud, he must now face the fact that numerous developments have created a "reality" so overwhelming, he is now vulnerable to a total nervous breakdown. The assault on his self-esteem, the increased awareness of a growing powerlessness has left him defenseless, for the most part, against external deception, but more importantly, has increased his own self-deception as he tries to cope.

The unprecedented development of the State and technology, for example, has practically taken morality out of the hands of the individual. It must be remembered that self-esteem is a moral appraisal, and morality pertains only to the volitional, that which is open to man's choice. An unbreached rationality—i.e., an unbreached determination to use one's mind to the fullest extent of one's ability, and a refusal ever to invade one's knowledge or act against it—is the only valid criterion of virtue and the only possible basis of authentic self-esteem. Today, much individual choice is gone. For example, peace is maintained between Russia and the United States not because these countries are moral, but because not to do so would mean total destruction by nuclear power. And with the State entering more and more areas of our lives such decisions on euthanasia, abortion, gambling are removed from the individual's control. The State determines what is important to its growth (what is moral) and simply enforces it. As a consequence, individuals are frustrated and feel powerless as volitional choice—self-esteem diminishes.

The biggest single factor overall, however, to impact on self-esteem seems to be change. The roaring current of change is so powerful it has overturned institutions, shifted our values, and shriveled our roots. Alvin Toffler calls it "Future Shock." But change itself is not new. The qualitative difference between this and all previous lifetimes, is that we have not merely extended the scope and scale of change, we have radically altered its pace. We have in our own time released a totally new social force—a stream of change so accelerated that it influences our sense of time, revolutionizes the tempo of daily life, and affects the very way we "feel" the world around us. The way we "feel" today is the distinction that separates truly contemporary man from all others, for behind the acceleration lies impermanence and transience, its psychological counterpart.

Indisputably, technology is the major force behind accelerative change; it is the engine driving this prodigious monster. To understand technology, however, the old image of clanking machines and smoky steel mills must be jettisoned, for it no longer accurately symbolizes technology. It is even misleading. Technology which includes technique are *ways* to breed fish, plant forests, light theaters, count votes or teach history. Their measure is always efficiency. Further, technology makes more technology possible, it makes for innovation. And when machines or techniques are combined in new ways, it makes for even greater technological innovations to the point that man's total intellectual environment is altered.

But there are also other factors impacting on him and making him even more vulnerable. The entire knowledge system in society is undergoing violent upheaval. We are increasing the rate at which we must form and forget our images of reality. Every person carries within his head a mental model of the world — a subjective representation of external reality. This model consists of tens upon tens of thousands of images. If society itself were standing still, there might be little pressure to update his own supply of images, to bring them in line with the latest knowledge available in society. Mostly, man's response to the quantity of change and its pace has become increasingly thwarted, ineffective. Of course, as radio, television, newspapers, magazines and novels sweep through society, as the proportion of engineered messages received by the individual rises, we witness a steady speed-up in the average pace at which image-producing messages are presented to the individual. This sea of coded information now surrounds him and begins to beat at his senses unmercifully. Man has become so overstimulated that he is on the verge of blowing a fuse. This has led to a sense of helplessness, a feeling of being out of control, to an enormous feeling of frustration and anxiety, to being powerless, and overall to a lack of self-esteem.

Even the growth of the "Affluent Society," as Galbraith tags it, has impacted negatively. The more conflicting, harsher, puzzling and confusing life has become, the more affluence has allowed us to "escape" to more and more privacy, so that we have become alienated and isolated from one another. In fact, we are pursuing loneliness!

In a typical middle class home today, the father, mother and one or two of the teenagers in the same family may have their own phones. Each child may have their own room, with their own toys, etc. It is possible for a family to live under the same roof and not bump into each other. Automobiles increase isolation as they pass like strangers in the day or night. All in all, a great many people have become so voluntarily confined to their homes that they literally have withdrawn from neighbors and community.

The end result is a society in breakdown. Individuals no longer able to cope appropriately. We turn off, we role play, we pretend, we drug out, we fail miserably; we become helpless, powerless and totally vulnerable. Externally, we become prey to propaganda to relieve terrible anxiety; internally, we become victims of narcissism, a totally self-centered universe so accurately depicted by Lasch in "The Culture of Narcissism," and characterized by others as the "me" generation.

The failure of the individual to control all these factors — to make volitional choices based on accurate information — has impacted severely on his sense of self-esteem. It has debilitated his sense of personal efficacy and sense of personal worth. It has destroyed his self-confidence and self-respect. It has created the enormous doubt that one is competent to live and has even diminished the sense that one is worthy of living.

It has opened the floodgates to not only propaganda and narcissism, but to the deception of bullshit. Where propaganda and narcissism may function to relieve anxiety, bullshit is a definite attempt to gain more power, i.e., control over the situation, another person or institution. As a matter of fact, the greater the loss of self-esteem, the more expansive the use of BS in society.

In order to begin to regain control and efficacy — self-esteem — it is essential that we examine the process and impact of each of the factors we have touched upon. A good beginning will be to view a character in fiction who, while making the transition from victim to perpetrator, discovers the power and secret of BS. Because the scene is set at the West Point Academy, it will also give us an insight to the institutionalization of BS, as well.

THE CORE OF BS RELATIONSHIPS

In the novel, "Dress Gray," Lucian K. Truscott IV has quite insightfully revealed the core of bullshit relationships. The setting of the highly structured West Point Military Academy is very much like viewing an organism under a microscope. The Academy is rigid and unbending without, but within is a perverse fluidity which functions with its own peculiar logic.

The character, Slaight, a cadet new to West Point is particularly good for illustration because he goes from being a victim to a perpetrator, and as he does he reveals insights on BS unique to that environment. His first general observation is regarding the fact that appearance is quite often stronger than reality, and that it must be constructed and maintained in order to be effective. Slaight says:

"... One's image was composed of both myth and reality. Myth served as a shield to protect reality. Construction and maintenance of one's image was necessary (because) in myth could be found a power that reality often lacked."

The quintessence of bullshit, however comes in the following passage and reveals the connection between the individual cadet and the military institution.

"But from the inside there was this subliminal anxiety, just beneath the surface of cadet lives; pent-up frustrations and doubts, imperfections that had to be hidden, contained, controlled, checked and balanced by self-confidence which appeared to come from nowhere, but which really came from West Point itself, from the United States Military Academy, from the final truth that you were a god-damned Cadet, and when push came to shove you dropped all your doubts and insecurities and believed all the bullshit. West Point said it was so, and you believed it: you were better than the rest of them, all those fuckers outside, everybody who didn't know the definition of gray, all the nongrads, and the civilians and the politicians, the goddam enemy."

The very first clue that the victim is a mirror to the perpetrator, and that a common bond exists between them comes when Slaight says:

"... Leadership (was) the thing West Point had to offer. The system counted subliminally but necessarily on human imponderables. West Point knew you'd end up loving those whom you were trained to despise and abuse — in this case, your own plebes . . .

. . . lying awake at night, thinking to himself . . . actually getting down and goddamn thinking about it (he) loved those beans. Every sorry-assed one of them. He loved them because they depended on him, like some kind of father or mother . . . He loved them because down deep, very deep inside, they were him. He was a bean. He was a plebe. *He was a fuck-up no-good-for-nothing-piece-of-shit, and goddamn if he didn't remember what it was like!*" (Italics mine)

205

Up to now Slaight has been gaining insight into himself, the Academy, and the game of bullshit. Now, however, he learns one of the secrets of BS; that one must pay dues to enter the hierarchy.

"In return for receiving the secret gift the academy had to offer, a special knowledge of the inner workings of power among men, *one had first to surrender himself and become powerless.* (Italics mine)

The secret that Slaight really learns relates to Principle One that states bullshit, most often, starts at the top and filters down. If one is at the bottom and submits, "paying dues," it is possible to gradually work one's way up in the hierarchy so as to ulti- mately be able to dispense BS effectively and with impunity.

But now Slaight sums up his insights regarding the awesome synergistic power of bullshit, as well as the self image it generates for the bullshtter of being a superior person. It is the other side of the coin of being a victim, of lacking self-esteem; and of being a perpetrator, and enlarging one's ego at the expense of the victim.

"But there's a bottom line to bullshit, and the bottom line says we're better than the rest of them. We're special. We're being let in on The Secret. I found my own private version of that bottom line and explored it, and discovered they're right. I am special. I am better. That bothered me. But it isn't what scared me . . .

. . . Hell, believing the bullshit is okay. Every goddamn place pushes one version of it or another. Up at Harvard, they think an MBA is a master key to the vault in the Chase Manhattan Bank. Fuck. The secrets of clubs at Yale like Skull and Bones are darker than the cracks inside King Tut's tomb . . . Once I'd accepted the fact I believed the bullshit, I started testing it from both ends. I tested the bullshit itself: Are we in fact better? And I tested my belief in it. Fucking-A if the equation didn't balance!

. . . That's when I got scared. Once the fucker balanced, I had nothing left to test with. I started crowding the edge. Down near the end, I was just whipping it on, firing blind, running amok. And it was working, clicking, like it was coming straight out of a field manual. But it wasn't. It was coming out of me, and that's when I knew something West Point never prepared me for. I was using power that was coming from me. I didn't understand it, thus I couldn't control it. Everything here at West Point is so goddam rational you get used to it. You depend on it. And this feeling of power that came from nowhere, it was crazy, I guess the feeling

206

was, it controlled me . . . *I didn't know what you call it. Strength.*
Power. Magic. Sport. But . . . you could fuckin' see it!"

Self-esteem is the common factor that binds victim and perpetrator. When Slaight was the bullshittee (the cadet), his feelings
were of being a "fuck-up and a dullard and a worthless no-good-
for-nothing-piece-of-shit." When he is promoted and becomes
the bullshitter, his perception of himself shifts to where he says,
"I am special. I am better." He now sees himself as a superior
person to the rest, to the "outsiders." Prior to this feeling of
superiority, Slaight realizes that the system of bullshit exacts a
price: before one secures power (a special knowledge of the inner
workings of power), one had to first surrender oneself and
become powerless. This marks the difference between the two
positions.

What is interesting, however, is that in both facets of the par-
ticipant, regardless of the fact that the bullshitting aspect is the
dominant one, it still remains true that both parts of the psyche
lack self-esteem. The bullshitter's image of himself as better,
superior, is still predicated on a false action—deception. It is not
based on any true accomplishment, or anything of real quality. It
is just the other side of a counterfeit coin passed off as a gold
coin. It is not of substance and it lacks true value. In addition,
the superiority is temporary, and if the bullshitter's efforts are
not kept going constantly his shell will collapse, possibly shatter-
ing him forever.

SELF-ESTEEM AS A MORAL APPRAISAL

Branden is emphatic in stating that "There is no value-
judgement more important to man—no factor more decisive in
his psychological development and motivation—than the estimate he passes on himself . . . The nature of his self-evaluation
has profound effects on a man's thinking, processes, emotions,
desires, values and goals. It is the single most significant key to
his behavior. To understand a man psychologically, one must
understand . . . the standards by which he judges himself."

And whether man identifies the issues explicitly or not, he
cannot escape the feeling that his estimate of himself is of life
and death importance. No one can be indifferent to the question
of how he judges himself: his nature does not allow him this
option because man experiences his desire for self-esteem as an
urgent imperative, as a basic need.

207

So intensely does a man feel the need of a positive view of himself, that he may invade, repress, distort his judgement, or disintegrate his mind in order to avoid coming face to face with facts that would affect his self-appraisal adversely. A man who has chosen or accepted irrational standards by which to judge himself, can be driven all his life to pursue flagrantly self-destructive goals — in order to assure himself that he possesses a self-esteem which in fact he does not have.

In order for man to know he is "competent to live and worthy of living" he must make efficacious choices based on accurate reality. The choices must be right. Also, he cannot exempt himself from the realm of values and value judgements. Whether the values by which he judges himself are conscious or subconscious, rational or irrational, consistent or contradictory, life-saving or life negating — every human being judges himself by some standard; and to the extent that he fails to satisfy that standard, his sense of personal worth and self-respect suffers accordingly.

Man needs self-respect because he has to act to achieve values — and in order to act, he needs to value the beneficiary of his action. In order to seek values, man must consider himself worthy of enjoying them. In order to fight for his happiness, he must consider himself worthy of happiness.

The two aspects of self-esteem, self-confidence and self-respect, can be isolated conceptually, but they are inseparable in man's psychology. Man makes himself worthy of living by making himself competent to live: by dedicating his mind to the task of discovering what is true and what is right and by governing his actions accordingly. If man defaults on the responsibility of thought and reason, thus undercutting his competence to live, he will not retain his sense of worthiness. If he betrays his moral conviction, thus he commits treason to his own (correct or mistaken) judgement, and thus, will not retain his sense of competence.

Basically, man must make moral choices. It must be remembered that self-esteem is a moral appraisal. However, morality pertains only to the volitional, that which is open to man's choice. It is imperative, therefore, that the choices be made with an unbreached rationality — an unbreached determination to use one's mind to the fullest extent of one's ability, and a refusal ever to evade one's knowledge or act against it — for this is the only valid criterion of virtue and the only possible basis of authentic self-esteem.

But here is the rub: Branden, as so many others, has not

factored into the equation, the total transformation of man, society and values wrought by the unprecedented growth of the State, Technology and Affluence which has created so much change travelling at such an incredible pace that it has literally caused a mass breakdown of man (Future Shock). If the individual is not in control then what can he be responsible for? For sure, the transformation has decimated traditional methods of coping, and altered traditional values of living. It has also tilled the soil for the pervasive growth of bullshit. Let's take a look at how the breakdown has occurred.

THE EFFECT OF TECHNOLOGY ON SELF-ESTEEM

Change

The roaring current of change has been so powerful that it has overturned institutions, shifted our values, and shriveled our roots. Change is the process by which the future invades our lives. It is "future shock" — what happens to people when they are overwhelmed by change. It is about the ways in which we adapt — or fail to adapt.

The acceleration of change in our times is, itself, an elemental force, and this accelerative thrust has resulted in personal and psychological, as well as sociological consequences. It is clear that "future shock" is no longer just a potential danger, but a real sickness from which increasingly large numbers suffer. Should the rate of change continue as is, without any controls, it is likely that we are doomed to a continued and massive adaptional breakdown.

Western society for the past 300 years has been caught up in a storm of change; and far from abating it appears to be gathering even more force. The result of these changes as they sweep through highly industrialized countries with ever accelerating speed and an unprecedented impact are the curious social flora they have spawned from psychedelic churches, and "free universities," to science cities in the arctic and wife-swap clubs in California.

But a key, qualitative difference between this and all previous lifetimes is that we have not merely extended the scope and scale of change, we have radically altered its pace. We have in our time released a totally new social force — a stream of change so accelerated that it influences our sense of time, revolutionizes the tempo of daily life, and affects the very way we "feel" the world around us.

If acceleration is a new social force, transience is its psychological counterpart, and without understanding the role it plays in contemporary human behavior, all our theories of personality, all our psychology, must remain pre-modern. In all, by changing our relationship to the resources that surround us, by violently expanding the scope of change, and, most crucially, by accelerating its pace, we have broken irretrievably with the past. We have cut ourselves off from the old ways of thinking, of feeling, of adapting. We have set the stage for a completely new society that seems to have fractured man. It has left him desperate, lonely, empty, anxious, insecure, and confused, as well as angry and violent. Equally, it has left him more and more powerless.

Not everyone, however, shares these feelings. Millions sleep-walk their way through life as if nothing had changed since the 1920's, and as if nothing ever will. They have attempted to with-draw from it, block it out and, if possible, to try and make it go away by ignoring it. They see a "separate peace," a diplomatic immunity from change.

One sees them everywhere; old people, resigned to living out their years, attempting to avoid at any cost the intrusions of the new. Already-old people of thirty-five and forty-five, nervous about student unrest, sex, and drugs, feverishly attempt to per-suade themselves that, after all, youth was always rebellious and that what is happening today is not different from the past. However, even among the young we find an incomprehension of change: students so ignorant of the past that they see nothing unusual about the present.

The disturbing fact, however, is that the vast majority of peo-ple, including educated and otherwise sophisticated people, find the idea of change so threatening that they attempt to deny its existence. They have a vague "feeling" that things are moving faster despite their denials. Doctors and executives complain they cannot keep up with the latest developments in their fields. Hardly a meeting or conference takes place today without some ritualistic oratory about the "challenge of change." Among many there is an uneasy mood — a suspicion that change is out of con-trol. Even the people who understand intellectually that change is accelerating, have not internalized that knowledge, do not take this critical social fact into account in planning their own per-sonal lives.

C.P. Snow, the novelist and scientist, also comments on the

new visibility of change. "Until this century . . .," he writes, social change was "so slow, that it would pass unnoticed in one person's lifetime. That is no longer so. The rate of change has increased so much that our imagination can't keep up." "Indeed," says social psychologist Warren Bennis, "the throttle has been pushed so far forward in recent years that no exaggeration, no hyperbole, no outrage can realistically describe the extent and pace of change . . . In fact, only the exaggerations appear to be true."

Technology: The Motor of Change

The great growling engine driving this prodigious monster of change is technology. This is not to say that technology is the only source of change in society. Social upheavals can be touched off by a change in the chemical composition of the atmosphere, the alterations in the climate, by changes in fertility, and many other factors. Yet, technology is indisputably the major force behind accelerative thrust. However, the old images of technology must be jettisoned. Technology — systematic treatment — which includes technique are ways to make chemical reactions occur, ways to breed fish, plant forests, light theaters, count votes or teach history. There is almost no area that is not subject to technology. Technology's primary characteristic and measure is always efficiency. The old image of technology as clanking machines and smoky steel mills is misleading. In the age of technology the assembly line — the organization of armies of men to carry out simple repetitive functions — has become an anachronism.

A thumbnail account of the progress in transportation can well dramatize the development of technology and the acceleration it has caused. It has been pointed out, for example, that in 6000 B.C. the fastest transportation available to man over long distances was the camel caravan, averaging eight miles per hour. It was only in 1600 BC. when the chariot was invented that the maximum speed rose to roughly twenty miles per hour. It then took until approximately the 1880's to reach the speed of one hundred mph with the advanced steam locomotive. However, it took only fifty-eight years from that time to quadruple that limit, so that by 1938 airborne man was cracking the 400 mph limit. It took just a mere twenty years more to double that speed limit. By the 1960's rocket planes approached speeds of 4000 mph, and men in space capsules were circling the earth at 18,000 mph.

211

Whether we examine distances traveled, altitudes reached, minerals mined, or explosive power harnessed, the same accelerative trend is obvious. The pattern, here and in a thousand other statistical series, is absolutely clear and unmistakable. Millennia or centuries go by, and then, in our own time, an explosion of the limits, a fantastic spurt forward.

The reason for this is that technology feeds on itself. Technology makes more technology possible, as we can see if we look for a moment at the process of innovation. Technological innovation consists of three stages linked together with a self-reinforcing cycle. First, there is the creative, feasible idea; second, its practical application; and third, its diffusion through society. The process is now completed and the loop closed, the diffusion of technology embodying the new idea, in turn, helping to generate new creative ideas.

The computer, for example, made possible a sophisticated space effort. Linked with sensing devices, communications equipment, and power sources, the computer became part of a configuration that in the aggregate forms a single new super machine—a machine for reaching into and probing outer space. But for machines or techniques to be combined in new ways, they have to be altered, adapted, refined or otherwise changed. So, the very effort to integrate machines compels us to make still further technological innovations.

It is vital to understand, moreover, that technological innovation does not merely combine and recombine machines and techniques. Important new machines do more than suggest or compel changes in other machines—they suggest novel solutions to social, philosophical, or even personal problems. They alter man's total intellectual environment—the way he thinks and looks at the world. They also determine his behavior. So far, man has pretty much failed in his adaptation to technology. It forces him to react constantly. And with each failure to cope, he becomes psychologically shattered. The rising rate of change in the world around us disturbs our inner equilibrium, altering the very ways in which we experience life. Acceleration without translates into acceleration within. The accelerative thrust in the larger society crashes up against the ordinary daily experience of the contemporary individual. For the acceleration of change shortens the duration of many situations. This not only drastically alters their "flavor" but hastens their passage through experiential channels. Compared with life in a less rapidly changing society, more situations now flow through the channel in any given interval of time—and this implies profound change in human psychology.

While we tend to focus on only one situation at a time, the increased rate at which situations flow past us vastly complicates the entire structure of life, multiplying the number of roles we must play and the number of choices we are forced to make. This, in turn, accounts for the choking sense of complexity about contemporary life. Moreover, the speeded-up flow-through of situations demands much more work from the complex focusing mechanisms by which we shift our attention from one situation to another. There is more switching back and forth, less time for extended, peaceful attention to one's problem or situation at a time. This is what lies behind the vague feeling noted earlier that "things are moving faster." They are. Around us. And through us.

There is, however, still another, ever more powerfully significant way in which the acceleration of change in society increases the difficulty of coping with life. This stems from the fantastic intrusion of novelty, newness into our existence. Each situation is unique. But situations often resemble one another. This, in fact, is what makes it possible to learn from experience. If each situation were wholly novel, without some resemblance to previously experienced situations, our ability to cope would be hopelessly crippled.

The acceleration of change, however, radically alters the balance between novel and familiar situations. Rising rates of change thus compel us not merely to cope with a faster flow, but with more situations to which previous personal experience does not apply. We no longer have the luxury of thinking about something, making a decision about it, and utilizing this effort in application to similar instances. Now, it is necessary to take each situation and repeat the process each time, and with the rapid flow of the new, unique confrontations it is not only difficult but oftentimes impossible.

THE IMPACT OF DESOCIALIZATION ON SELF-ESTEEM

Affluence

The reaction of many of these victims has been denial, specialization, reversion and super-simplification—classical techniques for coping with overload. All of these techniques for coping evade the rich complexity of reality. They generate *images* of reality. The more the individual denies, the more he specializes at the expense of wider interests, the more mechanically he reverts to past habits and policies, the more desperately he over-simplifies, the more inept his responses to the novelty and choices flooding into his life. The more he relies on these strategies, the more his behavior exhibits wild and erratic swings and general instability. Information scientists recognize that some of these strategies may, indeed, be necessary in overload situations. Yet, unless an individual begins with a clear grasp of relevant reality, and unless he begins with clearly defined values and priorities, his reliance on such techniques will only intensify his adaptive difficulties.

These preconditions, however, are increasingly difficult to meet. Thus the future shock victim who does employ these strategies, experiences a deepening sense of confusion and uncertainty. Caught in the turbulent flow of change, called upon to make significant, rapid-fire-like decisions, he feels not simply intellectual bewilderment, but disorientation at the level of personal values. As the pace of change quickens, this confusion is tinged with self-doubt, anxiety and fear. He grows tense, tires easily. He may fall ill. As the pressures relentlessly mount, tension shades into irritability, anger, and sometimes, senseless violence. Little events trigger enormous responses; large events bring inadequate responses.

And finally, the conclusion and uncertainty wrought by transience, novelty and diversity may explain the profound apathy that desocializes millions, old and young alike. This is not the studied, temporary withdrawal of the sensible person who needs to unwind or slow down before coping anew with his problems. It is the total surrender before the strain of decision-making in conditions of uncertainty and over choice.

Affluence makes it possible for the first time in history, for large numbers of people to make their withdrawal a full-time proposition. The family man who retreats into the evening with the help of a few martinis or beer and allows televised fantasy to narcotize him, at least works during the day, performing a social function upon which others are dependent. His is a part-time withdrawal. But for some (not all) hippie dropouts, for many of the surfers and the lotus-eaters, withdrawal is full-time and total. A check from an indulgent parent may be the only remaining link with the larger society.

Another effect of capitalism, now an "affluent society," as Galbraith so aptly describes it, is that not only does it generate a prodigious desire for products utilized in private ways, but it is responsible for all the instant products—instant coffee, tea, soup, and so on. In turn, contemporary man is constantly looking for instant sex, instant love, instant success—instant gratification. He feels this is his inalienable right! As a result, his self-centered impatience has given rise to a moral looseness allowing an uninhibited envy and greed. A "something for nothing" attitude underlies his approach; further, if you can't get something for nothing with shrewdness, then steal it. Greed or envy is precisely what the bullshitter looks for in a one-on-one, situation. He knows that once he baits his "hook," greed will take over. It works almost all the time. Some would say people are gullible; the bullshitter knows they are greedy. On a broader scale, however, this deterioration is reflected in the fact that contemporary man values celebrity more than fame, a "winning image" rather than accomplishment, spectacle rather than sport, flash rather than real light.

The Pursuit of Loneliness

Buffeted, frustrated, fearful, and overwhelmed on the one hand, and indulged and self-indulgent on the other hand, the end result is that contemporary man has become alienated and driven into isolation. Loneliness is now one of the predominant problems of society. Philip E. Slater, in "The Pursuit of Loneliness" makes the forceful point that contemporary man is chasing loneliness. He is pursuing it albeit unconsciously, and partly as an adjunct of capitalism. He describes it thus: "It is easy to produce examples of the many ways in which Americans attempt to minimize, circumvent or deny the interdependence upon which all human societies are based. We seek a private house, a private means of transportation, a private garden, a private laundry, self-service stores, and do-it-yourself skills of every kind. An enormous technology seems to have set itself the task of making it unnecessary for one human to ever ask anything of another in the course of going about his daily business. Even within the family, Americans are unique in their feelings that each member should have a separate room, and even a separate telephone, television and car, when economically possible. We seek more and more privacy, and feel more and more alienated and lonely when we get it. What accidental contacts we do have, furthermore, seem more intrusive, not only because they are unsought

215

but because they are unconnected with any familiar pattern of interdependence."

Our encounters with others tend increasingly to be competitive as a result of the search for privacy. We less often meet our fellow man to share an exchange, and more often encounter him as an impediment or a nuisance: crowding the highway when we are rushing somewhere, cluttering and littering the beach or park or world, pushing in front of us at the supermarket, taking the last parking place, polluting our air and water, building a highway through our house, blocking our view, and so on. Because we have cut off so much communication with each other, we keep bumping into each other, and thus a higher and higher percentage of our interpersonal contacts are abrasive. Since our contacts with others are increasingly competitive, unanticipated and irritating, we seek still more apartness, accelerating the trend.

Daily newspapers increasingly report the impersonal aspect of much killing that occurs. The impersonality of killing in war is now not only common knowledge but has become common practice in society. One radical caused an uproar when he accurately pointed out that in America, violence was as American as apple pie! Perhaps Americans enjoy the mass impersonal killing of people who cannot fight back because they themselves suffer mass impersonal injuries from mechanical forces against which they, too, are powerless.

There are two main causes for the increase of violence in America. The first arises from our tendency to handle interpersonal conflict by increasing individual autonomy, which simply attenuates the directness of these conflicts. The clashes between people that are thereby avoided rebound upon us by a very circuitous route. We create elaborate mechanisms to avoid conflict with our neighbor and find as a result that we are beleaguered by some impersonal far-off agency. When we fight with our neighbor, we can yell at each other and feel some relief, perhaps even make it up or find a solution. But there is little satisfaction in yelling at a traffic jam, or a faulty telephone connection, or an erroneous I.B.M card, or any of the thousand petty (and some not so petty) irritations to which Americans are daily subject. Most of these irritations are generated by vast impersonal institutions to which the specific individuals we encounter are only vaguely connected. We not only feel helpless in relation to their size and complexity, but the difficulty of locating the source of responsibility for the problem is so overwhelming that attempts at redress are often abandoned even by middleclass persons, and the poor seldom even try. It seems we can do little to relieve these feelings of vague expressions of futile exasperation at "the system." The energy required to avoid even the most obvious forms of exploitation by commercial enterprises in our society would not permit the individual to lead a normal active life. Like "Looking-Glass Country," it takes all the running one can do to stay in the same place.

Powerlessness has always been the common lot of mankind, but in the preindustrial age one could at least locate the source of injury. If a nobleman beat you, robbed you, or raped your womenfolk, you hated the nobleman. If a hospital removes a kidney instead of an appendix, or when there is only one kidney to remove (accidents that occur far more often than most people imagine, particularly to patients in public wards), who do we hate? The orderly who brought the wrong record? The doctor who failed to notice discrepancies? The poor filing system? The more we attempt to solve problems through increased autonomy the more we find ourselves at the mercy of these mysteries — impersonal and remote mechanisms that we have ourselves created.

PSEUDO SUBSTITUTES FOR SELF-ESTEEM

Propaganda

As a result of his total vulnerability, contemporary man, in his fractured, insecure, bombarded, powerless state, is an excellent candidate for propaganda which rushes in with its predetermined symbols, beliefs, structure and objective, to fill the emptiness — the vacuum.

Jacques Ellul says, "Man is not automatically adjusted to the living conditions imposed upon him by society — the increasing pace, the working hours, the noise, the crowded cities, the tempo of work, the housing shortage. Then there is the difficulty of accepting the never changing daily routine, the lack of personal accomplishment, the absence of an apparent meaning in life, the family insecurity provoked by these living conditions, the anonymity of the individual in the big city and at work. The individual is not equipped to face these disturbing, paralyzing traumatic influences. Here again he needs a psychological aid; to induce such a life, he needs to be given motivations that will restore his equilibrium. One cannot leave modern man alone in a situation

217

such as this. What can one do? One can surround him with a network of psychological relations (human relations) that will artificially soothe his discomfort, reduce his tensions, and place him in some human context. Or one can have him live in a myth strong enough to offset the concrete disadvantages, or give them a shade of meaning, a value that makes them acceptable. To make man's condition acceptable to him, one must transcend it, and this is the function of propaganda."

Let us recall some frequently analyzed traits of the man who lives in the western world and is plunged into its overcrowded population: let us accept as a premise that he is more susceptible to suggestion, more credulous, more easily excited. Above all, he is a victim of emptiness—he is a man devoid of meaning. He is very busy, but he is emotionally empty, open to all entreaties and in search of only one thing—something to fill his inner void. To fill this void he goes to the movies—only a very temporary remedy. He seeks some deeper and more fulfilling attraction. He is available, and ready to listen to propaganda. He is the only man (The Lonely Crowd), and the larger the crowd in which he lives, the more isolated he is. Despite the pleasure he might derive from his solitude, he suffers deeply from it. He feels the most violent need to be re-integrated into a community, to have a setting, to experience ideological and effective communications. That loneliness inside the crowd is perhaps the most terrible ordeal of modern man; that loneliness in which he can share nothing, talk to nobody, and expect nothing from anybody, leads to severe personality disturbances. For it, propaganda is an incomparable remedy. It corresponds to the need to share, to be a member of a community, to lose oneself in a group, to embrace a collective ideology that will end loneliness. It also corresponds to deep and constant needs, more developed today, perhaps, than ever before: the need to believe and obey, to create and hear fables, to communicate in the language of myths.

Narcissism

In what may seem like a paradox, however, contemporary man has also gone to an internal psychological defense—narcissism. The external result which has become quite extensive has developed into a "Culture of Narcissism" according to Christopher Lasch, transforming the substance of politics, education, art and sport—all of life—into a total new entity with a totally new set of values. This transformation has vitiated and made tinsel-like the substance of these activities. In regard to the individual, Lasch says, "In the last twenty-five years, the borderline patient, who confronts the psychiatrist not with well-defined symptoms but with diffuse dissatisfaction, has become increasingly common. He does not suffer from debilitating fixation or phobias or from the conversion of repressed sexual energy into nervous ailments; instead he complains of a 'vague, diffuse dissatisfaction with life' and feels his 'subtly experienced yet pervasive feelings of emptiness and depression,' *violent oscillations of self-esteem,*' and 'a general inability to get along.' He gains 'a sense of heightened self-esteem only by attaching himself to strong, admired figures whose acceptance he craves and by whom he needs to feel supported.' Although he carries out his daily responsibilities and even achieves distinction, happiness eludes him, and life frequently strikes him as not worth living." (Italics mine)

Psychoanalysis, a therapy that grew out of experience with severely repressed and morally rigid individuals who needed to come to terms with a rigorous inner "censor" today finds itself confronted more and more often with a "chaotic and impulse-ridden character." It must deal with patients who "act out" their conflicts instead of repressing or sublimating them. These patients, though often ingratiating, tend to cultivate a protective shallowness in emotional relations. They lack the capacity to mourn, because the intensity of their rage against lost love objects, in particular against their parents, prevents their reliving happy experiences or treasuring them in memory. Sexually promiscuous rather than repressed, they nevertheless find it difficult to "elaborate the sexual impulse" or to approach sex in the spirit of play. They avoid close involvements, which might release intense feelings of rage. Their personalities consist largely of defenses against this rage and against feelings of oral deprivation that originate in the pre-Oedipal stage of psychic development.

Often these patients suffer from hypochondria and complain of a sense of inner emptiness. At the same time, they entertain fantasies of omnipotence and a strong belief in their right to exploit others and be gratified. Archaic, punitive, and sadistic elements predominate in the superegos of these patients, and they conform to social rules more out of fear of punishment than from a sense of guilt. They experience their own needs and appetites, suffused with rage, and they throw up defenses that are as primitive as the desires they seek to stifle. Man has gone into EST and other similar "self-realization' disciplines which have an underlying aggressiveness. It first annihilates the self-esteem of the individual (if there was any to begin with), and then a narcissistic refocus occurs in which the individual is at the center, now able to utilize the inherent aggressiveness of narcissism, to manipulate others to their advantage.

Studies of personality disorders that occupy the borderline between neurosis and psychosis, though written for clinicians and making no claims to shed light on social or cultural issues, depict a type of personality that ought to be immediately recognizable, in a more subdued form, to observers of the contemporary cultural scene: facile at managing the impressions he gives to others, ravenous for admiration but contemptuous of those he manipulates into providing it; unappeasably hungry for emotional experience with which to fill an inner void; terrified of aging and death.

Because the intrapsychic world of these patients is so thinly populated — consisting of the "grandiose self," in Kernberg's words, "the devalued, shadowy images of self and others, and potential persecutors," — they experience feelings of emptiness and inauthenticity. Although the narcissist can function in the everyday world and often charms other people (not least with his pseudo-insight into his personality), his devaluation of others, together with his lack of curiosity about them, impoverishes his personal life and reinforces the "subjective experience of emptiness." Lacking any real intellectual engagement with the world — notwithstanding a frequently inflated estimate of his own intellectual abilities — he has little capacity for sublimation. He therefore depends on others for constant infusions of approval and admiration. He "must attach (himself) to someone, living an almost parasitic existence. At the same time, his fear of emotional dependence, together with his manipulative, exploitative approach to personal relations, makes these relations bland, superficial, and deeply unsatisfying."

The narcissist comes to the attention of psychiatrists for some of the same reasons that he rises to positions of prominence not only in awareness movements and other cults but in business corporations, political organizations, and government bureaucracies. For all his inner suffering, the narcissist has many traits that make for success in bureaucratic institutions which put a premium on the manipulations of interpersonal relations, discourage the formation of deep personal attachments, and at the same time provide the narcissist with the approval he needs in order to *validate his self-esteem*. Peter L. Giovacchini confirms these types of patients suffer "pervasive feelings of emptiness and a deep *disturbance of self-esteem.*" (Italics Mine)

Although the narcissist may resort to therapies that promise to give meaning to life and to overcome his sense of emptiness, in his professional career, the narcissist often enjoys considerable success. The management of personal impressions comes naturally to him, and his mastery of its intricacies serves him well in political and business organizations where performance now counts for less than "visibility," "momentum," and a "winning record." As the "organization man" gives way to the bureaucratic "gamesman"—the "loyalty era" of American business to the age of the "executive success game"—the narcissist has come into his own.

SELF-ESTEEM: MAN AS SOVEREIGN

The defense of contemporary man to cohere himself by internalization—narcissism—and the intense undermining of reality by modern technology, has not only produced a distorted over-specialization in the individual, but a distorted view of the world. This in turn transformed the substance of life, particularly values, into a new entity that reflects the narcissist's emptiness. Politics has been transformed to theatricalism, sports to spectacle, truth to credibility, and so on; in other words, the trivialization of almost everything. Further, it has corrupted authority and a host of other values. We no longer pay attention to the substance of things, only the appearance. The corrupted world of "appearances", triviality, glitter, emptiness, and falseness—illusion—is the result of our pitiful response to a technology that is out of our control, and to a state that has grown so large and impersonal that it is also out of our control. Contemporary man, trying to find some defense or other, has failed badly. Neither propaganda nor narcissism has worked effectively. The results have been devastating. In effect, modern man is psychologically shattered. For years now, he has been extremely vulnerable to whatever new development came along.

It is out of this background that bullshit has been able to flourish. Our value system is so out of whack it is almost impossible to find its center. Obfuscation is so total, internally as well as externally, that we no longer see reality, let alone have the ability to function by a human-index value system—a system that would place the individual at the apex. Technology has overwhelmed us with change, leaving us in fear, loneliness, insecurity,

221

and confusion. It has made us feel helpless, puny and insignificant. It has made us mean and insensitive. It has robbed us of self-esteem — a sense of self-worth.

The state, as co-conspirator, including the institutions of business, education, even family and psychiatry, has conditioned the individual to support its needs. As a matter of fact, it has not only conditioned the individual to its needs but has actually reshaped him to fit. In the process it has left man a victim. In his desperate search for self-esteem he has gone to desperate means including bullshit. He has taken the lead of religion, the state, and technology to try and gain some little measure of control and power by the use of bullshit. As a consequence, he himself continues to contribute to the further erosion of civilization; he also continues to add to his own victimization.

In decoding the psychology of bullshit it is hoped that a more effective method to true self-esteem can be achieved that will result in a permanent benefit to society and civilization. It must be a self-esteem based on the reality that one is *competent* to live and *worthy* of living. Man must stop being a victim, or continuing the victimization by his own self-deceptions. He must choose and the choices must be right (based on reality, not confusion or illusion), so that it leads to a self-respect caused by the achievement of true values — values that enhance the individual as a sovereign human being. In his sovereignty, he must see clearly and seek to gain control, thus controlling and changing the environment and institutions surrounding him, so that they conform and function to his new sense of self-esteem, self-confidence, and self respect rather than he to their devouring needs. He must see clearly, regain control and power, and become sovereign once more.

CHAPTER X

BULLSHIT IN POLITICS

Why Politics?

In an effort to convey a simple definition of philosophy to the "man on the street," some astute person said, "Once you strip away the mystique and pretention, philosophy is simply a point of view toward life. Every man on earth has a philosophy—the way he sees events and people. He may not organize it into a system of thought, or articulate it in the form of tenets, but he does draw conclusions from his experience as to what it means to him. This perspective then is his philosophy, his meaning of life."

By the same token, politics is simply a way to maintain, enlarge, or redistribute power. Although politics has the appearance of permitting equitable solutions through "negotiation," in reality, it is force and violence (the implied or actual use of it) that are the true movers which determine "solutions." As politics progressively gained ascendency over war and force, and became the primary tool in resolving conflict, it seemed to acquire a "shine," if not a "nobility," marking the progress of civilization. Politics was also thought to be a more efficient, economical and humanistic method of problem solving often leading to long term solutions, and thus held in high esteem. We even reached the point of viewing politics as an art and a science, teaching political science or statesmenship at revered institutions of higher learning.

Unfortunately, no matter how much we laud politics and polish its image, we never seem to be able to remove its tarnish. If we were to poll the man on the street, he would surely, overwhelmingly, tell you that when politicians aren't lying outright, they are bullshitting. This view is so commonly held that even the dictionary defines politics . . . "as sometimes crafty or unprincipled methods." The implication seems to be that politics and deception are synonymous; that at its core, as a crucial element of its foundation – as integral to its function – is deception. And yet politics remains the predominant instrument utilized to prevent violence. So, though it is impugned, it remains the method. Why? Does it have the qualities of efficiency and economy that override its negative aspects? Maybe it's because it seems to characterize a quality inherent in democracy (Or, is it like our morality of creating God in our own image that we have once again deceived ourselves into believing politics is the best, the only method, by which to solve our problems?)

Historically, it is interesting to note that Machiavelli, a realist, writing "The Prince" in 1532, has since that time, been reviled by many because he stripped away the misconceptions of how politics and power actually work. Machiavelli has borne so unsavory a reputation that the word "Machiavellian" has become embedded in our language as synonomous with Mephistophelian – a notion that the devil himself had become familiarly known as Old Nick only because Niccolo had been Machiavelli's first name. Was it because he revealed "secrets;" that politics and power function on hypocrisy, venality, flattery, lying, corruption – deception? Maybe it was because he directed advice on controlling people to kings – rulers – the already powerful? Or was it because he took away our crutches and made us face many of the illusions we hold regarding politics and power? Whatever the reason, we have moved away from Machiavelli, to the other extreme of imbuing politics with an idealism. In addition, we have also come to view politics as a universal panacea; that is, as able to solve all of our problems. As a result, we now politicize everything from freedom, justice, peace, prosperity, happiness, sex, business, to health, housing, education and religion. Religion, of course, has always been synonomous with politics, and in the past *was* actually politics. Interestingly, politics in the past was the preserve of the higher echelon, the powerful. In that time it was seldom, if ever, part of the common man's day to day existence. But now, the general population has suffused everything with politics and dragged it screaming into the political arena.

FACTORS INCREASING POLITICIZATION

The State

As a consequence, according to Ellul, "as the public increasingly turned to the state for a solution to those problems, the more they had to surrender their power to the state; in turn, the state not only deprived them of any control whatsoever over the problem, they could not deliver a solution even if it had tried. There is no political solution for these problems; there is none for genuine political problems. *A genuine political problem consists of truly contradictory given facts, i.e., that it is insoluable in the precise meaning of the term.* So, while arithmetical problems can have a solution, political problems have none." Political problems merely permit *equitable settlements*. And "equitable" settlements are most often dependent on positions of power (who has or implies the most ability for force and violence). So, while the state, as a result, has grown to enormous proportions, instead of solutions, it has created additional problems of equal proportion to its size. (Italics Mine)

Technology

What are the factors that have brought about this total change to politicizing everything? There is no one answer, of course, but among the most prominent has been technology. It starts with the fact that technology has reduced the size of the world in both distance and in the ability to be in almost instant contact with each other. The advent of the automobile, train, airplane and spacecraft, makes it possible. One can be in France or England via the Concorde in a matter of a few hours; the moon and other planets via space-craft in days. More importantly, the telephone, radio, and television, now transmitted via satellite to the remotest areas of the world, has turned the world into what Marshall McLuhan has described as a "global village."

In addition to the "global village" brought about by technology, nation-states have had to change their form in other ways. Toffler points out that European countries grudgingly but inevitably have been driven to create a Common Market, a European parliament, a European monetary system, and specialized agencies like CERN—the European Organization for Nuclear Research. He sees from the explosion of transnational corporations to transnational associations, a set of developments all moving in the same direction; nations less able to take independent action, losing much of their sovereignty. "What is being created," he says, "is a new multilayered global game in which not merely nations but corporations and trade unions, political, ethnic and cultural groupings, transnational associations and supranational agencies are all players." So, beyond media and technology, there is an actual shrinking of the world, as well as a need for constant interaction and dependency upon one another. Communications (technology) has not only brought the remotest parts of the world together, it has created a cross-influence and a standardization.

Many years ago I attended school in Mexico and lived with 20 to 30 students from all parts of Mexico. I was surprised to find they spoke many dialects which made it difficult for them to understand each other. In contrast, in the United States where our media were highly developed and available to most, even though we had regional dialects, we could still understand one another without too much problem. Radio and television had brought us together so we could make language uniform enough to eliminate that problem. The development of media and our accessibility to it is astounding. Television is so accessible that almost every family in the country has a television set. A sporting event like the Super Bowl will boast some 60 million sets tuned in at one time. When President Kennedy's death and funeral were televised, the total number of sets and people watching could easily have been twice that number. It is well-recognized that most people today consider media a necessity, not a luxury.

Overall, the effects of television have been many. However, we shall stay with the one effect that is relevant to our subject; almost everything in the world has become fodder for our viewing. Along with breakfast or supper, we have war in living color-guns, bombs, mutilation; crime in all its gory detail; accidents and disasters; riots, demonstrations, revolutions; we also view the most intimate events possible—the birthing of a baby, divorce, sex, psychiatric sessions, surgery—nothing is excluded. Everything is fair game in the inexorable need of the media to feed itself—and us. This need is so voracious, all types of activity and events, including many political conflicts, are actually designed for mass media presentation.

MEDIA FORMATION OF POLITICAL FACT:
PUBLIC OPINION

Technology has rapidly increased the creation and formation of public opinion, always a significant factor in the politicizing of anything. Ellul says, "As a result of the global interconnectedness established by a network of communications systems, every economic or political fact concerns every man no matter where he may find himself. A war in Laos, a revolution in Iraq, or an economic crisis in the United States will have direct consequences for many in all parts of the world. The second element in this new situation is that governments being based on people, the people are called upon to give their opinion on everything; it is therefore necessary that people know the global facts. How does the public know the facts? Such knowledge can no longer be obtained directly; it is knowledge conveyed by many intermediaries. After a kind of transformation, such information eventually becomes public opinion. But precisely because of public opinion's importance, it can be said that a fact does not become political except to the extent that opinion forms around it and it commands attention. A fact that does not command attention and does not become a political fact ceases to "exist" even as a fact, whatever its importance may be . . . nowadays a fact is what has been translated into words or images; what has been worked over to give it a general character very few people can experience directly; what has been transmitted to a very large number of individuals by means of communication; *and to which has been added a coloring that is not necessarily present in the eyes of those who experience it*." (Italics mine)

Today, the methods of creating such "facts" have been developed to a high degree of sophistication. Obvious emotional appeals are avoided; the objective is a tone that is consistent with the prosaic quality of modern life—a dry, bland matter-of-factness. Accurate details are used to imply a misleading picture of the whole. Truth is made the principal form of falsehood. The important consideration is not whether information accurately describes an objective situation but whether it sounds true. And trading on the public's "honest desire to be informed"—the craving for facts which feed the illusion of being well-informed—we are simply fed misinformation clothed in obfuscatory jargon. "This language," says Lasch, "surrounds the claims of administrators and advertisers alike with an aura of detachment. More importantly, it is calculatedly obscure and unintelligible—

qualities that commend it to a public that feels it informed in proportion as it is befuddled." Overall, the intent is to create a set of impressions for other than the apparent motivation. It is to divert the public away from what the true motivation of the perpetrator may be.

But even the "good" guys, those fighting for freedom, justice, a clean environment, or peace, must strive to secure public opinion for their side. To be effective, they must also "play" to the media; occasionally it happens inadvertently, but more and more it must be done by design. In the entire Civil Rights struggle, nothing was more effective than Bull Connors and his policemen letting loose their nightsticks, the high-pressure water hoses, and the trained attack dogs on the Black demonstrators. The national revulsion and outrage against racism and this type of repression was immediate. In a prior time, this identical situation would have occurred and except for those who witnessed it locally, it would have passed quickly without any further response. By the same token, the slaughter of seals in Canada, environmental issues, issues of safety—all issues that get media exposure and crystalize public opinion become important and must be acted upon. To have no public exposure is tantamount to not existing. No longer does the substance of an issue determine its importance; media exposure gives it importance. This is one of the many reasons government and other big power sources monopolize the media. In holding the key to media, they control it, and in controlling the media they control public opinion. However, many dissident groups have become sophisticated to the technique and would not think of fighting a battle unless they had a chance for media coverage. I don't mean to imply that cases would not be fought if there were no media exposure—the inherent inequity, injustice and unfairness alone drive these groups to fight the battle anyway—but these groups now have the additional awareness that the game has changed and has new rules. So, even if the conflicts in Vietnam, El Salvador, South Africa, the Middle-east, or the battles for better wages, housing, jobs, tolerance, and so on were not covered by media, they would still of necessity be fought. However, today these groups would try in some way to "play" or "stage" it so that media could record and televise it.

THE THEATRICALIZATION OF POLITICS

In 1968, Jerry Rubin and Abbie Hoffman made it clear that a theatrical conception of politics had driven more rational conceptions from the field. "Yippie is gestalt theater of the streets," Rubin claimed, "compelling people by example to change their awareness." They wore Paul Revere costumes, judicial robes in the courtroom, and in general disrupted the court proceedings resulting from their arrest at the Democratic National Convention in Chicago in 1968. While these actions may seem rather extreme and bizarre, they are really off-shoots of other accepted behavior such as the show of war weapons in a parade and political baby kissing, which are done to create favorable public opinion. The Yippies simply took their actions out of the stereotypical mode for identically the same reasons. The most crucial issues of today—abortion, ERA, nuclear energy, racism, foreign policy, crime, unemployment, inflation—cannot be fought in Congress or the courts alone; to be effective, they must be fought in the media as well. The deciding factor in many of these issues has become public opinion. If anything uniquely distinguishes this generation, it is that publicity confers status, importance, credibility, and validity; without publicity, the issues, cause, or even the person (celebrity) fades into "non-existence."

The practice is now so common, even local politicians on a township or city level use it instead of dealing with issues of substance. However, it doesn't stop there. This process has filtered down to almost everyone from individuals in police departments to school systems, community groups, unions and business. "Jet-setters," as well as the man in the street, vie with each other for celebrity. Where in the past it was an isolated person who would jeopardize his life for recognition, today it is a common occurrence extending to "stunts" of climbing buildings, all the way to assassinations. It seems nothing can stop the rush for "instant fame," which can and does occur overnight (with enough media exposure), and disappears just as quickly.

TRANSFORMATION OF SUBSTANCE

Truth has degenerated into credibility, facts to statements that sound authoritative without conveying any information. Ron Zeigler, Nixon's press person, once demonstrated the use of these techniques when he admitted that his previous statement on Watergate had become "inoperative." Many commentators assumed that Zeigler was groping for a euphemistic way to say that he had lied. What he meant, however, was that his earlier statements were no longer believeable. Not their falsity but their inability to command assent rendered them "inoperative." The question of whether they were true was beside the point. There are far more serious effects caused by this technique which transforms substance and policy into something far more sinister. For example, the object of American policy in fighting the war in Vietnam was defined from the outset as the preservation of American credibility throughout the world. This consideration, which amounted to an obsession, repeatedly overrode such elementary principles of statecraft as avoidance of excessive risks, assessment of the likelihood of success and failure, and calculation of the strategic and political consequences of defeat. Not only were the economic consequences disastrous, but the loss of lives and prestige incalculable.

Vietnam and the American Public

Politically, the need to appear dominant and in control—winners—affected presidents Kennedy, Johnson and Nixon to such a degree that deception, including outright lying, became the modus operandi in regard to Vietnam, and to the American public as well as to the world. Thus, American casualties were not only high, they were "obscene"—sacrificed to credibility and public relations. The TV show, "60 Minutes," ran a segment on General Westmoreland and his military intelligence personnel who reported to him that there was a build-up of North Vietnamese and Chinese forces to approximately 500,000 men, and that they were to be involved in an upcoming offensive against American forces. While General Westmoreland and President Johnson were posing for newspapers and television, they were stating to the American public that our forces were winning the war; and in order to allay the public's alarm at the number of American soldiers in Vietnam, said that the number of our military had been stabilized. According to the CBS report, to maintain this image, Westmoreland and his staff arbitrarily reduced the number of Communist forces in the upcoming battle from 500,000 to 250,000. As a result, the American defense prepared for battle at the lesser number of enemy; therefore they were underprepared and undermanned; the consequences were thousands of unnecessary American deaths and casualties, as well as defeat. Sadly, no one has been accused of murder or prosecuted for criminal behavior!

In the language of the Pentagon Papers "relevant audiences" have to be cajoled, won over, seduced. They confuse successful completion of the task at hand with the impression they hoped to make on others. American officials blundered into the war in Vietnam because they could not distinguish the country's military and strategic interest from "our reputation as a guarantor," as one of them put it. More concerned with the trappings than with the reality of power, they convinced themselves that failure to intervene would damage American "credibility." They borrowed the rhetoric of games theory to dignify their obsession with appearances, arguing that American policy in Vietnam had to address itself to "the relevant audiences" of U.S. actions — the Communists, the South Vietnamese, "our allies (who must trust us as underwriters)," and the American public.

England vs the Falklands

In April 1982, Great Britain sent an armada of forty war vessels to recapture the very small Falkland Islands taken with force by Argentina. Great Britain gave many reasons for the necessity of sending the fleet; there were British subjects on the island who were under British rule and wished to remain so; the British had been sovereign in the Falklands for approximately 150 years; that under United Nations, aggression of this sort was totally prohibited. However, disregarding the right or wrong of either party, and taking into consideration that both parties were certainly utilizing the action to divert their own citizens away from the horrendous internal problems each country faced, the significant thing that remained was that in the eyes of the world, Britain had been publicly humiliated; its image as a world power had been diminished. And before Britain would tolerate this blow to its prestige, it would go to war. The true issue here was public opinion, the image the British people, as well as the rest of the world, held of Great Britain. This image was by far more important than the actual territory, or the 1600 British subjects there. Britain, in the past, had relinquished colonial territory, although reluctantly, but never under such public humiliation. So, even as the ships sped toward the Falkland Islands, the real battle was being fought on world-wide media.

This points up the necessity to play the media game, and how it transforms the issue of substance to one of appearance. The

231

transformation of substance to image, as a result, has had a devastating effect on values. It has for the most part vitiated substance and led to serious consequences. In this case, although I believe the conflict might have been resolved by negotiation, there was also an equal chance for war between these two countries which is actually what did occur.

U.S. vs U.S.S.R./Superideology Allies?

Sometimes the transformation of substance is so subtle, yet widespread, it literally escapes the attention of most, yielding a profound effect. Toffler describes such a situation between the United States and Russia for dominance in Africa, Asia, and Latin America. While it seems the United States and Russia are coming from totally different ideological camps, they are nonetheless promoting the same *superideology*. "By the middle of the nineteenth century," he says, "every industrializing nation had its sharply defined left wing and its right, advocates of individualism and free enterprise, and its advocates of collectivism and socialism . . . . The battle of ideologies, at first confined to the industrializing nations themselves, soon spread around the globe. With the Soviet Revolution of 1917, and the organization of centrally directed worldwide propaganda machines, the ideological struggle grew even more intense. And at the end of World War II, as the United Sates and the Soviet Union attempted to reintegrate the world market — or large parts of it — on their own terms, both spent huge sums to spread their doctrines to the world's *non-industrial peoples*. (Italics mine)

On the one side were totalitarian regimes, on the other so-called liberal democracies. Guns and bombs stood ready to take up where logical arguments ended. Seldom since the great collision of Catholicism and Protestantism during the Reformation had doctrinal lines been so sharply drawn between two theological camps.

What few noticed in the heat of this propaganda, however, was that while each side promoted a different ideology, both were essentially hawking the same superideology. Their conclusions — their economic programs and political dogmas — differed radically, but many of their starting assumptions were the same. Like Protestant and Catholic missionaries clutching different versions of the Bible, yet both preaching Christ, Marxist and anti-Marxists, Capitalist and anticapitalist, American and Russians marched forth into Africa, Asia, and Latin-America — *the non-*

industrial regions of the world—blindly bearing the same set of fundamental premises. *Both preached the superiority of industrialism to all other civilizations.* Both were passionate apostles of indust-reality." The struggle for power—to bring non-industrial nations under their particular wing of influence—has been the goal, despite the vast appearance of differences. Not only has this battle been fought with guns (both countries contributing armaments and expertise), but the battle is constantly being fought in the media for world opinion. (Italics mine)

The United States at present is heavily involved in all of Latin-America with economic aid, armaments, and advisors. It has been most embarrassing to the United States to reconcile our human rights stand with our support of the military right—the fascists—who have thrown all human rights out the window. Yet, we clumsily try to rationalize the action of the right so their act will be acceptable to the American public and world opinion. In order to do this, we have lumped the leftist struggle into the general terrorist bag, along with discredited terrorists. We have once again villainized the victims. So, when the left opposed the elections in El Salvador, they were shown to be against the democratic process. On the other hand, Russia is no innocent either. They, in fact, are extremely sophisticated and are able to keep the parties we support constantly on the defensive. But make no mistake, regardless of who takes what side—the ultimate battle is that of industrial nations. We are both hawking the same superideology; only the appearances are different. We may talk about equity, justice, peace and freedom, but in the end it is money and power that are the objectives which will come from industrializing non-industrial countries.

Technicalities vs. Issues

Anthony E. Shorris in an article in "The New York Times" reveals yet another way the politics of bullshit comes into play. He points up that the politics of issues has given way to the politics of process. Policy choices—the difficult decisions concerning the distribution of wealth, provision of services, and the tax burden—seem much less visible today. Instead, politicians deal with process questions. Management is the central issue today for presidents and mayors, for congressmen and councilmen. *But management is not an issue.* Education, sanitation, poverty, and national defense should be the subjects of debate. However, it seems that Democrats and Republicans alike have come to agree that management is the key to the solution of our problems. Terms such as "the bottom line," "cash flow," and "cost-benefit" have entered the vocabulary of elected officials. But who is to determine the cost-benefit of health care for the poor, free education for our children, and safe streets? Choices must be made; improved management and administrative techniques as the focus of political dialogue have become a substitute for the substance of politics. The politics of management presupposes the existence of a general consensus of policy. Fundamental issues need not be raised; therefore existing patterns continue and the embarrassing consensus—maintain the status quo—is hidden. The politics of process are ultimately very conservative, very deceptive, for it diverts one away from the necessity for substantive choices.

In another area, law has suffered the same deterioration. Law has largely become transformed to procedure. The party that can delay or postpone a case repeatedly (usually the rich and powerful), and force financial attrition on the other party, becomes the victor. For example, when an insurance company delays a settlement, or the case from coming to court for several years, while the victim may be a paraplegic as a result of the accident, the advantage definitely falls to the insurance company. Another instance is when a murderer goes scott free because of improper technical procedure; at the least he can get a retrial, the delay which plays to his favor. Where the serious concern with the law was with its spirit or its letter, today it's with technical procedure.

In addition, once the courts were sacrosanct in regard to televising its proceedings. Although it is still experimental at this time, there is no doubt in my mind that it will become standard operating procedure in the future. Soon lawyers, judges, and all other participants will be playing to the camera, and a further degeneration will occur. There are those who say television in the courts will diminish much of the arrogance and corruption that presently exists, but I don't have much faith in that based on my knowledge of the effects of this process in other areas.

POLITICS AND TECHNOLOGY: A NEW PERSPECTIVE

Can the tide of technology—media—largely responsible for much of the over-politicization of everything, as well as the increase of BS in politics—the distortion, the dishonesty, the degeneration of substance—be stemmed, or at least controlled? It is obvious to me that neither technology, nor the changes due to it, can be reversed. It would be naive, if not reactionary, to suggest that we severely limit or remove media from our lives. Even if this were possible, society would revolt against it. While some see television as a narcotic, others view it as a key to freedom. Thus, if we cannot control or restrict media, would it at least be possible to depoliticize much of the activity we have thrown into the political arena? Again, the answer seems to be negative.

It is well to understand that though we exist in a totally political world, as well as a world of technology which has changed the "game" as it is played, political, social and cultural change have always occurred regardless of whether media existed or not. In other words, as long as inequality or oppression exists, people will fight for equality—a balance—against its oppressors. The United States broke away from the English without benefit of the media; the French Revolution and the Russian Revolution did the same. The leftists in El Salvador would continue to fight the military rightist even if the media didn't cover it. While the way the game is played may have changed, it still needs "real" participants and "real" causes. It is interesting to note, too, that the media is far more important to those in control than it is to the opposition. And that is because the oppressed, in every instance, outnumber the oppressors. While force can maintain control for a limited time, eventually, if the oppressor doesn't or cannot "con" the oppressed into "loving" them, it will be overthrown. In order for the oppressor to maintain control, the media is absolutely essential for the widespread deployment of their "brainwashing." Lasch points out that the idea that politics turns on self-interest, the careful calculation of personal and class advantage, does justice to the irrational elements that have always characterized the relations between the dominant and subordinate classes. "It pays too little heed to the ability of the rich and powerful to identify their ascendency with lofty moral principles, which make resistance a crime not only against the state but against humanity itself. Ruling classes have always sought to instill in their subordinates the capacity to experience exploitation and material deprivation as guild, while deceiving themselves that their own material interest coincide with those of mankind as a whole." Flo Kennedy in "The Pathology of Oppression" puts it another way; "Society (the rich and the powerful) have a diabolical way of making the good guys bad and the bad guys good. It's called *villainizing the victims.*" And as long as there is inequity and oppression there will be conflict; however, when the bullshit in politics breaks down, the oppressed eventually triumph. No matter how much firepower the French or Americans used in Algeria or Vietnam, or the political bullshit that was fed to the American and French people, the end result was a defeat. No matter how President Reagan tried to cut and deprive our senior citizens of Social Security, they still rose to defeat him on the issue. History verifies many other examples. While political bullshit may control the situation for certain periods, the damage and destruction it causes begins to feed back on itself to the point where the chickens come home to roost.

No. We should not withdraw from politics, no matter how tarnished it may be. Yes, we must take politics off the pedestal we have placed it on. It cannot solve all of our problems. However, we must free political affairs from the myths that clothe them so that we see them in their proper perspective. Democratic behavior presupposes that a man knows that opinions are unstable, that a pure system cannot be attained, that justice cannot be had in politics. He therefore should admit that political debate has a limited scope. This suggests we might look to the many political issues we have thrown into the political arena, and see instead if there are other ways to negotiate an equitable settlement. For example, much of the phenomenal Japanese productivity in business is due to a personal and cultural respect and trust between employer and employee. At the moment, and due to a terrible recession, American business and the unions are finally resolving their adversary stance and pulling together so that much of American industry, as well as the public, can survive. I'm sure the same effort can be successful in the political area. But first we must free political thoughts from myths and illusions, even while the media is doing nothing but engaging in myth creation. The press can exist only if it attributes to any event it picks, an element of passion and myth that completely prevents individuals from knowing or understanding anything. We must strive not only to depoliticize much of our contemporary activity, but more importantly, we must demythicize—we must see through the illusions—we must see through the distortions—images colored to divert one away from the true, accurate motivations of those pushing anything. The minority opinion, the less powerful groups, will quite often, if you look to it, reveal by what it opposes, the true motivation of those in power. By correctly pinpointing accurate motivations, one can cut though the bullshit in politics, to what is the truth.

CHAPTER XI

BULLSHIT MORALITY, OR THE MORALITY OF BULLSHIT

THE ORIGIN OF MORALITY: A PERSONAL THEORY

Is the term "morality" just a matter of semantics for the purpose of a cynical smile, or is the implication serious and meaningful? In order to answer properly I will present a theory and view of morality that is, without question, an oversimplification, but nonetheless, a different perspective which may shed some light on this perplexing subject. No doubt there will be those who take exception to my view and I welcome their thoughts. Morality has taken a back seat for much too long now. It needs to be brought more vitally to the forefront.

MAN VERSUS NATURE

One thing we know for certain: morality can be dated with the very recent advent of man: an extremely short period in the context of the creation of the world. In the millions of years prior to man, it was nature that determined who and what lived, and how they lived. Nature's law of survival of the fittest told us that those things that could change and adapt survived—those that couldn't perished. For example, dinosaurs, according to one naturalist, perished during an extremely cold period. Their physiology was totally dependent on solar heat, which all but disappeared during this particular period for some reason.

We also know that in nature living things feed off each other in a way that keeps nature efficient and balanced. Survival of the species being paramount, a species seldom preyed on itself. All this is to say nature ruled and these organisms had to conform to survive. In essence, these organisms could only *react* to nature. Man, however, because he could think and abstract knowledge, gradually came to control and dominate nature. But until the time man's dominance over nature actually occurred, he, too, could only *react*. Mainly, he tried to appease nature's power with ritual, sacrifice, gifts, incantation, obeisance; in other words, he tried to "con" nature. However, these methods were not efficient enough so he had to try to find a better way to minimize the fear of nature's power. Man, therefore, turned to conning himself!

DISPLACING NATURE THROUGH SELF-DECEPTION

With his superb imagination and unlimited ability for self-deception he created a supernatural personage in his own image that in effect displaced nature! The supernatural personage (God in man's image) went through many transformations, of course, and fought many battles with other God-like personages and things, but God in man's image emerged dominant and victorious. This God was imbued with supernatural abilities; he was "spiritual" (beyond the limits of flesh), fearsome (able to punish), eternal and all knowing. Since man could not completely escape his own dimension (not even in his imagination) the supernatural also wound up being imbued with many of man's lesser characteristics. He was petty, vindictive, righteous, biased, demanding, jealous, and self-centered.

RELIGION AND MORALITY

The next step in this process was for man to bend his creation (God in man's image) to his advantage. Therefore, he now claimed the supernatural had selected him as the "chosen." Henceforth, might and right would be on his side. But there was a split between the groups of men who claimed, in their interpretation, that they were the chosen. This led, of course, to the conflicts between different religions for dominance, but overall the concept of God in man's image was reinforced.

This explanation, while a total oversimplification, does serve to date morality as well as offer a plausible reason for it, to wit: to gain control and dominance for those who originally created

238

"God" and his tenets. In other words, if you were first with the rules—morality—you led and dominated: otherwise you followed and took a lesser position. In addition to the illusion of God in man's image displacing nature's power, it also replaced reality, corrupting almost every action of man that followed.

MORALITY: THE POWER TOOL

An important element of morality during this period was "persuasion" which contained a factor of fear almost more fearsome than death. It was man's imagination which could create a dimension far greater than reality. As a matter of fact, it was surreal, and the "hell" was infinitely more painful than reality. But along with the "hell," the supernatural was also benevolent and the subject could benefit from it if he conformed. Of course, those who would not conform by "persuasion" were often punished with death by the supposed keepers of the "sacred trust."

This methodology still operates in very much the same manner today although it has become infinitely more sophisticated. The few who are the keepers of the "word" (the power) rule the mass. In ruling, those in power maintain their power and continue to enlarge upon it. To take a moment away from the religious and focus on the secular, it is amazing to me that most people do not recognize their own power. If nothing else, their power of sheer numbers. For example, tenants outnumber landlords, depositors outnumber bank owners, workers outnumber management. In fact, it would be relatively simple to overturn the power structure except that the individual is so "brainwashed," he keeps himself subjugated, believing the power structure is invincible; that they have some "sacred" mandate to rule.

History also shows that as each center of power developed it became institutionalized with its own hierarchical structure, making it virtually impregnable. However, when these centers of power could not convince other centers of power of their righteousness, they would revert once again to the "primitive" method of force; hence, the many religious wars. When politics began to supplant religion, the war cries were simply exchanged for issues of nationalism, freedom, or territorial imperatives. But whatever the reason, it was always based on a morality that imbued each party with a righteousness. Many fought out of fear of punishment from "God," or their government, but they were also propelled by a "sincere belief" in their mission and this proved to be the strongest motivation. The foundation of this motivation was morality. It was made to fit the advantage of a particular circumstance, an individual party, or group. In this context then, morality can be seen as being relative. It can be and is manipulated.

UNIVERSAL MORALITY: A CONTRARY VIEW

There are those, however, who maintain that a Universal Morality exists, and is essential to a continuing civilization: they say it is people who are imperfect, not the ideas of Universal Morality. In other words, if the war of the Crusades was over human weakness (intolerance), it does not invalidate the idea of tolerance, nor in this instance, the Christian faith. The implication is that the faith is not responsible for the behavior of its adherents; that the validity of the idea can and does stand apart from its practitioners! Not only is there a dichotomy between these viewpoints that is difficult to resolve, but now, along comes Jacques Ellul, a French philosopher in two absolutely brilliant works, "The Technological Society," and "The Political Illusion," who maintains that neither of these viewpoints is determinant because technology and the state have transformed morality into a new entity. And without the individual being aware of it, morality has slipped out of his control (if he ever had it), and has become the prerogative of the state and technology which fashion a morality to serve its rigid needs, not the individual. The tail now wags the dog rather than the dog wagging the tail.

HOW THE GROWTH OF THE STATE ALTERED MORALITY

Ellul maintains the change regarding the state is the result of the total politicization by the individual of every issue that arises. It is the act of suffusing everything with politics and dragging it into the political arena. In our modern world, contrary to what was the rule in all previous ages, everything is politicized: men seek political solutions for everything, whether the problem be freedom, justice, peace, prosperity, morality, or happiness. As a result of this politicization, and of the orientation of all thought and energy to politics, men increasingly turn to the state for a solution to these problems. This has led to a boundless inflation of the state's size and power. We therefore make the state guardian and executor of all values — which, as a result, wither away.

240

Ellul says, "To have true choice in a political decision, the possibility must exist of combining various given factors and even facts of differing nature. And to make it really political, these given factors must not be imaginary, theoretical, or ideal, but must correspond to reality—either to facts or to real beliefs. But one of the considerable limitations of political choice is the elimination of what can be called values from the collective conscience (the current mentality, the spontaneous attitudes of the man in the street) . . . No matter how shocking or unlikely this may appear, the man of our day, indifferent to values, has reduced them to facts. Justice, freedom, truth now have new connotations: justice means happiness produced by equal distribution of material goods; freedom has come to mean high living standards and long vacations; and truth, more or less, has come to mean exactness with regard to facts . . . Strangely enough, politicians sometimes consider themselves liberated—more independent and more effective—when values have been jettisoned and they find themselves engaged in pure realism, cynicism, and skepticism . . . Despoiling politics of values means to relegate it to the domain of pure facts, which gives politics a chance to act without moral rules, to be sure, but at the same time considerably reduces its choices and decisions . . . Naturally, if we judge in this fashion, we are thinking of believed, adopted values, accepted by all or almost all in a society or nation . . . (Today, however) these values are thought to be part and parcel of an antique mode of thought, existing only as appearances to which credence is no longer given, having been rediscovered as "Sunday sermons" that nobody considers worth basing his conduct. And yet the "liberation" from the tutelage of values only leads to submission to a more stringent necessity, which is, however, felt less because it no longer leaves any choice."

Among the many examples, for instance, Nixon O.K.'d the bombing of Cambodia because he saw it as a necessity. The fact was that the North Vietnamese were receiving supplies through Cambodia. By Nixon having established it as a fact, his action became a necessity and was fulfilled. To take this action, Nixon had to jettison the value of human lives and reduce the context to a military and political fact. But this procedure was costly because he had to keep it from Congress, damaging the trust and credibility necessary between these two branches of government. He also had to lie to the American public which damaged trust and credibility there. One can almost consider this process a forerunner of Watergate, and Watergate the result of this pro-

241

cess. Nonetheless, Nixon saw these circumstances as a fact and a necessity and subsequently was unapologetic regarding them, as well as Watergate. On the other hand President Carter was castigated by many because he chose to uphold the value of the 50 people who were held hostage in Iran. Many felt that President Carter in making this choice, if not jeopardizing the other 200 million people, had at the least, damaged our world image as one of the most powerful nations on earth. Many felt we should have bombed Iran out of existence despite the fact we might have lost the 50 hostages.

It is interesting to note that Israel which prides itself on having a "soul," that is, being morally superior to many other nations, does not have this problem. Israel has reduced this type of situation to fact: the survival of the state is supreme; it is more important than any single individual. Its citizenry understand this; as a consequence, when a similar situation like Iran arises, it is understood that Israel must take any action necessary, even if it results in the death of individuals. It doesn't mean that Israel won't try to rescue hostages as it did in Entebbe, but should they try and fail and some die — well, that's the cost. What would be worse is the damage the state would incur if this type of action went unanswered. However, the main difference between Israel and the United States is that Israel is practicing what it preaches; it has stated the facts straight-forwardly and acted accordingly. One can take exception to the choice, even deplore the result of this policy, but you can't accuse Israel of being dishonest or hypocritical to its citizens.

THE STATE: A NEW MORALITY

In addition to understanding how the state became so large and powerful, it is important to now understand that the state functions totally by its own rules and ignores to a great extent the politician and the individual. The politicians we have elected to represent our beliefs and values have largely been rendered impotent by the state. They are actually powerless because they must rely on the bureaucrats to execute what they initiate. The bureaucrats, in actuality, are the true powers within the state. An analysis of the development and the structure of bureaucracy would take too long to explain here, but Ellul in "The Political Illusion" does a thorough and convincing job and I refer you to this work. Suffice it to say, bureaucracy has become like a robot which suddenly has a mind of its own and no longer follows instructions input to it. For example, although politicians create legislation, it must be executed by bureaucracies. Since the bureaucracy follows its own center of power for the most part, and its own rules of survival, bureaucracy can hinder greatly, if not fatally, much legislation by simply delaying implementation, executing poor implementation, or doing no implementation. It can grind things to a halt. Much Civil Rights legislation is typical of this process. It is now years later and many of these laws are still not completely instituted, vitiating their impact.

Somehow, the public generally refuses to believe this reality, and insists on functioning under the illusion that individual politicians can make a difference in the overall direction the government travels. The state as represented by the bureaucracy is so powerful, and works so inexorably by its own internal rules, that it even renders the President impotent. What is true for the politicians is true for the public. It is no longer the state which serves the public, it is the public who serves the state. Michael Elkins in a "New York Times Magazine" article quotes Meron Benvinisti, a historian who was born in Jerusalem where he has lived over 48 years. He says, "We had a dream, to create a new, healthy, and just society in Palestine, and that could only happen if we got our state. Well, we got the state in 1948, but then what happened to us — as to many other national liberation movements — *is that the state as means became an end* — and the emphasis on building the society, which was the object of the whole enterprise, was ignored." In other words, the state as an autonomous, all consuming monster follows its own needs, creating its own rules and morality which serve its survival and growth. It is no longer concerned with the public except as a cog in its machine. The politicians in the machine are like live pilots in the cockpit of a plane flying on automatic. They look like they're controlling the plane, but in reality the plane is flying on its own and following predetermined actions and routes. So, in effect, the state having created its own morality will tell the public they cannot be individually violent, yet they must kill for the state should it be necessary in police action, a riot, or a war. They tell the individual he may not steal or cheat, yet the state appropriates, at the point of a gun if necessary, much of your hard earned money which it spends on anything it chooses, regardless of your feelings or beliefs. In effect, by politicizing everything and looking to the state for all the solutions, we have relinquished our power to it, causing the state to become the monster described. For the most part, it has taken morality out of the individual's hands, and determined it so that it serves the needs of the state. The law, as an aspect of morality has also been perverted by the state. Recently, on the television show, "60 Minutes," two parents whose son was murdered by a mental patient irresponsibly released from a Massachusetts mental institution, were not allowed by the State of Massachusetts to sue the state. The parents then went to the Supreme Court, which would not even hear the case. The parents were not primarily interested in winning damages, but felt if the case were heard, it might eventually help reduce such criminal irresponsibility in the future and save other innocent lives. However, their purpose did not suit the state's purpose, and the parents were not allowed in court. This may sound like an aberration but it is not. Overall, our willing surrender to the state for the solution to all our problems, the reduction of values to facts due to the nature of politics and the state, and the inherent need of the state to follow its own rules for survival and growth, create a morality unique to the state, and is in opposition to any other morality based on the individual and the humanistic.

DISPLACING THE STATE MORALITY THROUGH TECHNOLOGY

By the same token, technology — nuclear power, space exploration, satellite communications, new discoveries in biology — has made it mandatory that politicians as well as the bureaucrats depend on technology for its specialized knowledge. As a matter of fact, they (the state) has become subjugated to technology. Technology, like the state has also reduced values to facts and has added the iron measuring rod of efficiency. Technology, too, has its own inflexible operating rules by which it functions that run roughshod over every area, ultimately demanding subservience. It, too, obviates the individual. More, it creates the the type of individual which will best serve its purpose.

There are many who perceive technology to mean machines. This perception is almost totally inaccurate and certainly inadequate within the context we are speaking. Jacques Ellul says, "Whenever we see the word technology or technique, we automatically think of machines . . . it is a mistake to continue this confusion . . . Technique has now become almost completely independent of the machine. As a matter of fact, the machine is now entirely dependent upon technique, and represents only a small part of technique. Technique integrates the machine into society. It constructs the kind of world the machine needs and introduces order where the incoherent banging of machinery heaped up ruins. It clarifies, arranges, and rationalizes; it does in the domain of the abstract what the machine did in the domain of labor. It is efficient and brings efficiency to everything.

Technique (technology) refers to any complex of standardized means for attaining a predetermined result. When we look at the technical man we see his fascination with results, with immediate consequences of setting standardized devices into motion. He cannot help admiring the spectacular effectiveness of nuclear weapons of war. Above all, he is committed to the never ending search for "the one best way" to achieve any designated objective.

When technique enters into every area of life, including the human, it ceases to be external to man and becomes his very substance. It is no longer face to face with man but is integrated with him, and it progressively absorbs him. In this respect technique is radically different from the machine. This transformation, so obvious in modern society, is the result of the fact that technique has become autonomous. Technique tolerates no judgement from without and accepts no limitation.

Ours is a progressively technical civilization: that is, the ever expanding and irreversible rule of technique is extended to all domains of life. Whether it be science, economics, politics — all are subject to the rule of technique. It is a civilization committed to the quest for continually improved means to carelessly examined ends. Indeed technique transforms ends into means. What was once prized in its own right now becomes worthwhile only if it helps achieve something else. And conversely technique turns means into ends. "Know-how takes on an ultimate value."

When, in morality, we evaluate means as being as important as ends, we must now understand that technology has changed that: now the means contain the inherent ends, i.e., nuclear bombs determine there be "peace," not man, nor politicians, or hardly governments. Any other choice but "peace" would mean total devastation for all. Technology has prodigiously increased our means of action and has made it impossible for us to claim any control whatsoever over those means. Rather they control us. The intensity of these means of action and their immediate and constant presence in our lives provoke, without our wanting it or even being conscious of it, a definitive primacy of action over thought, meditation, choice, judgement.

The means determine the ends; by assigning us ends that can

be attained and eliminating those considered unrealistic because our means do not correspond to them. At the same time, the means corrupt the ends. We live at the opposite end of the formula that "the ends justify the means." We should understand that our enormous present means shape the ends we pursue. Consequently, as technology more and more controls man, the less man makes his own choice in all areas including morality.

Ellul concludes, "Morality judges moral problems; as far as technical problems are concerned, it has nothing to say. Only technical criteria are relevant. Technique, in sitting in judgement on itself, is clearly freed from this principle obstacle to human action . . . thus, technique theoretically and systematically assures to itself that liberty which it has been able to win practically. Since it has put itself beyond good and evil, it need fear no limitation whatsoever. It was long claimed that technique was neutral. Today this is no longer a useful distinction. The power and autonomy of technique are so well secured that it, in its turn, has become the judge of what is moral, the creator of a new morality. Thus, it plays the role of creator of a new civilization as well. This morality—internal to technique—is assured of not having to suffer from technique. In any case, in respect to traditional morality, technique affirms itself as an independent power. We no longer live in that primitive epoch in which things were good or bad in themselves. Technique is neither, and can therefore do what it will. It is truly autonomous." Morality it seems, is now in the domain of both the state and technology upon which it depends, and appears to be out of the individual's control.

THE MORAL CRUX:
MAN WITHOUT VOLITIONAL CHOICE.

What is certain though is that the role of the state and technology is little known by the public. And if a poll were taken, I am certain that an overwhelming percentage of the people would say that it is they who control the state and technology, not vice-versa. This means the general public is functioning under a terrible illusion, the subject of which has already caused tremendous change and damage to the quality of our life, particularly in the area of morality. The rape has been so swift it has been almost imperceptable.

And when one considers the effects of functioning under the previous illusion perpetrated by religion, an illusion that still prevails today, one has to ask, was there ever a true morality? A true morality implies that one sees the issues accurately and that a real choice exists. One must also ask, has morality ever had an intrinsic value of its own, above and beyond its use as a tool in the hands of the power structure?

The result of religion with its base of arrogance and intolerance has kept the world divided and at war. The state-created morality has done no better with its nationalistic thrust. The best that can be said for technology is that with the creation of nuclear weapons, total destruction has been forestalled for the time being. And even that seems precarious. These illusions have resulted in the unregulated growth to monumental proportions of big religion, big states, big business, big technology. They are dominant, each vying to put the individual to their use as servants. The individual must follow their dictates and demands or perish. We have literally become prisoner/slaves. The cell of our imprisonment may be well-padded, and we may be "willing" prisoners, nonetheless, we *are* prisoner/slaves. *And that is because we do not have a true choice.* If "morality" has led us to this point, what good can it be? Does it have an intrinsic quality which can validate it? Are we somehow overlooking that quality? The answer is yes . . . Providing . . . !

The intrinsic value of morality lies in the fact that the individual *must make a choice* for the good, the constructive, the humanistic. It is this volitional act that is the essence of morality. It assumes the individual has studied the choices, and made a decision for those particular values. However, for the process to be valid, the choosing must be between true values or beliefs that are based on reality. It cannot rest on the illusion of having a choice, nor on the deceptive values which have been presented for choice, but are really like props in a play. These props are there for appearance sake and only to suggest the real thing within a real context. It is important that one see morality as an ever active *process* rather than as a set of dogma, even nice sounding dogma. It is a process in which an examination, exploration, analysis is ever constant and upon which a true choice is made between true values: a choice that will favor the good, the constructive, the humanistic; that will enhance life and humanity. Therefore, "morality" stemming from religion must be stripped clean of the illusion it has created, and be seen for what it actually is; a control mechanism in the service of power. It must be held responsible for the negative results it engenders. It must assume responsibility in society in the areas of the financial, the political, the social where it functions. For example, religious entities should pay taxes like every other institution. It should be designated as a formal political party since it functions that way. It should not be allowed to hide behind the apron of "morality."

MAN AS SOVEREIGN

Regarding the state and technology, we must see it for its potential danger; as necessary but a thief of true values of freedom, justice, the pursuit of happiness. We must jettison the illusion we are controlling these monsters and face up to the fact they are controlling us. We must also face up to the fact they have taken morality out of the individual's hand and determined a "morality" to serve its own needs which are anti-humanistic.

The individual must relinquish these illusions, make true choices based on true values, and then weigh his decision toward the constructive and the humanistic. Equally important, the individual must overturn the power structure so that he once again controls them so that they are in his service rather than he in their service.

This is all well and good, but how does one begin? The first step that must be taken is the examination of what bullshit morality has created and recognize the results as a form of reality. This is similar to a patient who says he suffers terrible pain but for which the doctor can find no biological basis. Is the pain still real? Most doctors today agree if the patient is perceiving it as pain and feeling it as pain, then it is real. Therefore, we must examine this reality — bullshit morality — and see if we can generate a morality of bullshit. That is, can something positive and constructive be fashioned from this negative and destructive pile of manure. If we can take fecal wastes and turn them into fertilizer to enhance better growth of plants, then we can take fecal morality and do the same. It is interesting to note that this process, which is a part of a larger system of sanitation, creates a cleaner, safer, more productive environment which enhances life in general.

Science, for example, has had to face the issue of whether there should be unbridled scientific exploration regardless of what ends it produces. It has always been a constant concern. However, since science has come under the yoke of technology, that concern was removed because the measure of science is now efficiency, not morality. If we can recognize how prevalent this

248

situation is, and see the need for its control and limitation, we may have a start.

If we see clearly that big business has resulted in practices of corruption of the individual, the law, the environment, and in many cases causes deaths by its irresponsibility, maybe there is a way to control big business. Maybe big business should not be big but a series of smaller businesses. At the least, maybe management should be made responsible for their actions and criminally prosecuted for their irresponsibility. Maybe it is the whole system of business which is oriented toward profit rather than social good that must be changed?

The state with its inherent bureaucracy must be examined in regard to the loss of individual freedom and justice. We must look hard at our intrusion into the affairs of other countries, of our attempts to "destabilize" those countries. Maybe we must simply depoliticize many things and decentralize the state.

As for religion, frankly, I don't know what can be done. Religion is like a universal narcotic with so many people dependent on it for support, I doubt they could relinquish it. However, I would try to deinstitutionalize it by subjecting it to the responsibility other organizations have to assume, such as taxes. I would also limit its political activity.

A clue to this method would be to see who and what the power was attacking. It will tell you where to look for the positive. For example, religion attacks sex and abortion, yet does not support day care centers for working mothers. The government spends millions of dollars for the military but attacks the poor on welfare (President Reagan even tried to steal social security until the old people really put up a stink): worse, the state will deny the individual the right of violence in their struggle for social change, yet will use violence to control them.

Business wants high profits but attacks labor in order to pay the least amount in wages. Business also fights safety regulations in automobiles, mines, factories; also, environmental controls. It opposes socialism for the poor but not for itself. It accepts government largesse in the aerospace, automobile industries, and in big business farming.

The success of this method presumes the individual sees clearly and exactly what these organizations are and what results they produce. It presumes illusions have been removed. In addition, it presumes true choices between true values have been made. When, and if, this process is effected, is the point at which we have arrived at a true morality—one that gives the individual the power to once again control those who should be serving him rather than he them. True morality makes the individual sovereign.

THE FULL CIRCLE

Pragmatically, if I were to stop at this point, I would be guilty of creating bullshit. This would be so because if an individual or even a million individuals were able to accomplish a true morality, realistically, they would still not be able to unseat the power structure. Power is always loath to relinquish its power. In most instances it will defend its power to the death with force. At this point, history tells us change will most frequently occur only if an equal or superior force opposes it. So, if force is necessary to oppose and unseat power, we are back to square one. We have to rationalize our use of force with a morality that justifies it. And should the force opposing the entrenched power structure be victorious, history teaches us another lesson of irony; the victor may not be any better than the defeated, and in many cases, is actually worse, for it (the new power) begins to follow its own needs and dictates. Yet, it is logical that the only way to oppose and control the newly created entity, is by the individual in his morality who makes a true choice based on reality, a choice that in its goodness, constructiveness and humanistically oriented way will control the negatives of impersonal entities such as the state and technology. It seems to me to be a moral imperative that the individual regain control over those forces so they will be utilized to his benefit, and in a responsible way. Is this realistically possible? I honestly don't know. When Danilo Dolce, a potential Nobel Peace Prize winner, was asked if his philosophy might not be too idealistic, he replied, "Is illusion the same as a dream? You must free yourself from illusions but you can't live without dreams." I believe nothing is created in a vacuum, not even the negative. By examining processes, one can discover how it might have come to be, and from that, how one can change it to be what one wants it to be. But first, we must accurately see bullshit morality (the illusions), from which we must try to fashion a morality of bullshit (a reality), that will hopefully lead us to a true morality (making a true choice based on true values based on reality). True morality is each individual's responsibility. It is not a set of dogmas but a volitional process that keeps the balance of life tipped to the side of the individual human. It is life enhancing, constructive and humanistic. It sees the individual as sovereign.

CHAPTER XII

THE END/THE BEGINNING

Several years ago, a motion picture impacted on the American consciousness to forever change our attitude toward the media. It brought out into the open the deception and manipulation (the bullshitting) of the public which has so confused and frustrated us. The film, of course, was not only about the media, but about the media as a microcosm of all business and society. However, there were many who rejected the film because they thought it was unrealistic and extreme. They just could not believe the scenes depicted were possible.

"Network" is Paddy Chayefsky's searing, savage, satirical look at the misuses and abuses to which the power of television can be put when those in command become crazed with greed and starved for profit. It is also about power. The power to control the mind. Specifically, the question Chayefsky poses is: how far is an ailing network prepared to go in the exploitation of the public's "tastes" and "trends" to regain and hold its vast audience?

Howard Beale, an anchorman whose low rated news slot, is about to be canceled, cracks up on screen and tells his audience he is going to "blow" his brains out right on the air a week from today . . . next Tuesday. There is an uproar. They get Beale off the air immediately but he pleads with his boss to let him go back on and apologize and make a brief farewell statement. "I have eleven years at this network, Max," he says. "I have some standing in this industry. I don't want to go out like a clown."

Out of regard for their old friendship, Schumacher, Beale's boss, agrees to give Beale two minutes on television to bow out

251

with dignity. That evening Beale reappears on his show and begins. "Good evening. Yesterday I announced on this program that I would commit public suicide, admittedly an act of madness. Well, I'll tell you what happened. I just ran out of bullshit . . ." Although there is chaos in the studio, Schumacher refuses to cut him off the air. "I'm leaving him on," Schumacher shouts into one of the telephones. "He's saying life is bullshit and it is. So what are you screaming about?" and Beale continues on the air explaining exactly why he feels life is bullshit, ending with "I don't have any bullshit left. I just ran out you see . . ." For saying that life is bullshit on TV, Beale becomes something of a folk hero. Quickly cashing in on his notoriety, network executives take over Beale and his news program, advertising him as The Mad Prophet "inveighing against the hypocrisies of our time" and urge him on to continue doing "his angry man thing."

Beale is a hit. Ratings go through the roof. But Beale is really on the brink of madness. Some would say he is sane and the rest of the world is mad. In one of the most intense moments in the film, Beale says to his audience, "We all know things are bad. Worse than that. They're crazy." and he proceeds to list some of them: shopkeepers forced to keep guns under a counter, punks running wild in the streets, the dollar doesn't buy a nickel's worth, the air is not fit to breathe and the food not fit to eat while we, the people, sit in front of our TV sets listening to a newscaster telling us that today we had fifteen homocides and sixty-three violent crimes as if that's the way things are supposed to be. "All I know," says Beale, "is first you've got to get mad. You've got to say, 'I'm a human being, goddammit. My life has value.' I want you to get out of your chairs and go to the window," he exhorts his unseen audience. "Right now, I want you to open it and stick your head out and yell. I want you to yell: 'I'm mad as hell and I'm not going to take it anymore!'"

The glorious and exhilarating scenes that follow in an accompanying thunderstorm — when inspirited by Beale's message, window after window go up all over New York and people call out from their hearts, "I'm mad as hell and I'm not going to take it anymore," — is like a magnificent volcano erupting its suppressed energy skyward into a constellation of light and force that will change its surroundings.

Although the public response to Howard Beale's plea to get angry was fictional, fiction and the artists who create it, not only have a way of mirroring everyday life, but of foretelling events long before their occurrence. In the films of Stanley Kubrick,

"Dr. Strangelove," "Clockwork Orange," "2001," he pointed to the insanity of nuclear energy in the wrong hands, senseless, impersonal violence as commonplace, and technology ultimately wagging the human being instead of humans controlling technology. Reality has made these and other artist's perceptions accurate to an uncanny degree. "Network," too, has been prophetic. The public has become "mad as hell" and they are not willing to take it anymore. It is not just people in the United States who are calling for a nuclear freeze but the world. It was not our leaders who put an end to the Vietnam War but the public. It is the "mad as hell" public that is demanding that science, technology, the military, corporate America, be more responsible. The point is that what seemed etched in stone and irreversible was changed. However, what must be changed and how it must be changed demands that we first clear away the bullshit surrounding these life and death issues.

When Schumacher, the news executive, answers to higher ups after allowing Beale to continue on the air where he tells his audience "he's just run out of bullshit," he says to them, "Well, life is bullshit," implying that is a truth. But life is not bullshit. There is bullshit in life but that does not synonymize life as bullshit. Life is important, constructive, joyous, enlightening, caring, and a lot of other things of value. Sure, bullshit has trivialized it, corrupted it, made it cynical and false, and as I pointed out at the beginning of this book, cancerized the body, but we are not yet dead. And as long as you, I, and the other person refuse to bullshit, there will always be enough of us to reverse this trend. But it has to start with you and I as individuals, because while we cannot control others we can control ourselves. And more importantly, within each of us is the power to be moral and exercise a choice for good.

There was a time I opted on the side of bullshit. I said to myself, if that is the way the game is played, then I'll play it by their rules. And I was successful by material standards. I had a luxurious home, fancy automobiles, the best hi-fi equipment, beautiful clothes, security and position. But — I had become cynical. I could no longer accept other human beings at face value. I could no longer genuinely interact with them. I had become emotionally stunted. As a matter of fact, when I shaved in the morning and had to look at myself in the mirror I did not like that person.

I remember a sit down dinner party of friends and family. The surroundings were attractive and comfortable, the table laden with exquisite foods, and most everyone in good cheer, and yet I felt lonely, alienated, and isolated. Even though my guests and family wished me well, I could not accept their feelings as genuine. I had become so cynical I constantly questioned their motives, suspecting some base or greedy reason for their "play acting." At that moment, I knew I was in deep trouble. While I had solved the practical problems of life, I had done it at the expense of family and friends. I could no longer accept their direct, sometime simple, honest communication, nor their love.

In the long trek back to emotional health, I finally evolved the philosophy that one could function and prosper in this world without becoming one of them—the bullshitters. I could not remain "innocent," of course, nor naive, nor could I remain blinded to the true intentions or motivations of other people. In other words, I had to see clearly and accurately and defense myself properly. If I became involved with a bullshitter I had to walk away from the situation. If I could not walk away from it, I had to bring reality and truth to the forefront as quickly as possible and let the chips fall where they may. If my life and livelihood were involved, then I had to measure the loss of my power, integrity, self-respect and dignity against any material gain I was to make. Most often, I concluded the price was too high to pay.

But more importantly, I also found there are many, many people who share my philosophy and values. There are people who believe in honest communications, true and loving feelings, who have maintained integrity, self-respect and dignity.

The struggle, however, has to begin with you. The ultimate bullshitter is the person who bullshits himself. While the saying, "To thine ownself be true," may be a cliche, it is nonetheless the best advice one could be given. If you are straight, truthful and honest with yourself, it is much easier to be truthful and honest with the next person.

This is not the complete solution, of course, because bullshit has become firmly entrenched and institutionalized. When Howard Beale's ratings went up as a result of his disclosure to commit suicide publicly, along with his speaking "honestly," the TV network took that and corrupted it by calling him "The Mad Prophet" and allowed him to go fully into madness before millions of viewers. It did not matter to them whether they sold "honesty," madness, violence, or manure, as long as it brought advertising dollars. Anything for a buck. So, whether it is television networks, government, business, education, religion, the military, science or technology—anything that has become institutionalized—the only way they are going to change is if you, along with millions of others, demand the change. The vicious circle can be broken, but only if it begins with you—to thine ownself be true. Get angry! Stop bullshitting and stop others from bullshitting. See clearly and accurately and face them with the truth!

BIBLIOGRAPHY

Becker, Ernest / "The Denial of Death" / 1973 / Macmillan Company, Inc. / New York

Sally Bedell / Don Kowet / "Anatomy of a Smear" / May 29–June 4, 1982 / TV Guide / Triangle Publications Radnor, PA

Berle, Adolf A. / "Power" / 1967 / Harcourt, Brace & World, Inc. / New York

Bernays, Edward L. / "Public Relations" / 1952 / University of Oklahoma Press / Oklahoma

Berne, Eric / "Games People Play" / 1964 / Grove Press / New York

Block, Arthur / "Murphy's Law" / 1977 / Price-Stern-Sloan Publishers Inc / Los Angeles, California

Block, Arthur / "Murphy's Law—Book Two" / 1980 / 1980 / Price-Stern-Sloan Publishers Inc / Los Angeles, California

Block, Joel D. / "Friendship" / 1980 / Macmillan Publishing, Inc. / New York

Bloom, Murray Teigh / "The Trouble With Lawyers" / 1969 / Simon and Schuster / New York

Bok, Sissela / "Lying" / 1978 / Pantheon Books / New York

Bowyer, J. Barton / "Cheating" / 1982 / St. Martin's Press / New York

Brackman, Jacob / "The Put-On" / 1967 / Henry Ragnery Company / Chicago, Illinois

Branden, Nathaniel / "The Psychology of Self-Esteem" / 1969 / Nash Publishing Corporation / Los Angeles, California

Branden, Nathaniel / "The Disowned Self" / 1972 / Nash Publishing Corporation / Los Angeles, California

Brooks, John / "Showing Off In America" / 1979 / Little Brown and Company / Boston

Browne, Harry / "How I Found Freedom In An Unfree World / 1973 / The Macmillan Company / New York

Buscaglia, Leo / "Love" / 1972 / Fawcett Crest Books / New York

Carr, Albert Z. / "Business As A Game" / 1968 / Signet Books / New York

Chapman, A.H. / "The Games Children Play" / 1971 / G.P. Putnam's Sons / New York

Elkins, Michael / "Self-Searching In Israel" / March 7,1982 / New York Times Magazine / New York

Ellul, Jacques / "The Technological Society" / 1964 / Alfred A. Knopf / New York

Ellul, Jacques / "Propaganda" / 1965 / Alfred A. Knopf / New York

Ellul, Jacques / "The Political Illusion" / 1967 / Alfred A. Knopf / New York

Epstein, Joseph / "Ambition" / 1980 / E.P. Dutton / New York

Farb, Peter / "Word Play" / 1974 / Alfred A. Knopf / New York

Fisher, Milton / "Intuition" / 1981 / E.P. Dutton, Inc. / New York

Freudenberger, Herbert J. / "Burn Out" / 1980 / Doubleday & Co., Inc. / New York

Galbraith, John Kenneth / "The Affluent Society" / 1958 / Houghton Mifflin Company / Boston

Galbraith, John Kenneth / "The New Industrial State" / 1967 / Houghton Mifflin Company / Boston

Galinsky, Ellen / Between Generations / 1981 / Times Books / New York

Gall, John / "Systemantics" / 1975 / The New York Times Book Company / New York

Garrity, Joan / "Total Loving" / 1977 / Simon and Schuster / New York

Ginott, Haim G. / "Between Parent & Child" / 1956 / Macmillan Publishing Company / New York

Ginott, Haim G. / "Between Parent & Teenager" / 1969 / Macmillan Publishing Company / New York

Ginott, Haim G. / "Teacher & Child" / 1972 / Macmillan Publishing Company / New York

Goldberg, Herb / Robert T. Lewis / "Money Madness" / 1978 / William Morrow & Company / New York

Heller, Robert / "The Great Executive Dream" / 1972 / Delacorte Press / New York

Herzog, Arthur / "The B.S. Factor" / 1973 / Simon and Schuster / New York

Kordo, Michael / "Success" / 1977 / Random House / New York

Korda, Michael / "Power" / 1975 / Random House / New York

Lambdin, William / "Doublespeak Dictionary" / 1979 / Pinnacle Books Inc. / Los Angeles, California

Lasch, Christopher / "The Culture of Narcissism" / 1979 / W.W. Norton & Company / New York

Maccoby, Michael / "The Gamesman" / 1976 / Simon and Schuster / New York

Machiavelli / "The Prince" / 1952 / Oxford University Press reprinted by The New American Library of World Literature / New York

McDonald, Frank / "Provenance" / 1979 / Little Brown & Company, Inc. / Boston

Musashi, Miyamoto / "The Book of Five Rings" / 1982 / Bantam Books / New York

Miler, Wackman, Nunnally, Saline / "Straight Talk" / 1981 / Rawson, Wade Publishers, Inc. New York

Packard, Vance / "The Status Seekers" / 1959 / David McKay / New York

Peters, Laurence J. / "The Peter Principle" / 1969 / William Morrow and Company / New York

Ringer, Robert J. / "Winning Through Intimidation" / 1973 / Fawcett Books / New York

Ringer, Robert J. / "Looking Out for #1" / 1977 / Fawcett Crest Books / New York

Ruben, Harvey L. / "Competing" / 1981 / Harper & Row Publishers, Inc. / New York

Seabury, David / "The Art of Selfishness" / 1937 / Simon and Schuster / New York

Smith, Manuel J. / "When I Say No, I Feel Guilty" / 1975 / The Dial Press/New York

Slater, Philip E. / "The Pursuit of Loneliness" / 1970 / Beacon Press/ Boston

Toffler, Alvin / "The Third Wave" / 1980 / William Morrow & Company / New York

Truscott IV, Lucian K. / "Dress Gray" / 1979 / Doubleday & Company / New York

Walker, Alexander / "Stardom" / 1970 / Stein and Day Publishers / New York

Wareham, John / "Secrets of a Corporate Headhunter / 1981 / Atheneum / New York

Whitside, Thomas / "The Block Buster Complex" / 1980 / Wesleyan University Press / Middleton, Connecticut

Wright, J. Patrick / "On A Clear Day You Can See General Motors" / 1973 / Multimedia Product Development, Inc. / Chicago, Illinois